PREFACE

Before reading this book, you've probably had moments of curiosity about Korean culture.

Why does the Korean flag look like it has a Pepsi logo? Why do so many Korean kids share the same last names—Kim, Lee, and Park?

If you're a K-Drama fan who watches variety shows too, your fascination with Korea may have grown even deeper. What does *Korea* actually mean? Who are the people on Korean banknotes? Why do Koreans love kimchi so much—and why with everything?

Koreans also have their own way of figuring each other out. Forget small talk; they often ask your age, or even blood type. (Yes, blood type! Some still believe it reveals personality—Type A perfectionists, Type O easygoing.) And now it's all about MBTI—from ENFP to ISTJ, it can even hint at workplace or dating compatibility.

You might also wonder why you suddenly become a year (or two) older upon arriving in Korea. Why all the drama in street tent bars (*pojangmacha*)? How do Koreans drink so much soju from those infamous green bottles?

And, of course, the 2020s question: Why is K-pop so insanely popular? (Hint: it's not just BTS—NewJeans, Stray Kids, LE SSERAFIM, and a wave of global idols are leading the charge. And yes, what does "*Gangnam Style*" even mean?)

If you've seen *Squid Game* or *Parasite*, you know Korean entertainment is not just catchy—it's deep, emotional, and brutally honest. Even animation is joining the trend with shows like *K-Pop Demon Hunters*, blending Korean pop culture with global storytelling.

When you get lost in translation, a dictionary or app can help—but cultural gaps aren't that easy. You might guess right once, but miss the *why* behind Korea's customs and behaviors. No matter who you are—a K-Pop or K-Drama fan, an expat, a study-abroad student, or a second-generation *gyopo*—you no longer need to stay puzzled by the quirks that make Korea, well, Korea.

This book covers over 350 essential topics and FAQs, organized into 27 categories, exploring Korea through the *Five Ws* (Who, What, When, Where, Why) and *How*. By the end, you'll understand Korea—from history and values to food, slang, and modern trends. You'll also finally know why Koreans sit on the floor, why pouring with one hand is rude, and why K-Dramas' hidden cues make so much sense. After reading, dramas, movies, and K-Pop lyrics will feel completely different—and you'll spot the clichés before they happen!

Next time you hang out with a Korean friend, you can casually impress them—like explaining why people tap the neck of a soju bottle or why to turn away when drinking with elders. And if someone says you have a "small face," you'll know to proudly reply: "Thank you!"

Now, let's start with a perfect first example of Korean culture—the famous "*Ppali Ppali*" (빨리빨리) mindset. Hurry up and start reading!

ABOUT THE AUTHOR

Woosung Kang is an author based in Colorado and Seoul. He studied Business Management at the University of Denver and Consumer Psychology at New York University. Believing that the best way to share Korean culture is by first learning, appreciating, and respecting other cultures, he continues to travel the world to deepen that understanding. During his time in New York, he led a series of successful marketing campaigns promoting the beauty of Korean culture and appeared on television and radio to share his story. He is also the author of the bestselling series **The K-Pop Dictionary**, and since 2021, he has been a regular guest on KBS Radio's Through the **Multicultural Lens (다문화 돋보기)**, where he explores topics of cultural diversity and global communication.

E-mail: storyteller1634@gmail.com
Instagram: vivaretro0810

ABOUT THE EDITOR

Edward Leary is a K-Pop fan first and everything else second! Reporting K-Pop news for 7 years, Edward has shared his opinions and content through allkpop, kpopstarz, print magazines, and more. Residing in Korea, Edward is pursuing Korean Broadcasting as a TV personality to showcase his love of Korea through Hallyu. Using the name Hello Eddi, he has appeared in two K-Pop MVs, alongside MC-ing events, voice acting, and modeling in Korea.

E-mail: kpop.eddi@gmail.com
Instagram: Hello_Eddi

KOREAN CULTURE DICTIONARY
어서와! 한국문화는처음이지?

**From Kimchi To K-Pop And K-Drama Clichés.
Everything About Korea Explained!**

ISBN 979-11-93438-30-5

**Written and Compiled by WOOSUNG KANG
Edited by EDWARD LEARY**

초판 1쇄 2020년 11월 3일
초판 2쇄 2021년 8월 5일
개정판 1쇄 2023년 6월5일
개정2판 1쇄 2025년 11월11일

Printed in the Republic of Korea

www.newampersand.com

HOW TO USE THIS BOOK

We've written this book with people like you in mind, so having zero knowledge about Korea is absolutely fine! You can simply follow the sections in pre-set order and get done with the course. However, if you are the proud K-Culture know-it-all of your friend group you can put your knowledge to the test and even learn some new interesting facts to surprise your friends with by jumping between sections of your choice. We've cross linked important information so you are always guided in the right direction and will not get lost in the middle of the road. But, that's not all, folks! To maximize your learning, we've included the following in every section!

BOLD & *Italicized* — Important Names & Korean Terms You Should Know!

Taejo / Yi Seong-gye 태조 / 이성계

Taejo 태조, birth name **Yi Seong-gye 이성계** (1335 - 1408), was the founder and the first king of the Joseon Dynasty, reigning from 1392 to 1398, and was the main figure in overthrowing the Goryeo Dynasty. By the late 14th century, the Goryeo Dynasty was beginning to fall apart, with its foundations collapsing from years of war against the Mongol Empire. During the time, General Yi Seong-gye gained power and was respected for pushing the Mongol remnants off the kingdom and repelling Japanese pirates. When the newly rising Ming Dynasty demanded the return of a significant portion of Goryeo's northern territory, Goryeo was split into two factions – anti-Ming who argued to fight back and those who sought peace. Yi, the latter, however, was chosen to lead the invasion. At **Wihwado Island 위화도** on the **Amnok River 압록강**, he decided to revolt and withdrew the troops, and headed back to the capital. The military coup succeeded, and he dethroned the King. He first put a puppet king, but later exiled him, and ascended the throne, and began the Joseon Dynasty.

Epic Battle Scenes!

Myeongryang 명량
(*The Admiral : Roaring Currents*, 2014)

Yukryongi nareusha 육룡이 나르샤
(*Six Flying Dragons*, 2015, SBS)

K-Drama series about
Yi Seong-gye's Military Coup &
The Beginning of the Joseon Dynasty

Must-See Films, TV Shows & Documentaries!

WATCH!
What Korean *Hoesik* Is Like

Scan the QR Code To See This Clip!

HOESIK 회식 – THE DREADED COMPANY EVENT EVERYONE WANTS TO AVOID

EDUCATION IN KOREA

DRINKING IN KOREA

WOKRING IN KOREA

FUN AND QUIRKY
KOREAN SUPERSTITIONS AND BELIEFS

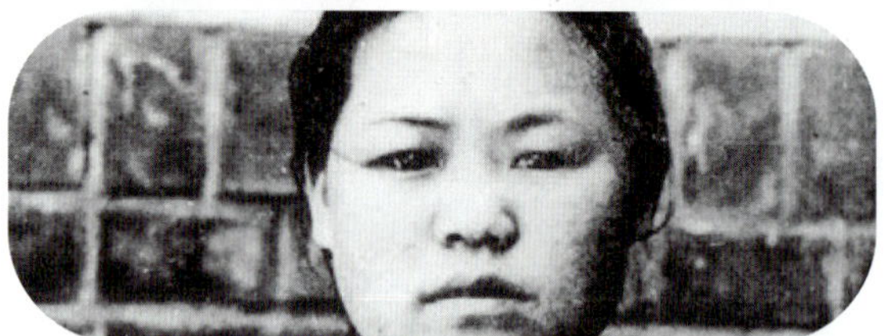

LOST IN TRANSLATION

KOREA IN THE DIGITAL ERA

HALLYU
KOREAN
WAVE

WHY
IS THERE A PEPSI LOGO ON THE KOREAN FLAG?

"Hey, nice work on the ambush marketing, Pepsi!"

When two groups of performers slowly merged to form a giant circle of perfectly interlocked red and blue symbols—strikingly similar to what you'd find on a Pepsi can—during the opening ceremony of the 2018 Pyeongchang Winter Olympic Games, social media exploded with a rush of tweets and posts from viewers around the globe.

2018 Pyeongchang WInter Olympic Games Opening Event
(SBS TV Screenshot)

13

How was Pepsi, whose name wasn't even on the sponsor list, able to make such a bold appearance—so much so that the world-(in)famous streaker Mark Roberts, who had crashed multiple Olympic events wearing a pink tutu and a monkey penis, would have been utterly overshadowed? Was the International Olympic Committee (IOC) blindsided by some elaborate ambush marketing stunt from Pepsi? The answer is a flat no. Pepsi had nothing to do with the performance, and it's safe to assume that 99.9% of those tweets were jokes. Still, this short-lived social media fad perfectly illustrates the common misperception about the uncanny resemblance between the Pepsi logo and the Korean flag.

So the big question is: How did Pepsi end up with what looks like a Korean symbol on its products—or did Koreans somehow "borrow" the Pepsi logo for their flag? I've heard many versions, but my favorite is the urban legend that a Korean billionaire once saved Pepsi from bankruptcy and demanded the Korean symbol be put on its cans in return.

In reality, the logo first appeared in the 1940s, during World War II, as a patriotic gesture meant to show support for American troops fighting abroad. The motif has endured with only minor tweaks—new fonts, slight size adjustments—over the decades. While it's fun to speculate, the Pepsi logo and the Korean flag are completely unrelated. The Pepsi logo, one of the most recognizable corporate trademarks in the world, features three colors—red, white, and blue (hint, hint!)—arranged in a sphere-like design.

HISTORY OF THE KOREAN FLAG

Meanwhile, the prototype of the modern-day Korean flag (oh, let me kindly remind you that there are STILL two Koreas at the time of writing, and throughout this book, unless otherwise noted, "Korea" refers to South Korea—our scary neighbor upstairs will be explicitly called out when needed) was first devised when the country was still under the **Joseon 조선 Dynasty (1392–1897)**, whose sovereignty was being increasingly threatened by Imperial Japan's ambitions in Asia.

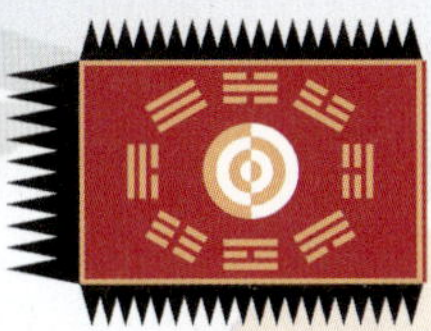 

In 1882, during the signing of the Joseon–U.S. Treaty, the need for a national flag suddenly became urgent, as there was none to represent the dynasty. To resolve the matter, delegate Lee Eung-jun 이응준, under royal order, modified the dynasty's royal standard, *eogi* 어기, into a national flag, which then stood side by side with the U.S. flag.

Later that year, on August 22, 1882, emissary **Park Yeong-hyo 박영효** rearranged the trigrams and produced a scaled model of the *taegeukgi* 태극기. (Taegeuk refers to the red and blue circle at the center of the flag, meaning "supreme ultimate," while *gi* 기 simply means "flag"—hence, the "supreme ultimate flag.") On January 27, 1883, the Joseon government officially promulgated the taegeukgi as the national flag.

When Emperor **Gojong 고종** proclaimed the Great Korean Empire, **Daehanjeguk 대한제국**, in October 1897, the *taegeukgi* continued to serve as the state's official flag.

During the Japanese occupation (1910–1945), a flag similar to today's South Korean flag was used by the Provisional Government of Korea based in China. After liberation and the establishment of the Republic of Korea in 1948, the current version was formally declared the national flag on October 15, 1949.

Like the Pepsi logo, the Korean flag has gone through tweaks and adjustments over time but has always remained the nation's most enduring symbol. That's why you'll often see the taegeuk incorporated into the logos of Korean companies today.

Government Emblem of South Korea

So, with that brief history lesson, I hope the Pepsi–Korea mysteries and conspiracies have been properly debunked and demystified. Now, let's take a closer look at the Korean flag itself and learn what all the symbols really mean!

WHAT DO THE SYMBOLS MEAN?

Let's start with the South Korean flag!

As we've already covered, the local name is *taegeukgi* 태극기, which literally means "supreme ultimate flag." The dominant background color is white, symbolizing brightness, purity, and peace. Koreans embraced these values so deeply that foreigners once nicknamed them the "white-clad people," since white was the most common color in daily attire, especially the *hanbok* 한복 of the 19th century.

At the center lies the circle, derived from the traditional philosophy of *yin* and *yang*. The red half represents positive cosmic forces, while the blue half represents negative ones, together forming a perfect balance. In essence, the *taegeuk* symbolizes the natural law of creation, where everything revolves around the interaction between yin and yang.

Surrounding the circle are four trigrams, called *geon* 건, *gon* 곤, *gam* 감, and *ri* 리. They represent the sky, earth, moon, and sun, as well as directions and seasons. (And yes, even if they don't look like they're arranged in the "right" order, this is the traditional way.) These trigrams complete the flag's theme of harmony and unity.

Why Were Koreans Called "White-Clothes People"? P. 200

BALANCE IN THE UNIVERSE

The laws of nature, where all creation revolves around the interaction of yin and yang.

HARMONY OF UNITY

The four trigrams form a harmony of unity, centered around the *yin–yang* symbol.

KOREAN MINDS

The bright white background reflects the national character of cherishing brightness, purity, and peace.

When World War II ended with the Allied victory in 1945, Japan relinquished its 35-year rule over the Korean peninsula. Under Allied arrangements, the Soviet Union occupied the northern half while the United States took control of the southern half.

Seeking to instill their socialist ideology, Soviet leaders rejected the idea of inheriting the traditional taegeukgi and opted to design a new flag. **Kim Il-sung 김일성**, then leader of North Korea, agreed, and in 1947 a new flag was dictated from Moscow. The North Koreans named it *ingonggi* 인공기, meaning "the flag of the people's republic."

The red star symbolizes Communism (a motif shared with the flags of the Soviet Union, Vietnam, and China) and the "bright future" of the people. The white circle behind it represents the universe. The dominant red field signifies the revolutionary spirit and the march toward Communism, while the blue stripes stand for the nation's supposed commitment to peace and friendship. Finally, the white stripes symbolize the purity of North Korean ideology as well as strength and dignity.

And with that, we've covered the ideas and meanings behind the flags of both Koreas. Hopefully, this served as a helpful introduction and gave you a glimpse into the ideologies each side has tried to represent through their national symbols.

Who Are The "Kim Dynasty"?
P. 222

SYMBOL OF COMMUNISM

The red star stands for Communism, while the white circle symbolizes the universe.

SPIRIT OF NORTH KOREA

The red field embodies the revolutionary spirit and the path to Communism. The blue stripes signify a proclaimed commitment to peace and friendship, while the white stripes represent purity, strength, and dignity.

FLAG DICTATED FROM MOSCOW

In 1947, under Moscow's direction, a new flag was created and named *ingonggi* 인공기, meaning "The Flag of the People's Republic."

KOREAN NAMES

WHY DO KOREAN PEOPLE ONLY HAVE LIKE… THREE LAST NAMES?

For this topic, let's start with a little trivia: what could the Korean proverb "**looking for a Mr. Kim in Seoul**" possibly mean? Well, keep this question in mind as you follow the story, and you'll figure it out by the end.

First, imagine flipping through a yearbook from a school with lots of Korean students. Go to the index and check the "K" section. Lo and behold—you'd see the descendants of the Kim family claiming the lion's share of the space.

The same is true for other common family names like Lee and Park. If you think back to the names of your Korean friends—or if you don't have one, just think of your favorite K-pop star—there's a good chance they're a Kim, Lee, or Park. And history and pop culture back this up: the first Korean in Major League Baseball was **Park Chan-ho**, the first Korean Olympic swimming gold medalist was **Park Tae-hwan**, and the first Korean to play for Manchester United was **Park Ji-sung**.

Notice that in Romanization, the family name comes before the given name. For clarity, I'll stick with the term family name from here on. Of Korea's past 12 presidents, 2 were Parks, 2 were Kims, and 2 were Lees. The current president of the World Bank? **Jim Yong Kim**. Olympic figure skating champion **Kim Yuna** (aka "Queen Yuna") is another famous example. Even **Kim Jong Un**, the "supreme leader" of North Korea, belongs to the Kim club. From Hollywood, you may recognize **Lee Byung-hun** (Terminator Genisys, The Magnificent Seven, G.I. Joe: Retaliation), **Lee Jung-jae** (Squid Game), **Lee Ki-hong** (The Maze Runner), and comedian **Bobby Lee** from MADtv.

Looking at this data, you might jokingly conclude: Parks make great athletes, Kims are great leaders, and Lees excel in entertainment. But that's not the real takeaway. The point is that Korea has only 286 family names (as of 2003, not counting naturalized citizens), and just three of them—Kim, Lee, and Park—make up more than 45% of the population (Kim 21.8%, Lee 14.8%, Park 8.5%).

For comparison:

- Russia has over 1,800 family names, with the most common (Smirnov) at only 1.8% of the population.
- In Japan, over 100,000 share the surname Sato, but even the entire top 10 names combined account for just 10% of the population.
- In the U.S., Smith is the most common, with 151,671 people—roughly 1% of the population.

If this were an investment portfolio, Korea's surname distribution would be the opposite of diversified. So what explains this disproportionate concentration? Are Korean families simply inbred? Is it a case of endogamy? At first glance, such speculation may sound plausible—especially knowing there are only 286 family names to go around. But here's where the concept of *bongwan* 본관 comes in. Bongwan distinguishes clans within the same family name by identifying the birthplace of the first ancestor who founded that line. According to a 2015 survey, there are 36,744 different *bongwan*.

So while two people may both be named Kim, if their paternal ancestors trace back to different founding places, they belong to completely different clans. Within each clan, there are further subdivisions into smaller factions. In this way, Koreans can tell the difference between families with the same surname, and the system prevents the entire nation from being one giant extended family tree.

Also, many Korean families—or their "lineage societies"—keep detailed records of their family history in a genealogy book called *jokbo* 족보. By checking your faction, you can see your familial status and your "generation level" (more on this later). Some onomasts—people who study proper names, especially of people and places—often compare bongwan to the European naming convention that incorporates a place of origin into a name (e.g., Olivia von Westenholz = "Olivia from Westenholz"). The difference is that the Korean system does not display the place label upfront, so it requires a bit more digging into one's family history. Oh, and here's an interesting fact: up until 2005, couples who shared both the same family name and bongwan were legally prohibited from marrying each other!

To put things into perspective, let's look at a real-life example.

All right, I'm sure you've figured out the answer to the Korean proverb quiz from the beginning. If not, the English equivalent of the proverb would be "finding a needle in a haystack."

WHY ARE THE KOREAN LAST NAMES 이 (YI) AND 노 (NOH) ROMANIZED AS "LEE" AND "ROH"?

Dueum beopchik 두음법칙 ("initial sound rule") is a Korean pronunciation rule designed to make certain Sino-Korean words, including family names derived from Chinese characters, easier to pronounce. It mainly affects words that begin with ㄹ (l/r) or ㄴ (n).

- When ㄹ (l/r) appears at the beginning of a word and is followed by the vowels ㅏ, ㅐ, ㅗ, ㅚ, ㅜ, or ㅡ (a/ae/o/oe/u/eu), it changes to ㄴ (n).
  - Example: Mr. 로철수 Roh Cheol-su → Mr. 노철수 Noh Cheol-su (When written in English, the original pronunciation "Roh" is usually retained.)
- When ㄹ (l/r) appears at the beginning of a word and is followed by the vowels ㅑ, ㅕ, ㅖ, ㅛ, ㅠ, or ㅣ (ya/yeo/ye/yo/yu/i), it changes to ㅇ (no initial consonant sound).
  - Example: 리철수 Lee Cheol-su → 이철수 Yi Cheol-su (When written in English, people often keep the original spelling—Lee, Ri, or Rhee—but some choose "Yi" to reflect the revised pronunciation.)
- In North Korea, these rules aren't generally applied when romanizing or even writing names because North Korean language reforms didn't adopt the same rules for initial ㄹ and ㄴ/ㅇ changes. They tend to preserve the original pronunciation of Sino-Korean characters.

WHY DO ALL KOREAN NAMES HAVE THREE SYLLABLES?

Now that we've covered the family name portion of a Korean name, let's turn to how a Korean first name is composed. If you've been following Korean celebrities for some time, you may have noticed a pattern: almost all Korean names have three syllables—one for the family name and two for the first name. For example, the famous K-Pop star **G-Dragon**'s Korean name is **Kwon (family name) + Ji-yong (first name)**. You might have wondered whether this structure is required by law, or if it's simply a social norm—remember the Korean proverb: "A cornered stone meets the mason's chisel."

To understand the reasoning behind this pattern, we need to refer back to the Korean genealogy system we just learned. A Korean family name indicates ancestral history, while the bongwan identifies the clan. But what about the first name? While the family name works vertically—showing lineage and ancestry—the first name works horizontally, providing information about one's generation.

Traditionally, members of the same generation and same sex share one syllable of their first name. This **"generational name"**, or *hangryeol* 항렬, is unique to each clan. The placement of this syllable—either the first or second syllable of the given name—is also determined and approved by the clan society (although this is often not strictly followed nowadays).

Think of it like a serial number on a manufactured product, which tells you when and where it was made. Similarly, the shared syllable indicates one's generational level. Thanks to such detailed record-keeping, members of the same clan—even distant cousins—can trace exactly how many generations they are removed from the clan's founding ancestor, thereby determining both their generation level and relative rank. Because of this system, it's possible for a younger person from a higher-ranking generation to receive honorifics from an older person from a lower-ranking generation. This can be confusing and even comical, even for average Koreans. The remaining syllable of the first name is usually chosen freely by the parents.

Here's another real-life example:

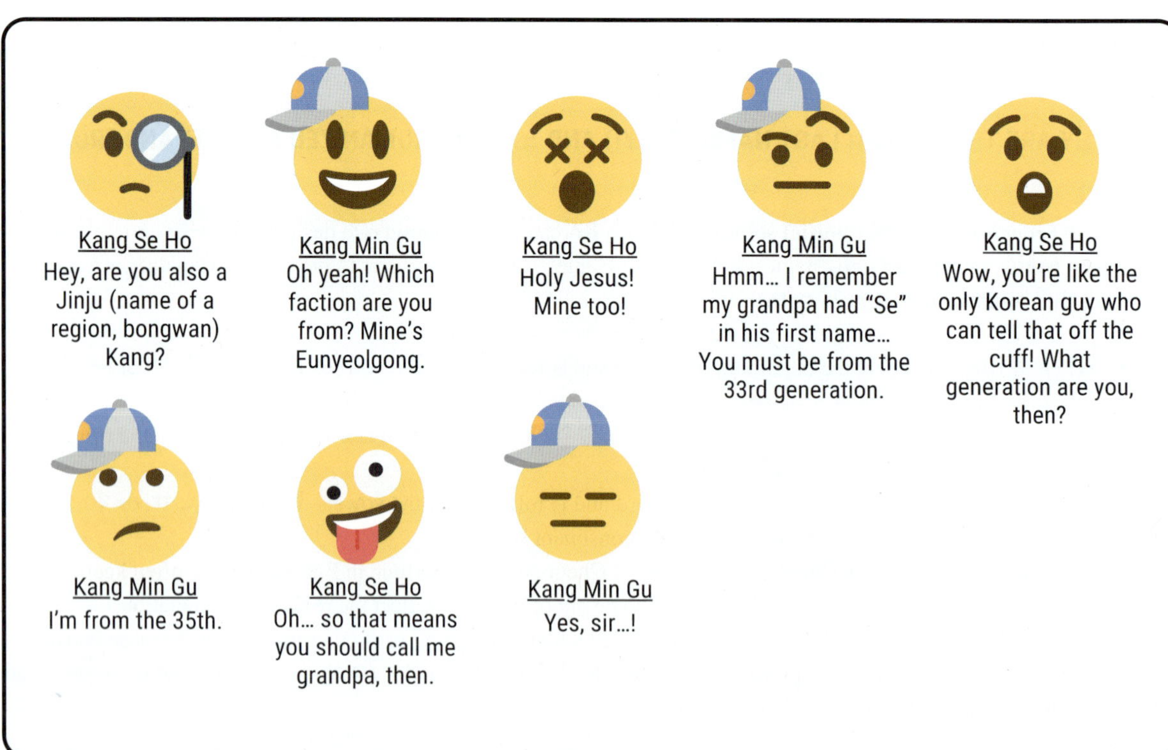

With the nation's relentless push for modernization and the Korean lifestyle rapidly shifting from collectivism to individualism, many traditional values and cultural practices are weakening. As a result, the syllable-sharing tradition in first names is being observed less and less. (However, if you come from an extremely orthodox clan, they might still "throw the book" at you.)

It's also important to clarify that the three-syllable naming system is not a legal requirement. Different combinations are perfectly fine. For example:

- Two-syllable names: 1-syllable family name + 1-syllable first name (e.g., Kim Hwan)
- Two-syllable family names: Sunwoo, Namkung
- Four-syllable names: 2-syllable family name + 2-syllable first name (e.g., Sunwoo Hyun-soo)

DO KOREAN PEOPLE HAVE A MIDDLE NAME?

Often, Koreans applying for English-based documents—like an international driver's license—find a syllable missing from their name. This "mysterious disappearance" usually happens because people mistakenly treat the second syllable of their first name as a "middle name" in English forms. For example, if your name is Kim Yong-jin, it may appear as Yong Kim, Yong J. Kim, or Yong Kim, because the middle name is often initialized or omitted in American English systems.

What causes this confusion? As an educated reader, you've probably guessed: it's the spacing between the two syllables of the first name.

A popular solution is either:

1. Inserting a hyphen between the syllables (Yong-jin Kim)
2. Eliminating the space entirely (Yongjin Kim)

Both methods work well, but the hyphen method is better for guiding pronunciation. For example, without a hyphen, Yongil could be read as "Yon Gil" or "Yong Il," but a hyphen clarifies it. For those wondering if there's a difference between hyphenated and no-space versions, they are essentially the same—the choice is stylistic.

Hong Gil-Dong - The John Doe Of Korea
P. 239

WHAT DOES A KOREAN NAME STAND FOR? HOW CAN I DECODE IT?

Now that we've successfully learned the structure of a Korean name, let's keep the momentum going and move to another popular topic: what does a Korean name actually mean, and how can you decode it? To understand this, it's important to know that over 70% of the Korean vocabulary is based on *hanja* 漢字 한자 (Chinese characters borrowed from Traditional Chinese and incorporated into Korean with Korean pronunciation). Korean names are no exception. A typical Korean name has an underlying hanja character, which represents a meaning (an ideogram), while *hangul* 한글, the Korean alphabet, represents the pronunciation (a phonogram).

For example, someone named **Lee Mi Hwa** might have the following *hanja*:

이 Lee 李 ("Jeonju" (place)) + 미 Mi 美 ("beautiful") + 화 Hwa 花 ("flower")

This shows that knowing only the *hangul* pronunciation of a name reveals only half the story, because many *hanja* characters share the same pronunciation but have different meanings. Here's a simple illustration:

A: Hi! My name is Lee Mi Hwa. Nice to meet you.
B: Are you serious? Mine is too! What hanja characters do you use for your name?
A: Mi, meaning "enchanting," and Hwa, meaning "harmony." And yours?
B: Wow, that's beautiful! Mine is Mi, meaning "beautiful," and Hwa, meaning "a painting." Yup! My dad was an amazing painter!

This example isn't meant to suggest that you need to share your hanja with someone you've just met. Simply exchanging the hangul name is sufficient. The point is that knowing the exact hanja characters and their meanings is necessary to fully understand one's name.

In fact, you'll sometimes see Korean business cards, especially from older generations, showing a name in both hangul and hanja. This bilingual practice also appears on official documents, such as identification cards. Also, recently, there's been an increase in cases where names, excluding the surname, are given using "pure Korean" words. This eliminates the need for complex kanji. Examples include purely Korean names like **Mireu 미르,** meaning "dragon") or **Garam' 가람**, meaning "river", which don't use hanja at all.

AND THE LONGEST KOREAN NAME AWARD GOES TO...

The longest Korean name is also made purely from Korean words:

Park Ha Neul Byeol Nim Gu Reum Haet Nim Bo Da Sa Rang Seu Reo U Ri
박하늘별님구름햇님보다사랑스러우리

It's a tongue-twisting, 17-syllable long name meaning: "more beautiful than the star, the sun, the moon, and the cloud in the sky." Think your baby has a chance to set a new record? Sorry to burst your bubble, but it's not possible. Current law limits the number of syllables in a first name to five max. Lastly, let's talk about the power of habit. In real-life conversations, Koreans will often shorten a lengthy name into the familiar three-syllable format for convenience—usually after becoming well acquainted. For example, the above name would simply be shortened to Park Ha Neul.

All right! I hope this has answered all your questions about Korean names. As you can see, a Korean name can be as simple as a pair of syllables, yet it contains a huge amount of family history and tradition. Now that you know how to decode a Korean name, try to discover what your favorite Korean stars' names really mean!

DO KOREANS SPEAK CHINESE OR JAPANESE?

All right folks, let's be honest. Before you started paying serious attention to Korea, did you ever wonder what language Korean people actually speak—Chinese? Japanese? Or something else entirely? Truth be told, this is one of the most frequently asked questions I've gotten from foreign friends. (Other "runner-ups" include: "Are you from North or South Korea?" and "Do you know Karate?") And I'm sure many fellow Koreans have had a similar experience at least once in their lives. If your answer to the question above is a solid "yes," don't feel embarrassed—it's actually very common. This curiosity simply shows how undiscovered Korea still is compared to its neighbors, China and Japan. (Note to Korea: time to step up the marketing/PR game!). Hopefully, with books like this, things will start to change. Now let's dig into why this question keeps popping up.

WHY CHINESE CHARACTERS ARE SEEN EVERYWHERE IN KOREA?

The biggest source of confusion comes from the ubiquitous presence of Chinese characters in Korea. If you've ever visited historical landmarks such as **Gwanghwamun Gate (광화문)** or **Gyeongbokgung Palace (경복궁)**, you've probably noticed the majestic signboards written in elegant Chinese calligraphy. Even walking around modern-day Seoul, you can still spot shop signs and buildings featuring Chinese characters—enough to leave many visitors puzzled.

As always, a little history helps us make sense of the present. For centuries, while keeping their own spoken languages, many Asian countries—including Korea, Japan, Vietnam, and Mongolia—adopted Traditional Chinese characters as a kind of written lingua franca. This was similar to how Latin functioned in medieval Europe, or how English serves as today's global standard. (For reference: Simplified Chinese characters have only been in use in mainland China and some other regions since the 1950s, mainly to promote literacy.)

In Korea, *hanja* 한자 漢字, the Korean term for Chinese characters borrowed from Chinese but read with Korean pronunciation, was the only system of writing available until the invention of hangul in 1443, which was officially promulgated in 1446.

Gwanghwamun Gate

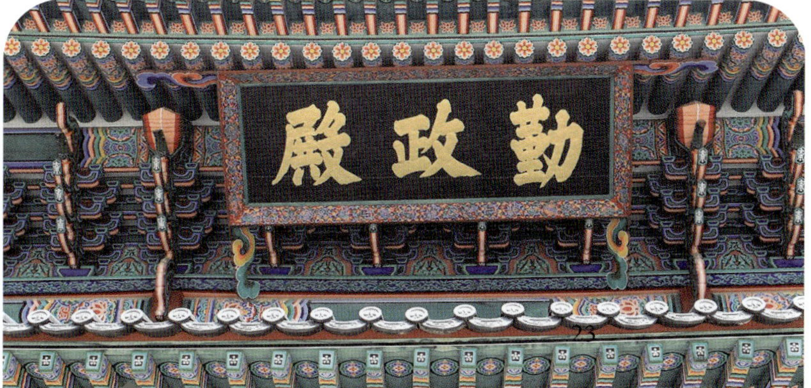
Gyeongbokgung Palace

WHO INVENTED HANGUL, THE KOREAN ALPHABET?

Beyond his long list of remarkable achievements, the main reason **King Sejong the Great 세종대왕 (1397–1450)** is revered as perhaps the greatest ruler in Korean history is his benevolence and compassion for his people. (Proof? Just look at the heart of Gwanghwamun Square, where his bronze statue stands in dignity, alongside Korea's greatest war hero, **Admiral Yi Sun-sin 이순신**.) Reflecting his down-to-earth character, King Sejong lamented that his people had to rely on the extremely complicated hanja for written communication. Learning hanja was a privilege reserved for the *yangban* **양반** (the nobility, scholars, and government officials), while the common people were too busy eking out a living—left as the illiterate majority of society. Even for those who knew hanja, being of foreign origin, it often failed to capture the full nuance of thoughts and emotions that could flow so naturally in spoken Korean.

More importantly, the lower classes had no real way to make their voices heard. Legitimate grievances (e.g., "I'm paying too much tax!") or ingenious ideas (e.g., "I know how to wipe out the enemies camped outside the fortress!") rarely reached those in power, since petitions required written hanja. Oral pleas were stopped by gatekeepers, and without proper recording, much of the hard-earned knowledge of ordinary people—such as farming techniques or folk remedies—was lost to posterity, a tremendous loss for society. Fortunately for Koreans, there was King Sejong the Great: a tireless scholar, a natural polymath who often surprised even the brightest experts, and above all, a practical problem-solver determined to walk the walk. Motivated by deep love and sympathy for his people, Sejong rolled up his sleeves and set out to fix the problem himself. He envisioned a uniquely Korean script that would be simple enough for even the uneducated to learn with ease.

After years of effort, he personally created a new alphabet of 28 letters (17 consonants and 11 vowels). Over time, 3 consonants and 1 vowel fell out of use, leaving today's hangul with 24 letters: 14 consonants and 10 vowels. He named it *hunminjeongeum* **훈민정음** ("The Proper Sounds for the Instruction of the People") and officially promulgated it on October 9, 1446. The preface to the proclamation still beautifully captures Sejong's benevolence and vision.

That was a moving introduction, wasn't it? His sincerity continues to resonate with us today. Now, let's take a look at how critics of the time received this groundbreaking invention.

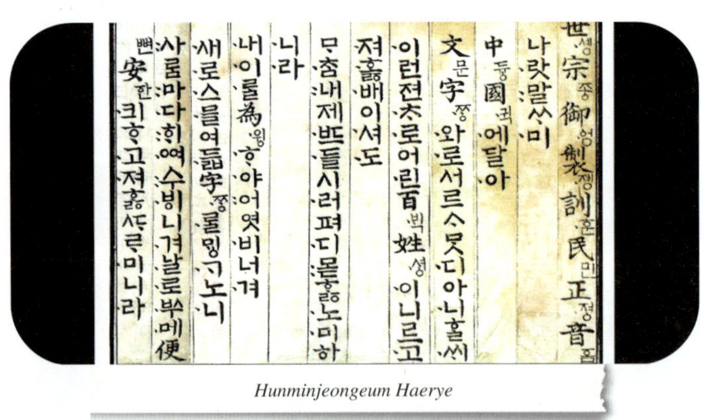

Hunminjeongeum Haerye

"A wise man can acquaint himself with them before the morning is over; even a stupid man can learn them in the space of ten days."

A commentary (basically a five-star review) written by scholars from the **Jiphyeonjeon 집현전** (Hall of Worthies) in the *Hunminjeongeum Haerye* **훈민정음 해례** ("Explanations and Examples of the Correct Sounds for the Instruction of the People") shows that King Sejong's plan to promote literacy among the commoners through an easy writing system got off to a great start—after all, when the nation's top scholars vouch for it, you know it's solid.

Korean Scholars Viewed *hangul* as a threat to their status

After the promulgation, however, the Korean alphabet faced fierce opposition from the literary elite and Confucian scholars of Joseon, who revered hanja (Traditional Chinese characters) as the only legitimate writing system and the true "language of scholars." More importantly, they saw hangul as a direct threat to their privileged status—fearing that enlightened commoners might one day spark a revolution.

But hangul gained traction in the late 16th century, when traditional poetry and hangul-based novels flourished. Centuries later, in 1894, the **Gabo 갑오** Reformists' drive for modernization, combined with strong support from Western missionaries, finally gave hangul its long-overdue boost: for the first time, it was used in official documents. A year later, in 1895, elementary schools began teaching texts written in hangul. And in 1896, ***Dongnipsinmun*** 독립신문 ("The Independence Newspaper") became the first newspaper ever published in hangul.

"The language of [our] people is different from that of the nation of China and thus cannot be expressed by the written language of Chinese people.

Because of this reason, the cries of illiterate peasants are not properly understood by the many [in the position of privilege].

I [feel the plight of the peasants and the difficulties faced by the public servants and] am saddened by the situation. Therefore, twenty eight [written] characters have been newly created.

[My desire is] such that, each [Korean] person may become familiar [with the newly created written language of Korean] and use them daily in an intuitive way."

- King Sejong the Great -

Newspaper from 1982 showing *gukhanmunhonyong*

Newspaper from 2018 published mostly in *hangul*

Since this period, hangul and hanja coexisted in a writing style known as ***gukhanmunhonyong* 국한문혼용**, a hybrid system where the two complemented each other.

During the Japanese Occupation (1910–1945), however, Japanese was imposed as the official language of Korea, and Korean was heavily suppressed. Early Korean literature was removed from school curricula, and publications in Korean were outlawed under the "cultural assimilation policy." Despite these harsh restrictions, hangul survived—taught in secret schools established by Koreans—and became a unifying force during the nation's darkest times. After liberation in 1945, hangul once again reclaimed its place as a core part of Korean culture.

A major shift came in 1968, when the government launched the **Exclusive Usage of Hangul Act**, a five-year nationwide project that abolished hanja education and promoted *hangul*. The policy had practical motivations: reading documents filled with hanja took too much time and effort, while the rise of computers favored the streamlined Korean alphabet with its 14 consonants and 10 vowels over the complexity of Chinese characters.

The project was carried out for practical reasons — reading and writing documents packed with hanja-based jargon required too much time and effort, while the rise of computer usage favored the simpler Korean alphabet with just 14 consonants and 10 vowels over the far more complex Chinese character system.

Yet despite these efforts, hanja could not be completely eliminated. The reason lies in the fundamental difference between the two systems: Chinese characters are ideograms (they represent meaning), whereas Korean characters are phonograms (they represent sounds). When text is written only in hangul, it often creates ambiguity in cases of homonyms.

For example, the Chinese words 最高 and 最古 are both pronounced ***choego* (최고)** in Korean, but one means "best" and the other "oldest." Without hanja, the distinction depends entirely on context, which can sometimes lead to confusion.

Because of this, some argue that hanja education should be reintroduced into the public school curriculum to strengthen comprehension and precision. Whether or not policymakers will act on this remains to be seen, but one thing is certain: hanja has been an indispensable part of Korean culture and is very likely to remain so in the future.

Looking back, *hangul* had one heck of a rocky ride, but the struggle was absolutely worth it. According to a 2002 CIA report, nearly the entire Korean population aged 15 and over can read and write, with literacy rates of 99.2% for men and 96.6% for women. These astonishing numbers reflect just how easy it is to master hangul—and they're also encouraging news for foreigners wondering if learning the Korean alphabet is within reach. The answer is a resounding yes: most people can learn to read and write hangul in just a day or two, sometimes even in a matter of hours. (Learning to speak Korean fluently, though, is a different story!)

The secret lies in hangul's scientific design and efficiency. Linguists around the world continue to praise it as one of the most logical and learner-friendly writing systems ever created. To honor King Sejong's legacy, UNESCO even established the King Sejong Literacy Prize, awarded annually to institutions, organizations, or individuals who make outstanding contributions in the fight against illiteracy.

If King Sejong were alive today, he'd no doubt be grinning from ear to ear, proud to see his people communicating freely through the alphabet he invented. Of course, someone would probably have to explain to him what a smartphone is first.

UNESCO KING SEJONG LITERACY PRIZE

an annual prize awarded to two institutions, organizations or individuals "for their contribution to the fight against illiteracy."

Story of King Sejong The Great and Hangul Creastion

Bburigipeun Namu 뿌리깊은 나무
(*Deep Rooted Tree*, 2011, SBS)

Who Are The People On The Korean Currency Notes? P. 199

Any *Civilization* fans?

King Sejong the Great, sitting on the Phoenix Throne at Gyeongbokgung Palace is the leader of the Koreans in *Sid Meier's Civilization V*!

THEN CAN KOREANS UNDERSTAND CHINESE, JAPANESE, AND VICE VERSA?

Having learned about the role of Chinese characters as the written lingua franca of Asia, you might assume that Koreans, Chinese, and Japanese people can communicate freely since they all adopted Chinese characters and share a large vocabulary derived from them. So, if you managed to order dim sum at a Chinese restaurant in Seoul, shouldn't you be able to do the same in Tokyo and Beijing?

The answer is: *partially yes, and partially no*. On the one hand, communication is sometimes possible through written Chinese characters, since they are ideograms that represent meaning (much like pictures). For example, a Korean traveler in China or Japan could write the character 水 (**"water"**) and easily get a glass of water at a restaurant.

But here's why it's only "partially yes." The **spoken** forms diverge due to grammar and pronunciation differences (even though Korean and Japanese share similar grammatical structures). For every Chinese character, there are two ways to read it in Korean: *hundok* (훈독, the native Korean reading) and *umdok* (음독, the Sino-Korean reading). Take 水 again: in Korean, it's pronounced *su* (수, *umdok*) or *mul* (물, *hundok*). In Mandarin Chinese, it's shuǐ, and in Japanese, it's *sui* (すい, *umdok*) or mizu (みず, *hundok*). With such variations, spoken communication quickly breaks down, even if the written character is mutually recognizable.

So, back to dim sum—if you want to try your favorite dish across three cities, you'll need to either (1) carry a flashcard with the Chinese characters (though this may confuse a Korean server, since hanja isn't commonly used anymore), or (2) be adventurous and learn the local terms. Just be prepared—you might end up with something unexpected (like chicken feet) if you get it wrong.

BUT I SEE KOREANS SPEAKING FLUENT JAPANESE IN MOVIES. HOW IS THIS POSSIBLE?

If you're a fan of historical Korean dramas set during the turbulent Late Joseon period or the Japanese Occupation (1910–1945)—titles like *Mr. Sunshine* (tvN, 2018), *The Age of Shadows* 밀정 (2016), or *Assassination* 암살 (2015)—you might have noticed that Koreans seem to switch effortlessly into Japanese. This can give the impression that Koreans are naturally bilingual or that the two languages are interchangeable.

The reason for the bilingual fluency of the Korean characters in the movies is due to the historical fact where the Japanese Imperialists obligated the Koreans to learn their language in school and even have their native Korean names converted to Japanese style during the **Japanese Occupation (1910-1945)**. Even today, there is a significant portion in the Korean population, especially those born during the time of Occupation, who are still able to carry out a conversation in Japanese – something that's been deeply ingrained in them.

But fast forward to present day Korea - only those who choose to learn it know how to speak Japanese, and Koreans are much more likely to know English than Japanese, as it is part of the school curriculum. Korean and Japanese are two distinctive languages, both spoken and written, and it's not possible to communicate directly without the help of a dictionary or a translator. For an average Korean, however, the Japanese language is probably the easiest foreign language to learn, thanks to the similarities found in their grammatical structure (syntax and morphology) and pronunciation.

Japanese Occupation - Sad History P. 212

Miljeong 밀정
(*The Age of Shadows*, 2016)

Amsal 암살
(*Assassination*, 2015)

Mr. Sunshine (tvN, 2018)

However, the sad history made an impact on the Korean language which still lingers on – a considerable amount of Japanese vocabulary and expressions (labeled "the vestiges of Japanese Imperialism" by Korean people) have become part of the Korean language, and they are still being used today unbeknownst to the Korean people's knowledge. But ironically, they help Koreans learn Japanese with relative ease (no need to memorize a new word!).

WHY DO K-POP GROUPS ALSO RELEASE ALBUMS IN JAPANESE?

Going to an ice cream parlor is exciting because of the variety—you get to choose from a wide range of flavors, and if you want, you can enjoy several at once. That's kind of what many K-pop groups do too: they often come in two flavors—Korean and Japanese. This naturally raises a question that K-pop fans around the world often ask: *Why do K-pop groups also release albums in Japanese?* We've already covered the historical relationship between Korean and Japanese, and we know that Koreans don't actually have a magical "language switch" they can flip on and off. So the answer isn't about linguistic convenience—it's about audience, culture, and market strategy. If we look at the matter from a business perspective, the answer is pretty obvious. With just over 51 million people, South Korea isn't a huge market compared to China (1.4 billion) and Japan (126 million). That's why many K-pop groups aim to expand their popularity beyond their home turf. On paper, China looks like the ultimate prize—imagine how much money you'd make if everyone there bought something as trivial as a toothpick!

But there's a catch: Mandarin Chinese isn't a language Koreans can pick up overnight. Japan, on the other hand, is a different story. Although the two countries have had a historically rocky political relationship (like cats and dogs), cultural exchange has remained strong. Add to that Japan's close proximity—just a short flight away—and the relative ease (compared to Mandarin, at least) of learning Japanese, and you've got a market that's both accessible and lucrative.

For K-pop groups looking to grow their revenue streams, Japan is the natural first step abroad. And seasoned idols know that promotions, advertising, and fan connections work far better when done in the local language—albums included. Plus, success in Japan, the world's second-largest music market, often brings even more global attention. So that's why K-pop albums often come in two flavors, Korean and Japanese. For fans, that's double the music to enjoy—though it might also mean double the spending!

What Is Hallyu (Korean Wave)? P. 252

kimchi

THE KOREAN SOUL FOOD

history of kimchi

What comes to mind when you think about Korean food? For most people, *kimchi* would rank right at the top of the list. This tangy, spicy fermented side dish isn't just food—it's an inseparable part of Korean identity (heck, it even has "Kim" in the name). According to research tracing its origins, kimchi's story goes back as far as the Three Kingdoms period (57 BC–668 AD), when it existed in a primitive form as simple pickled vegetables made for long-term storage. Back then, it was called *ji* (지), meaning "pickled." In the early **Joseon Dynasty (1392–1897)**, the dish took on new names—*chimchae* (침채) and *timchae* (팀채), both literally meaning "submerging vegetables (under saltwater)." Later, the word shifted to *dimchae* (딤채), before evolving through palatalization into *kimchae* (김채). Eventually, it settled into the form we know today: *kimchi*. (Here's to you, Charles Darwin!)

KIMCHI USED TO BE WHITE

Now, what color comes to mind when you think of kimchi? If you said red (who wouldn't?), it's probably because the types we encounter most often are the fiery *baechu* 배추 (commonly called "kimchi cabbage" today, though once known as Napa cabbage) kimchi and the crunchy *kkakdugi* 깍두기 (cubed radish kimchi). Their signature crimson hue comes from *gochugaru* 고춧가루 (chili powder), which is used generously in the seasoning.

But here's the twist—kimchi wasn't always this bold shade of red. In fact, chili peppers didn't arrive on the Korean peninsula until the late 16th or early 17th century. The most widely accepted theory is that they were introduced by the Japanese during their failed invasions between 1592 and 1598. For nearly 200 years, however, chili was considered toxic and stayed out of kitchens. It wasn't until the early 19th century that Koreans began embracing it as a staple seasoning. With the invention of *tongbaechu* 통배추 (whole cabbage) kimchi in the early 1900s, kimchi finally began to resemble the vibrant, spicy version we know today. Until then, *mu* 무 (radish) was the most popular main ingredient.

THERE IS EVEN A MUSEUM FOR KIMCHI

Established in 1986 with the mission of "displaying diverse aspects and stories of kimchi and enabling visitors to feel, experience, and enjoy it," the **Kimchikan Museum** (김치간) has enhanced its reputation as a prestigious institution promoting kimchi worldwide. In fact, CNN once selected it as "One of the World's 11 Best Food Museums." The museum consists of a media room, a souvenir shop, and special exhibition halls. Among its offerings, the kimchi-making experience program stands out as especially fun. Imagine—wouldn't the world be a much better place if people of all ages and backgrounds could come together to make kimchi while singing kumbaya?
(Visit *www.kimchikan.com* for more information.)

HOW MANY KIMCHI VARIETIES ARE THERE?

According to research, kimchi can be categorized based on (1) main ingredients, (2) form, and (3) supplementary ingredients. There are more than 200 varieties, and it's fascinating how regional kimchi reflects the characteristics of each area. For example, on Jeju Island, kimchi made with abalone has long been a local specialty, while in **Jeolla Province**, residents prepare kimchi with chili, ginger, and *yuja* (citron)—ingredients abundant in the region. Now imagine: if the King of Korea ordered you to make kimchi using ingredients unique to your hometown, what would it be like?

CAN KIMCHI REALLY STOP A PANDEMIC AND SAVE MANKIND?

When SARS (Severe Acute Respiratory Syndrome) and H5N1 Bird Flu swept across Asia—killing more than 700 people—many wondered how South Korea managed to remain largely unaffected (with only a handful of minor cases reported). Some speculated that kimchi might be the secret. The theory gained traction after the BBC reported on research by Korean scientists who fed kimchi extract to 13 infected chickens (ugh, I know… but as the Korean proverb goes, "bitter to the mouth, better for your health"). Astonishingly, 11 of the chickens recovered. The researchers themselves, however, admitted the results were not scientifically conclusive. While the link between kimchi and pandemic prevention remained murky, the winners were clear: domestic consumption surged, and sales of kimchi at Korean restaurants in China skyrocketed. (On a side note: Japan, not a major consumer of kimchi, fared just as well as Korea—so you be the judge.)

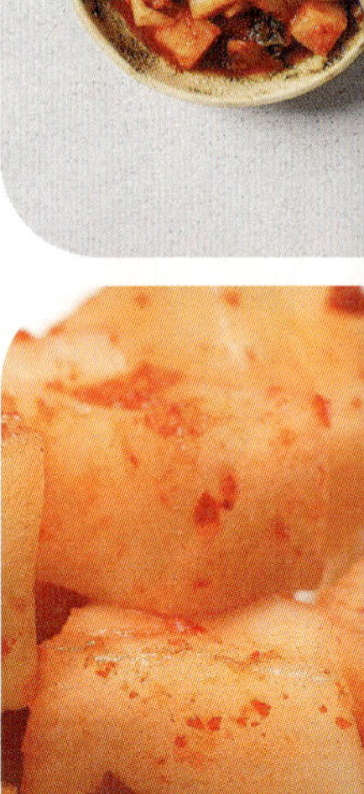

KIMCHI – CHOSEN AS '5 HEALTHIEST FOODS' BY HEALTH MAGAZINE BUT TOO MUCH OF A GOOD THING CAN MAKE YOU SICK!

In March 2006, Koreans' kimchi pride soared once again when Health magazine named it one of the world's five healthiest foods, alongside yogurt, lentils, olive oil, and soy. Kimchi was praised for its abundance of dietary fiber and vitamins A, B, and C, as well as its supply of lactobacilli (a.k.a. "good bacteria") known to aid digestion. To top it off, recent studies suggest it may even help prevent the growth of cancer.

But before you rush to crack open another jar—there's a flip side. Excessive consumption of kimchi has been linked to negative health effects, including a higher risk of gastric cancer, the most common type of cancer in Korea. The takeaway? Enjoy kimchi, but don't overindulge. As with anything, too much of a good thing can make you sick.

KIMCHI IS NOT A MEAL

But if you're the adventurous (or reckless) type and insist on overindulging in kimchi, here's another reason to reconsider—**KIMCHI IS NOT A MEAL**. I repeat: **KIMCHI IS NOT A MEAL**. Nobody in Korea eats it alone; it would be like having dill pickles as a full meal. Instead, kimchi is one of the many **banchan** 반찬 (side dishes) served alongside rice and soup in a typical **hansik** 한식 (Korean meal). This misconception has been reinforced by the Korean government's tireless efforts to promote kimchi as a representative Korean food—one of their favorite tactics is filming groups of foreigners trying kimchi and exclaiming "delicious!" on camera. The best way to enjoy kimchi? As a flavorful companion to other Korean dishes, like *bulgogi* and *japchae*. Mmm!

KOREANS CONSUME THIS MUCH KIMCHI ANNUALLY

So how much kimchi do Korean people actually consume? On the dining table of a typical Korean family, kimchi has its own reserved "parking spot," as most people eat it with every meal—and doubling down on the dosage is not uncommon. For example, adding kimchi on top of a spoonful of *kimchi bokkeumbap* 김치볶음밥 (kimchi-fried rice), which already has kimchi as the main ingredient, is a very common practice (think of dipping a chocolate ice cream bar in chocolate syrup). According to statistics released in 2013, the average South Korean consumes about 48 pounds (22 kg) of kimchi annually. For comparison, that's 3 pounds more than a large weight plate at the gym. Interestingly, this number actually reflects a declining trend in kimchi consumption, mainly due to changes in eating habits. As Koreans become more health-conscious, adopting a low-sodium diet has become a new trend, and naturally, people started cutting down on kimchi, which is high in sodium. Additionally, younger people, whose taste buds are well accustomed to Western food, no longer see kimchi as their BFF (Best Friend Forever). But that doesn't mean kimchi will lose its throne—Koreans remain attached to it, both physically and mentally. Many Koreans, even younger generations who have been traveling overseas for an extended period without eating Korean food, experience a mysterious "*kimchi craving*" that urges them to find the nearest Korean restaurant. So how do Koreans tame this craving when they are away from home, especially in places with no Korean restaurants? The answer: they pretty much take it everywhere with them.

KOREANS TAKE KIMCHI WITH THEM EVERYWHERE, EVEN TO SPACE!

When I say everywhere, I mean EVERYWHERE! At the height of the Vietnam War in the 1960s, South Korean troops—fighting as U.S. allies—were homesick, miserable, and low in morale. **Park Chung-hee**, then President of South Korea, realized that an uninterrupted supply of kimchi could lift their spirits and restore their fighting valor. So he personally wrote a letter to Lyndon B. Johnson, then President of the U.S., explaining what kimchi meant to South Korean troops and how it was directly tied to their combat readiness. Johnson agreed, and a direct supply of canned kimchi was sent to the battlefield.

Fast forward five decades: Korea sent its very first astronaut, **Yi So-yeo**n, to space. And what did she bring along? "Space Kimchi"—a special low-calorie, vitamin-rich, bacteria-free version (the bacteria are essential for fermentation on Earth, but scientists feared cosmic rays might mutate them). Not only that, the pungent smell was reduced by one-third to one-half while keeping the flavor intact. It was the moment kimchi went global… well, universal, rather.

"2014 Seoul Kimchi Making & Sharing Festival" by Republic of Korea
© Koreanet / CC BY 2.0 (Flickr)

KIMJANG - A UNESCO INTANGIBLE CULTURAL HERITAGE

Among all the reasons Koreans feel emotionally attached to kimchi, the biggest must be *kimjang* 김장—the tradition of making and sharing large quantities of kimchi to ensure every household has enough to last through the winter. Kimchi is a crucial source of nutrition during the cold months when food is scarce. Kimjang usually takes place between late November and early December, when the average daily temperature stays below 4°C (39°F) and nighttime lows dip below 0°C (32°F). If it's too warm, kimchi ferments too quickly; if too cold, it can freeze or turn sour. This labor-intensive practice brings Koreans together, involving families, relatives, and entire communities. Participants share in washing, salting, and seasoning the vegetables, and once the kimchi is ready, it is stored in earthenware jars buried in the ground up to the neck level to prevent freezing. In the end, kimjang is more than food preparation—it is a collective ritual that strengthens Korean identity, teaches the importance of sharing, and fosters harmony with nature. This is why **UNESCO** recognized kimjang as an **intangible cultural heritage** in 2013.

KIMCHI IS SCIENCE
KIMCHI REFRIGERATOR

Dimchae by Winia

Inheriting the cherished kimjang culture we've just explored, the "**Kimchi Refrigerator**" has become a staple appliance in Korean households today. That's right—a refrigerator made just for kimchi! At first, having a dedicated kimchi fridge in addition to a regular kitchen refrigerator might seem excessive, but once you see the science behind it, you can't help but nod in agreement. Its functions go far beyond simply keeping kimchi cool to prevent spoilage. It is a sophisticated machine carefully designed to emulate the optimal environment for storing and fermenting kimchi. Kimchi refrigerators are programmed to meet the unique storage and fermentation needs of different types of kimchi by maintaining colder, more consistent temperatures, higher humidity, and minimal air movement compared to conventional fridges—eliminating the old practice of burying jars in the ground. In short, the kimchi refrigerator is a perfect example of how tradition can evolve hand in hand with technology. At this point, I think we can all agree: Koreans really have kimchi down to a science!

YUGYO

THE IDEOLOGY OF
THE KOREAN PEOPLE

Kim Deuk-sin's *nosangsowondo* "Roadside Petitioners" (also known as *bansangdo,* meaning "nobles and commoners") depicts
men and women earnestly petitioning officials, blocking the path to the government office.

FROM BOWING TO RECEIVING STUFF WITH TWO HANDS, WHY DO KOREANS DO WHAT THEY DO?

Are you a PC user or a Mac user? On the outside, computers look pretty much the same—they all have a motherboard, RAM, hard disk, keyboard, mouse, and so on. But what really makes them different is the inside: the software, or the operating system, that governs how the hardware functions and how the user experiences it. When it comes to human civilization, the same idea applies. While all people are made of the same "parts," what sets cultures apart is their national philosophy—an invisible operating system that guides values, behavior, and social order. In East Asia, the countries belonging to the so-called "**Sinosphere**" (or "**Chinese-character cultural sphere**") adopted **Confucianism**—*yugyo* (유교) in Korean—as their core philosophy. Developed by the Chinese thinker Confucius, these principles became more than just a moral code: they evolved into the backbone of entire societies, shaping politics, governance, law, philosophy, and daily conduct. In short, Confucianism was not merely a philosophy—it became a civilization in itself. One reason it was so widely adopted is that it emphasizes hierarchy, obedience, filial piety, and loyalty—exactly the qualities a centralized government would value to maintain order. Among these countries, Korea embraced yugyo more deeply than any other, introducing Confucian principles as early as the **Three Kingdoms period (57 BC–668 AD)** and elevating them to their highest influence during the Joseon Dynasty (1392–1897). For centuries, Koreans lived by these teachings, treating them as sacred.

Now that we've covered the background, let's dive into how this philosophy explains everyday Korean customs—because once you understand Confucianism, you'll gain a whole new level of insight into why Koreans do what they do.

What Is The Three Kingdoms Period? P. 183

SAMGANG ORYUN 삼강오륜 (THREE CARDINAL PRINCIPLES AND FIVE ETHICAL NORMS)

A *yugyo* term referring to the code of ethics and practices that must be observed between the king and subject, the parents and children, the husband and wife, the adults and children, and friends.

Three Cardinal Principles

1.*Gunwishingang* 군위신강 (君爲臣綱): Focuses on *chung* 충 (loyalty). It's fundamental for a subject to serve its king.

2.*Buwijagang* 부위자강 (父爲子綱): Focuses on *hyo* 효 (filial piety to parents). It's fundamental for a son to serve his father.

3.*Buwibugang* 부위부강 (夫爲婦綱): Focuses on *yeol* 열 (faithfulness to husband). It's fundamental for a wife to serve her husband.

Five Ethical Norms

1.*Bujayuchin* 부자유친 (父子有親): There should be intimacy between parents and son.

2.*Gunshinyueui* 군신유의 (君臣有義): There should be a sense of righteousness between the king and his subjects.

3.*Bubuyubyeol* 부부유별 (夫婦有別): There should be a distinction between husband and wife.

4.*Jangyuyuseo* 장유유서 j(長幼有序): There should be order between an adult and a child.

5.*Bunguyushin* 붕우유신(朋友有信): There should be faith between friends.

> The modernization efforts in the 19th century caused the existing yugyo order to collapse considerably because Korean reformists blamed the misinterpreted and often abused *yugyo* customs for falling behind other advanced countries, and saw them as a major hindrance to the growth of Korean society. Some of them are:

Strict Hierarchy: Difficult to question superiors means loss of opportunities for possible innovation/improvement and slower decision-making processes.

Looking Down On Commerce and Favoring Scholars: Disrespect for manual labor, commercial and materialistic activities slowed down the progress in the field of natural sciences.

Patriarchal Society: Gender inequality leading to limited career opportunities for women and an uneven balance of domestic responsibilities.

Preferring Family/Personal Ties Over Formal Legality: Nepotism, factionalism, regionalism lead to corruption.1 Collectivism: Prioritizing the interest of a group at the expense of an individual's.

Because of this, in modern-day Korea, yugyo can also carry a negative connotation, often associated with something old-fashioned or restrictive. However, just like an operating system that improves through constant updates and patches, Koreans have adapted. While discarding outdated elements, they have continued to maintain a society deeply influenced by the core values of yugyo—respect, hierarchy, and social harmony—by integrating them into modern life in more flexible, practical ways. Now, let's take a closer look at some of the unique customs Koreans still practice today that are rooted in yugyo!

남녀칠세부동석 Namnyeo Chilse Budokseok

"A Boy And A Girl Should Not Sit Together After the Age Of 7"

You're watching yet another Korean "time-slip" drama. This time, Seho, a boy from modern-day Korea, accidentally stumbles into a time portal while searching for a secluded spot to take a bathroom break in the forest. Hours later, he finds himself in the Joseon Dynasty. As he struggles to figure out a way back, he meets a beautiful girl about his age, and the two begin to develop feelings for each other. One day, Seho finally musters up the courage to hold her hand in the middle of a busy street market. But she quickly pulls her hand away and whispers nervously, "I was taught that a boy and a girl should not sit together after they have reached the age of seven!" The camera zooms in on Seho's face, now bright red with embarrassment. This cliché is based on the yugyo notion *namnyeoyubyeol* 남녀유별 男女有別 ("There should be a distinction between male and female") which dictates the differences in the duties, roles, and space between genders. Stemming from the idea is *namnyeo chilse budongseok* 남녀칠세부동석 男女七歲不同席 – "A boy and a girl should not sit together after they have reached the age of 7." Some argue that the original meaning was not about sitting together but about not sharing the same bed. Either way, the intent was the same: to reinforce gender roles and social order—not necessarily to create inequality, but to maintain a structured society where everyone had clear responsibilities. Fast forward to modern-day Korea, and the idea feels almost comical. Just turn on any K-drama and you'll see couples holding hands, hugging, or even kissing in public. While younger Koreans are comfortable with PDA (Public Displays of Affection), their parents' generation might still find it awkward and raise an eyebrow.

WHY DO KOREAN PEOPLE ASK FOR YOUR AGE AT THE FIRST ENCOUNTER?

If you're meeting someone for the first time in Korea, don't panic if the very first question you hear is about your age.

While straight-up asking someone's age might feel too personal—or even offensive—in many cultures, in Korea it serves an important social purpose. As we've already covered, yugyo-based society is deeply hierarchical, placing a strong emphasis on the senior person's responsibility to look after the junior, while the junior is expected to show respect and discipline in return.

That's why "How old are you?" isn't just small talk—it's the quickest way to figure out how to navigate the relationship. One of the biggest perks of hanging out with older Korean friends is that they'll often insist on paying for the meal. In return, you can show respect by doing small things like setting the utensils or filling up the water glasses (many casual Korean restaurants run on a "self-service" system where you set the table yourself).

Of course, there are always a few mischievous types who try to game the system by lying about their age to gain the upper hand in the relationship. But nine times out of ten, the truth slips out when they run into a mutual friend who happens to be the same age. Cue another classic K-drama moment.

WIIY DO I GET A YEAR, OR EVEN TWO YEARS OLDER WHEN I LAND ON KOREAN SOIL?

And no, the sliding door you just passed through at Incheon International Airport wasn't a time-travel portal. The explanation isn't sci-fi at all—it's math (well, Korean math). Brace yourself, because there are actually **three different age-counting systems** in Korea.

First batter up! It's called *man-nai* 만나이 (*man* means "full" and *nai* means "age"). As you might guess, you only get older after a full year has passed since your last birthday—just like in most countries. This is what we'll call the "**International Age.**"

Next is *seneun-nai* 세는 나이 (*seneun* means "counting" and *nai* "means "age"), so it literally means "counting/counted age." Here's how it works: you're already 1 year old the moment you're born, and you add a year every New Year's Day, regardless of when your actual birthday is. So if you were born in December, by January you're suddenly 2 years old. This method is unique to Korea, which is why foreigners often call it the "**Korean Age.**"

Let's put this into perspective...

Suppose you were born on **December 31st, 2019.** The very first day of your life, you are

man nai – 0-year-old
seneun nai – 1-year-old (you're 1 year old as soon as you're born)

A day later, it's a new year. **On January 1st, 2020**, you are

man nai – still 0-year-old
seneun nai – 2-years-old (you get a year older with the year change)

On your first birthday, **December 31st, 2020**, you are

man nai – finally 1-year-old
seneun nai – still 2-years-old (birthdays don't add a year)

Again, with the year change a day later, on **January 1st, 2021**, you are

man nai – still 1-year-old
seneun nai – 3-years-old (you get a year older with the year change)

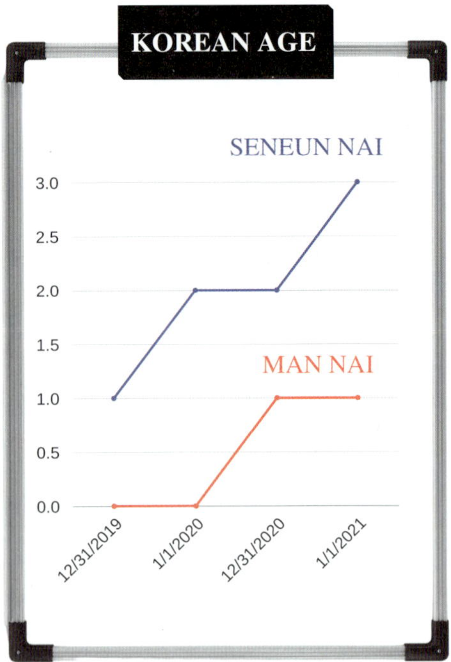

As you can see, two babies born on the exact same day can end up with an age difference of up to two years! Not exactly good news for anyone sensitive about their age. From a practical point of view, it's not even an advantage but rather a disadvantage—lumping a 1-month-old baby with an 11-month-old, or a 13-month-old with a 23-month-old, isn't fair when every single day makes a difference for infants.

So where did this practice come from? There are several theories about the origins of the "**Korean Age.**" Some say it reflects the ancestors' humanistic perspective, recognizing a fetus as a living being. Others argue that it simply stemmed from the lunar calendar system. While there's no definitive historical record, one thing is clear: this method wasn't unique to Korea. It was once widely used in many Asian countries, including China, Japan, Vietnam, and Mongolia, but today Korea is the only country where it still survives.

Here's the twist—legally, Korea only recognizes ***man-nai*** (the "**International Age**"). But because ***seneun-nai*** is so deeply ingrained in daily life, banning its use has proven nearly impossible. Back in 1962, when Korea switched from the traditional **Dangun Year** system (named after the legendary founder of **Gojoseon 고조선**, the first Korean kingdom) to the Gregorian calendar, the government ordered man-nai to be used exclusively. The result? People politely ignored it.

Alright, enough history—let's talk about the third system. Called ***yeon-nai*** (연나이, "**Year Age**"), this one simply subtracts your birth year from the current year. It's the standard used in certain laws, such as the **Juvenile Protection Act and the Military Service Act**. For example, no matter your actual birth date, if you were born in 2001, you became 19 years old on January 1, 2020. The appeal is convenience: by grouping everyone by birth year, it's easier to determine who qualifies for what. Compare this to the U.S., where ID checks hinge on the exact date of birth. In Korea, the moment your 18th year begins, you're good to go.

But unlike most cases where more options are better, having multiple age systems is… not. It leads to administrative errors, unnecessary social costs, and the everyday headache of figuring out which "age" someone is referring to. In short—***jjajeungna*** 짜증나 (annoying)!

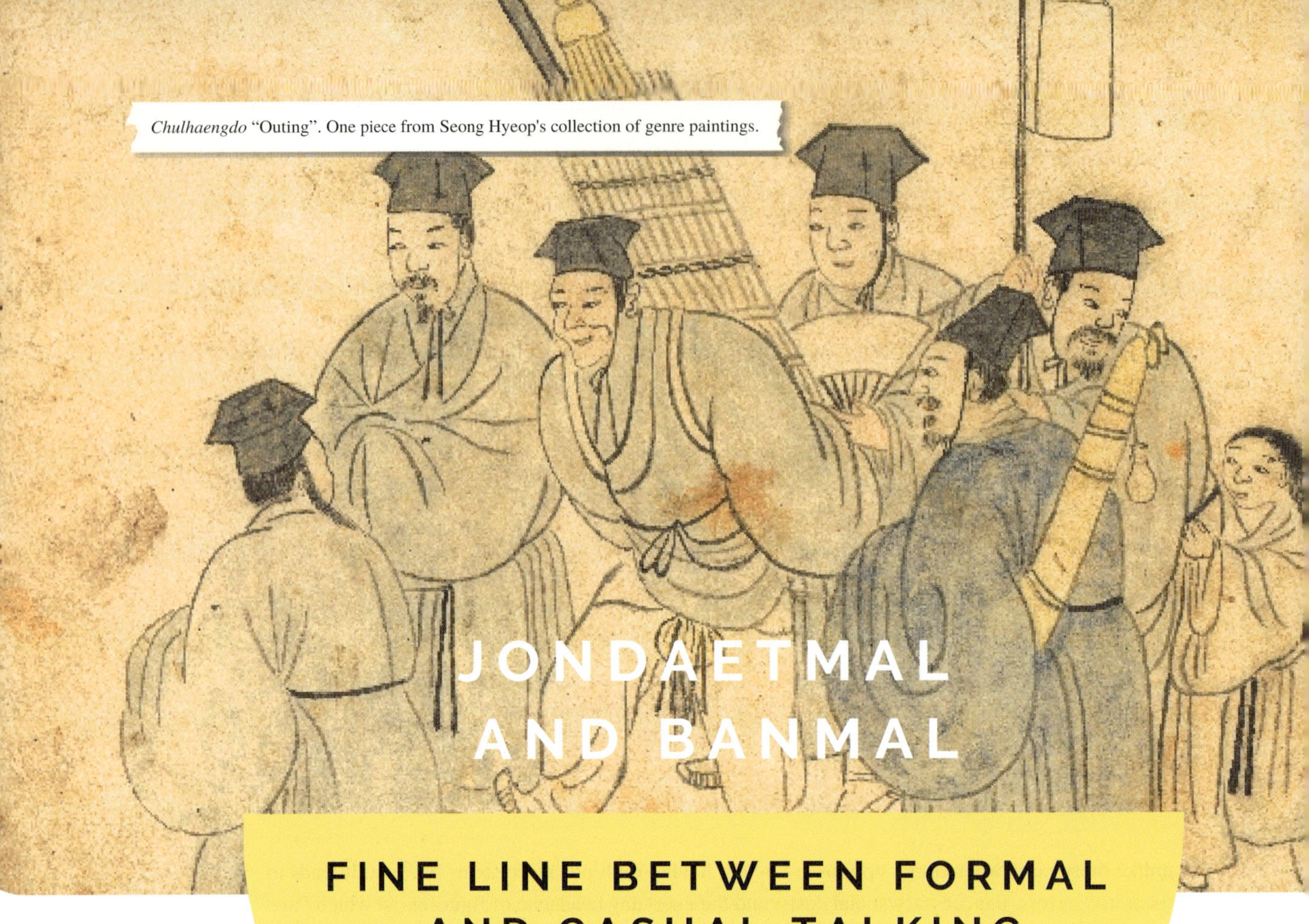

Chulhaengdo "Outing". One piece from Seong Hyeop's collection of genre paintings.

FINE LINE BETWEEN FORMAL AND CASUAL TALKING

We've just learned that age determines the relative hierarchy between people and how they interact with each other, but there's one more important factor to adjust—how they actually speak. If you've watched Korean dramas, you've probably noticed that Koreans use different forms of speech in different situations. But without cultural context, all the subtle nuances can get lost in translation, leaving you wondering: *"Why does the husband speak casually to his wife while she replies in a super formal way?"* or *"They all look about the same age, so why are some speaking formally while others aren't?"*

To begin with, there are two main types of speech. ***Jondaetmal* 존댓말** ("polite/formal speech"), which typically ends in *~yo, ~nida, ~kka*, is used when speaking to someone older, higher in rank, strangers, or anyone you aren't close to—even if you're the same age. It can also be used with someone much younger, like an elementary schooler, or much lower in rank, like an intern, if you wish to remain polite and respectful. Similar systems exist in other languages, such as tu vs. usted in Spanish or Japanese honorifics, but the Korean system is far more complex. It includes a myriad of honorifics to choose from, personal pronouns that get "upgraded" or "downgraded," and verb stems that change depending on who you're addressing. Even native speakers sometimes find it a puzzle.

On the other hand, ***banmal* 반말** ("informal/casual speech"), literally "half-speech," requires fewer words to convey the same message—for example: "May I please have a hot dog?" versus "Give me a hot dog." This is why Koreans sometimes say, *"Your speech is getting shorter,"* an indirect way of pointing out, *"Are you dropping formalities with me?"* Banmal is used with people younger than you, peers of the same age, those lower in rank, or anyone with whom you've built a sense of closeness and intimacy.

Now, pay attention to how I said it can be used—just because you're older or higher in rank doesn't automatically give you the right to drop jondaetmal. A person of character would first ask permission before switching to the informal banmal, so as not to offend the other party. Most of the time, the other person would gladly accept the request. Some think they have the right to skip this recommended due process and jump straight to banmal, but doing so can be seen as rude or even condescending, sometimes leading to conflicts. In other cases, Koreans are straightforward about when to drop formality—usually once they've developed enough closeness, or for convenience if they realize they're the same age. One might propose to "lower the speech" or *"drop the jondaetmal"* at that point.

Simply put, jondaetmal shows respect and politeness and creates a psychological barrier or social distance because of its restrictive feel, whereas banmal frees up the speaker, signaling friendliness and intimacy and bringing people closer. Noticing which form is used speaks volumes about a relationship, so pay close attention to any switches—they indicate a change in the underlying dynamic.

Let's look at a K-drama example. Youngho and Sumi work at the same company and feel an instant connection when they first meet. Not wanting to risk their professional careers, they stick to jondaetmal, keeping their distance. But the harder they try, the harder it gets. One night, Youngho, unable to contain his emotions, gets soaked in soju and shows up at Sumi's place. He surprises her by dropping the jondaetmal and speaking in banmal, telling her everything he feels and saying he wants them to be on a casual, banmal basis, just like any other couple. Sumi nods in acceptance—they are official.

Of course, it can work the other way too. Fast-forward to Youngho and Sumi's 10-year anniversary: instead of blowing out candles and drinking wine, they are standing in front of the divorce court in Seoul. They've grown apart and decided to separate. Youngho says, "Sumi… are you sure you want to do this?" and Sumi replies, "Of course, Mr. Kim, that's what we agreed on, isn't it?" Notice how Sumi reverts to jondaetmal—it signifies that she wants to keep a distance from him.

It's also interesting that social hierarchies are fully replicated and maintained through spoken language. Some critics argue this contributes to the generation gap in Korean society. Take Guus Hiddink, the Dutch football coach who led the Korean national team to the semi-finals during the 2002 FIFA World Cup. He noted that the strict hierarchy among players was stifling younger players' creativity. To fix this, he ordered everyone to "drop the jondaetmal" and call each other by their first names, putting everyone on equal footing. The move created an atmosphere of equality and solidarity—and it worked.

SOCIAL HIERARCHIES REPLICATED

What about family members? Many families allow children to speak in banmal to their parents, while others enforce a strict in-house rule requiring children to use jondaetmal. Typically, children start switching to jondaetmal as they grow up. Between husband and wife, the husband usually speaks to his wife in banmal, while the wife addresses him in jondaetmal—often because husbands are older. Of course, some couples choose to speak to each other entirely in jondaetmal, regardless of age difference. The options are flexible, and ultimately, it's up to you to decide how to navigate the speech levels in your household.

Why Do Korean People Prefer Addressing Someone by Their Title and Not Their Name?

In Korean workplace dramas like *Misaeng: Incomplete Life* 미생 (2014, tvN), everyone addresses each other using their titles—김 **과장** (Kim *Gwajang*, Section Manager Kim), 최 **부장** (Choi *Bujang*, General Manager Choi)—instead of their names. Is this a corporation's cunning plan to stifle individuality? If so, the TV series might have been a thriller rather than a drama.

Along with jondaetmal and banmal, appellations are another way Koreans maintain social hierarchies in spoken language. In the traditional Confucian (yugyo-based) Korean society, calling someone by their given name was considered impolite; a younger person addressing an older person by name was a major taboo. Older people, in turn, showed respect to younger adult males by using *jane* 자네 (a formal form of "you").

Many adult males, especially scholars, also had a *ho* 호, a pen name or alias used instead of their given name. For women, *daek* 댁 (a suffix indicating a married woman from a particular region) or *buin* 부인 (a suffix indicating the family she married into) was used. You may have noticed in Korean dramas that people often call each other familial terms —*hyung* 형 (older brother), *nuna* 누나 (older sister), *samchon* 삼촌 (uncle), *imo* 이모 (aunt)—even when they aren't related. This isn't literal; it's simply a way Koreans show affection and build rapport.

This tradition has persisted over time, and titles continue to serve an important role for Koreans who need to quickly assess and situate the people they meet. In the era of globalization, some companies have even adopted an "English-name-for-everyone" policy to transform the hierarchical vertical corporate culture into a horizontal corporate culture. You'll encounter these titles frequently in Korean dramas, and a handy table summarizing the most common appellations appears on the next page.

korean appellations

OO 엄마 EOMMA

E. Seho eomma
L. Seho's Mom
C. Mrs.
U. Between Neighbors

OO 아빠 APPA

E. Rina appa
L. Rina's Dad
C. Mr.
U. Between Neighbors

OO 댁 DAEK

E. Busan daek
L. Married woman who comes from Busan
C. Mrs.
U. Between Neighbors

OO 부인 BUIN

E. Kim-ssi buin
L. Wife of Kim Family
C. Mrs.
U. Between Neighbors

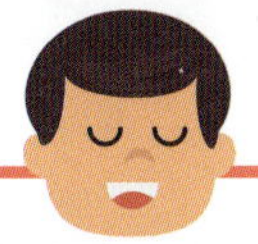

사장님 SAJANGNIM

E. KIM sajangnim
L. President/Owner
C. Mr. / Sir
U. To customer/client

어르신 EOREUSHIN

E. eoreushin
L. Elder
C. Sir
U. To a senior citizen

이모님 IMONIM

E. imonim
L. aunt
C. Ma'am
U. To summon a waitress at a restaurant

선생님 SEONSAENGNIM

E. KIM seonsaengnim
L. Teacher
C. Mr. / Sir
U. To someone older / Client

어머님/아버님 EOMONIM/ABEONIM

E. eomonim/abeonim
L. Mother/Father
C. Ma'am/Sir
U. To woman/man around your mom/dad's age / Your friend's mom/dad

형 HYUNG

E. Seho hyung
L. Older brother (M2M)
C. Brother
U. Older male friend

누나 NUNA

E. Rina nuna
L. Older sister (M2F)
C. Sister
U. Older female friend

아저씨 AJEOSSI

E. ajeossi
L. Middle-aged man
C. Mr.
U. To a male not close

아줌마 AJUMMA

E. ajumma
L. Middle-aged woman
C. Mrs.
U. To a female not close

오빠 OPPA

E. Seho oppa
L. Older brother (F2M)
C. Brother
U. Younger female friend

언니 EONNI

E. Rina eonni
L. Older sister (F2F)
C. Sister
U. Younger female friend

A genre painting depicting a noble family celebrating a holiday during the Joseon Dynasty (artist unknown)

WHAT DOES A KOREAN FAMILY LOOK LIKE?

No matter where you live, home is where the drama unfolds—and in Korea, it's also where many K-Dramas take root! While families everywhere share similarities, certain aspects of Korean family life are uniquely shaped by culture and history. Understanding what a traditional Korean family looks like—and how it functions—will help explain some of those K-Drama moments that may have left you scratching your head.

FAMILY STRUCTURE

Traditionally (during the Joseon Dynasty), the Korean family followed a patrilocal stem family system. This meant multiple generations often lived together under one roof—grandparents, their eldest son and his wife, and that couple's children. Since Korea was an agricultural society requiring a large labor force, big families with many children were not only common but essential for survival.

WHO WEARS THE PANTS IN THE KOREAN FAMILY?

The answer, traditionally, was simple: the men—ranked in descending order of age. This hierarchy stemmed from a strictly patriarchal system built on two major principles: men held authority over women, and elders held authority over the younger. Because only male children could continue the family line, sons were especially valued. Couples without a son often kept trying until they had one—leading to families with five, six, or even seven daughters before finally celebrating the birth of a youngest son.

Among the male children, the eldest son, *jangnam* (장남), was regarded as the major pillar of the family and received preferential treatment. He could inherit most, if not all, of the family estates and had the biggest voice in decision-making — a classic K-drama cliché where younger brothers complain to the old-fashioned father about unfair distribution, saying, *"Is jangnam the only son you have?"* But with great perks came great responsibilities. It was jangnam's duty to live with the parents after marriage, while younger sons were free to establish separate households. Moreover, jangnam was responsible for holding the *jesa* 제사 ceremony after his parents passed away. He was also expected to live near the parents' gravesite for quite some time following the funeral. In the case where there was no son, the grandson, *jangson* 장손, assumed the role of jangnam.

Up until the Goryeo Dynasty, women's status in the family was on par with men's. However, with the adoption of yugyo (Confucian) principles, their status declined significantly, with their roles mostly confined to the domestic sphere. This shift stemmed from the idea that there should be a strict distinction between male and female, which led to greater segregation against women. A key example of this is the doctrine of *samjongjido* 삼종지도, a Confucian moral code that defined the status and role of women in traditional society: *"Before marriage, a woman must obey her father; after marriage, her husband; and after her husband's death, her son."* This clearly illustrates women's restricted position during the Joseon Dynasty. Another example of gender inequality is that only the husband could legally divorce his wife. There were "seven valid vices" that served as grounds for divorce, known as *chilgeojiak* 칠거지악. These were: disobedience toward in-laws, inability to bear a son, adultery, jealousy, hereditary disease, talkativeness, and theft.

But there were exceptions — for example, if a wife had no family home to return to, if she stayed with her husband's family during the three-year mourning period for her parents-in-law, or if she had contributed to the family's rise from poverty to wealth, then divorce could be denied. Despite their lower status and limited roles, women were still regarded with reverence and respect within the household. As wives, they managed the family's finances and domestic affairs; as mothers, they oversaw the education and upbringing of their children. While daughters did not receive systematic yugyo (Confucian) education, their instruction focused on internalizing the virtues expected of women. At the same time, they learned practical household skills such as weaving from an early age. From childhood, boys and girls followed different educational paths, reflecting the gendered roles assigned to them in society.

Times have changed — and so has Korean society. What was once considered the unquestioned social norm is now often viewed as outdated. While many traditions, such as women's status in the family or the expectation to live near the parents' gravesite, have shifted dramatically, traces of yugyo ideas still linger in the lives of modern-day Koreans. For non-Korean viewers, this cultural residue can create confusion when watching K-dramas. But in a way, this imbalance offers an honest snapshot of a society in transition. Who knows — you might be witnessing a turning point in Korean history unfold before your very eyes!

JONGGA - THE HEAD HOUSE

Jongga 종가 refers to the head house of a clan, passed down exclusively through the eldest sons for generations. As the central household of the family line, the jongga bears the heavy responsibility of upholding strict traditions, maintaining discipline, and hosting important ancestral rites such as jesa (ancestral memorial ceremonies). While the burden is significant, the role is also a source of great pride, since the jongga symbolizes the continuity and authority of the clan. Because of this heritage, the jongga household often held the greatest influence within extended families and local communities. In modern Korean culture, the term has also taken on a broader meaning. It is often used to describe the "originator" of something. For instance, many restaurants promote themselves as the jongga of a particular dish, claiming to offer the "original recipe."

KOREAN ETIQUETTE BASICS

WHY DO KOREANS USE BOTH HANDS WHEN GIVING AND ACCEPTING THINGS?

Just like bowing, using both hands when giving or receiving something—even something as light as a piece of paper—to or from an older person or someone of higher status is considered a sign of respect. It's one of the very first manners Korean children are taught. How it's done varies depending on the situation. The most standard form is holding the item with both hands—this is the basic etiquette. But if the other person is a little farther away and you need to extend one arm to hand it over, you place your free hand under the wrist or elbow of the extended arm, as if supporting it. Another acceptable variation is placing the free hand lightly against your side, just below the armpit.

As for the origin of this very specific etiquette, some believe it comes from the traditional **hanbok** 한복, whose long, flowing sleeves often hung low. When pouring alcohol for someone, people had to hold the sleeve back so it wouldn't brush against the food. Over time, this habit evolved into the two-hand custom we see today.What about people your own age? If you're meeting for the first time, it's polite to use both hands. Once familiarity and closeness are established, however, it's perfectly fine to switch to using just one hand.

Hanbok - The Traditional Korean Clothes P. 154

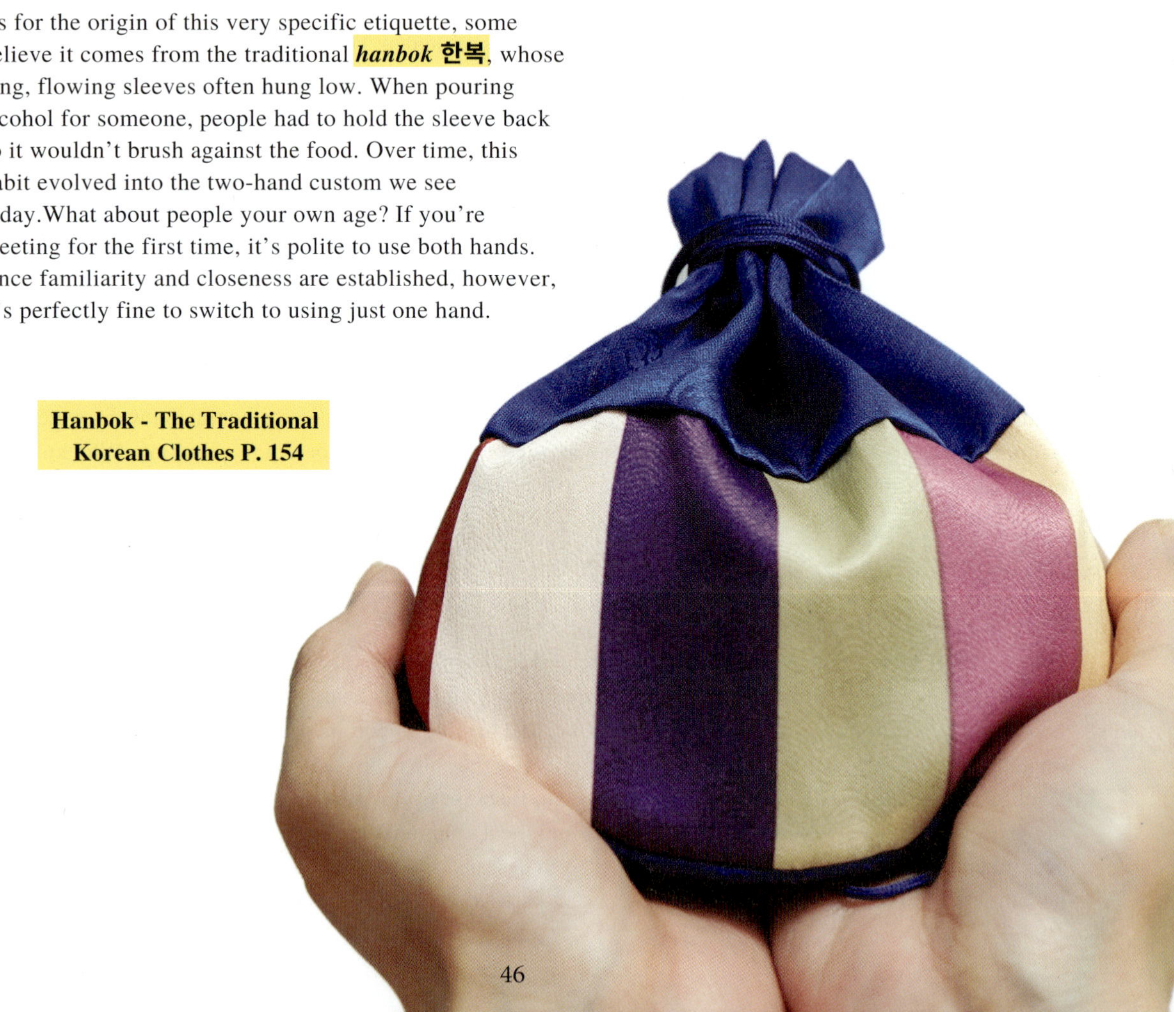

WHY DO KOREANS USE BOTH HANDS WHEN SHAKING HANDS?

This one is pretty self-explanatory and goes hand-in-hand (pun intended) with the topic we just covered. Use your right hand to shake, and place your left hand lightly under the wrist, elbow, belly, or even armpit of your right arm. Handshaking itself is a Western custom, and in the West, a one-hand shake is the standard. Koreans, however, added their own twist by incorporating both hands—and sometimes even combining it with a 90-degree bow. This is a good example of what scholars call cultural glocalization: blending a foreign practice with local customs.

DON'T PUT THE FEET UP ON FURNITURE OR SIT CROSS-LEGGED

Korean people find it rude and insincere because it looks disrespectful to the person you are having a conversation with. It's acceptable between friends.

DON'T TOUCH AN ELDER ON THE HEAD

Touching an elder's head—even if you're very close—is considered rude and should be avoided. The only acceptable context is between close friends of similar age.

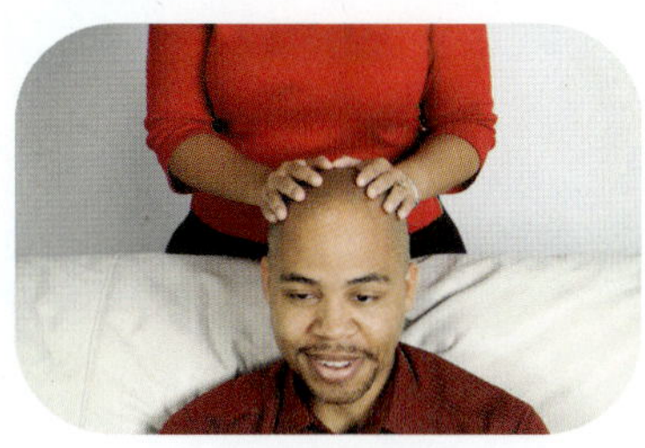

DON'T BECKON WITH PALM UP OR AN INDEX FINGER

The Korean gesture for "come here" is the opposite of the American style. Instead of palm-up beckoning with a finger, Koreans raise their hand to about head height, palm facing down, and wave the fingers in and out.

Never use just the index finger— it's considered insulting, as it is reserved for beckoning animals like dogs.

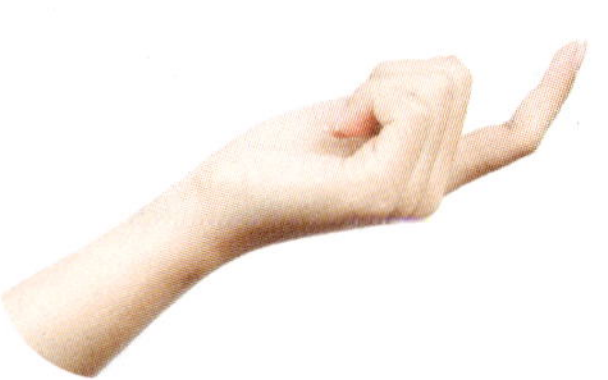

BUSINESS CARD ETIQUETTE

In Korea, business cards (*myeongham* 명함) are more than just contact details—they represent the person. For that reason, their exchange follows a precise etiquette:

- Giving and Receiving: Always use both hands. When giving, rotate your card so the receiver can read it immediately.
- Who Presents First?: Normally, the person of lower rank hands their card first. But if you're the visitor, it is polite to present your card first regardless of rank.
- When Receiving: Stand up (even if the other person is of lower rank), take the card with both hands, and avoid covering the name with your fingers. It is polite to quietly repeat the person's name and title to yourself.
- Afterward: Don't slip the card straight into your wallet or pocket. Instead, place it respectfully on the lower right corner of the table during your meeting, and only put it away when you leave.

THE ART OF BOWING

The fact that Koreans dominate Olympic archery proves they know how to handle a bow—but archery isn't the only kind of bow they excel at. Koreans are also masters of the many forms of *bowing*—from casual nods to belly-button bows, half-bows, and full prostrations. Let's explore them all!

Traditionally, every bow to an elder or in a formal ceremony begins with placing one hand over the other —left hand on top for men, right hand on top for women—and holding them below the waist.

This posture, called **gongsu** 공수, is also the default stance for showing politeness. Nowadays, however, many people simply keep their hands at their sides when bowing.

> **Koreans generally perform two main types of bows to express greeting, respect, apology, or gratitude: the standing bow and the sitting bow.**

Standing bows are used in everyday situations, while the more formal knees-to-the-ground sitting bows are reserved for special occasions such as traditional holidays, ceremonies, and *jesa* (ancestral rites). Because of the way traditional hanbok were designed, the form of the bow also differed for men and women.

경례
gyeongrye

STANDING BOW

The baekkop insa is a formal bow performed by service personnel, such as department store employees, when greeting customers. It is called the "belly-button bow" because the hands in *gongsu* position are placed politely at the level of the belly button.

반경례
ban gyeongrye
"Half-Bow"

Bend your waist
15 degrees

When returning a bow
Elder to a younger /
lower rank person /

평경례
pyeong gyeongrye
"Standard Bow"

Bend your waist
30 degrees

When greeting someone older
or higher in rank

큰경례
keun gyeongrye
"Big Bow"

Bend your waist 45 degrees

When you want to show
your utmost respect

의식경례
euisik gyeongrye
"90-Degree Bow"
"Folder Bow"

Bend your waist 90 degrees

Performed at ceremonies such
as a wedding and a memorial
ceremony

In Korean dramas, this bow is often exaggerated for comedic or dramatic effect—commonly by gangsters or junior employees trying to impress or please a boss. It is also used in situations where someone is asking for forgiveness or showing deep respect.

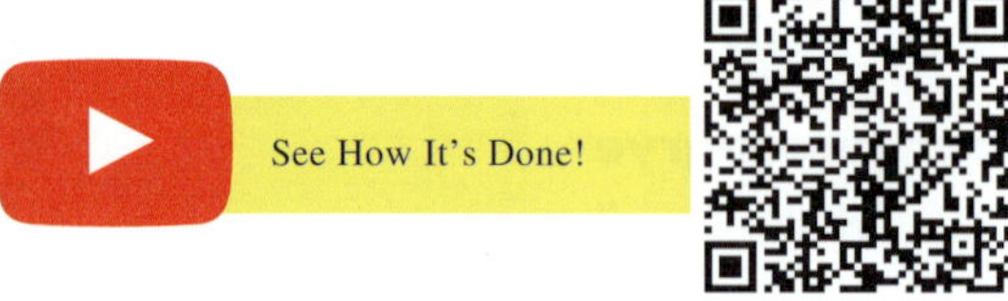

*For men, the left hand is placed over the right;
for women, the right hand is placed over the left.

큰절 keunnjeol "Full/Big Bow"

Most formal and polite.

To whom: Elders who don't have to reciprocate when they take a bow. Husband's lineal ascendants / Spouse's lineal ascendants / Collateral ascendants within the third cousins

When: Ceremonial events / New Year's Day / Ancestral rites / Seeing each other after a long time

평절 pyeongjeol "Standard Bow"

The standard bow. When greeting someone older or higher in rank. For males, it's performed in the same way as in a big bow, but you don't stretch out your *gongsu* hand at the beginning and you get up immediately when your forehead touches the back of your hand.

To whom: Someone who must bow back with the standard bow or the half-bow. Older adults, such as teachers, elders, superiors, spouses, older siblings, sisters-in-law / People of same age / Friends / If not related, and if the age difference is less than 15 years, they will bow to each other with the standard bow.

When: Seeing each other after a long time

반절 banjeol "Half-Bow"

Performed as a Return Bow to someone younger.

To whom: One's students / Friend's children / Children's adult friends / Younger siblings / Extended family members within 10 years of age difference

When: Upon taking a bow from a younger person

*If the younger person is a minor, then the older person can give a verbal greeting instead, but it's required to return a half-bow to an adult.

DON'T KOREANS MAKE EYE CONTACT?

Making eye contact is probably the most important aspect of interpersonal etiquette in Western culture, as it is a symbol of mutual respect and a way to build trust between people. For this reason, deliberately looking away or avoiding eye contact is considered rude or inappropriate, and could lead the other person to think that you are disinterested or insincere.

Meanwhile, in Korea, making direct eye contact can be perceived very differently. Especially in situations involving an older person and a younger person, the younger person tends to avoid direct eye contact, as it can be interpreted as hostile, defiant, or disrespectful. This is particularly true when an elder or higher-ranking person (e.g., a teacher) is scolding a younger or lower-ranking person (e.g., a student). If you look them directly in the eye while being scolded, you might hear:

"How dare you look me in the eye while I'm talking to you?" This is the opposite of Western expectations, where eye contact signals attentiveness and engagement. It's no surprise that this cultural difference is one of the most frequently discussed topics among Western English teachers in Korea, who often remark, "My students keep ignoring me when I scold them!"

You can also see the clash of cultures during drinking rituals. Watch closely – people from the West often maintain eye contact while clinking glasses (e.g., in Germany, breaking eye contact while raising your glass is believed to bring seven years of bad luck, and in Denmark, maintaining eye contact is considered a courtesy to the host). In contrast, Korean people usually focus on the glass itself rather than the person, reflecting a different cultural emphasis on respect and ritual over direct confrontation.

DOES A WILD ELDER ASK - "AIN'T YOU GOT NO PARENTS?"

"Ain't you got no parents?" is a cliché expression often used by angry elders when giving a lesson to an ill-mannered youngster. Like many idiomatic expressions, it shouldn't be taken literally – the elder is not actually interested in whether you have parents or how they are doing. Rather, it's a euphemistic way of saying,

"You're one rude son-of-a…!"

In Korean culture, proper character education is believed to start at home under the guidance of parents, and being disrespectful to elders goes against the yugyo principles that value reverence and obedience. Hence, the question indirectly asks whether the youngster has had the opportunity to learn manners and respect through proper upbringing.

WHY

IS SMOKING IN FRONT OF AN OLDER PERSON / HIGHER RANK FROWNED UPON?

Tajakdo "Threshing Rice" by Kim Hong-do

Before the late 17th century in the Joseon Dynasty, everyone could smoke freely without restrictions. However, as society became more patriarchal and hierarchical, it became necessary to distinguish smoking behaviors between social classes. Aristocrats used long smoking pipes as a status symbol, since owning such a pipe implied that a servant was available to light it. These pipes could be as long as 3 meters (10 ft), often made of precious materials and adorned with colorful decorations.

But appearances alone were not enough – strict rules and customs arose to maintain the class system and patriarchal authority, including:

- You can't smoke in front of your father or older brother, let alone elders."
- "It's rude to have your tobacco pipe visible when meeting elders on the street; you must hide it behind your back."
- "A woman shouldn't smoke in front of a man."
- "A commoner cannot smoke in front of a nobleman."

Although not legally enforced, these rules were passed down through social conventions and remain ingrained in Korean cultural etiquette.

ARE FEMALE SMOKERS FROWNED UPON?

One of Shin Yun-bok's album of genre paintings

Female smoking, especially in public, has long carried a social stigma in Korea and is still frowned upon in some contexts today. Initially, both men and women of all classes could smoke freely, but as patriarchy and hierarchy solidified, the noble class began regarding female smoking as vulgar, something only low-class commoners would do.

By the time Korea entered the modernization phase, which saw the collapse of the rigid class system, female smoking declined sharply, because doing so would imply low social status. This historical stigma explains why some older Koreans might still scold female smokers in public, exclaiming things like: "Only low-class commoner girls smoke!"

WHY ARE KOREANS THE SAME?

It's lunchtime at work, and the *bujangnim* 부장님 ("team manager") calls for a team lunch at a nearby Korean restaurant. Everyone's seated and ready to order, and the bujangnim starts off by saying, "All right, I think I will go with kimbap today! What do you all want, guys?" As if everyone had been craving kimbap all morning, they take turns saying, "I will go with kimbap, as well!"
On the surface, you might think Koreans are just a people of unity and teamwork! But underneath, it reflects the Korean tendency to conform to the norm. The proverb "an angular stone is bound to be hit by a chisel" (a nail that sticks out gets hammered) captures the Korean idea that values harmony and conformity, putting the group's interests before those of the individual. Good or bad? Like most things, it has its pros and cons.

On the positive side, it facilitates harmony and faster decision-making, but the downside is that it can stifle individuality and limit opportunities for innovation because it's difficult to "think outside the box." Some everyday examples are easy to spot on the streets of Korea:

- The "**long-padding craze**" that swept Korean teenagers—everyone wore similar long padded coats as if it were a school uniform.
- **Hairstyles that mimic popular TV drama characters**—once a series becomes a hit, the hairstyle is quickly adopted nationwide.
- The "**Honey Butter Chip craze**," where people lined up for days to get a newly introduced potato chip, and resale prices skyrocketed in a secondary market.

As you can see, Koreans love to feel part of a group. This sense of belonging gives them unity and security, and their effort to keep up with trends is part of that drive. While some see this conformity as a threat to individuality, companies have learned to capitalize on it.

Knowing that Koreans are among the trendiest early adopters in the world, many global corporations use Korea as a testbed for upcoming products, gauging their potential success. The logic is simple: if it becomes a hit in Korea, it's likely to succeed globally too.

WHAT IS
SAVING FACE?
KOREAN PSYCHOLOGY EXPLAINED

"Did you have to correct my mistake in front of my business partners? I totally lost my face today!"

"Thank you for talking me up to my girlfriend today. You really saved my face!"

The word "face" here is a conceptual representation of social standing, reputation, honor, influence, and dignity – known as **chemyeon** 체면 – and it is extremely important in Korean culture. As noted previously, Korean society is hierarchical, and social dynamics are determined by the relationships among members of a circle. Because of this, how one is perceived by others is crucial, and maintaining one's reputation in public is just as important as not making others lose face.

To navigate this, it's best to engage in indirect expressions when interacting with others. For example, when refusing or rejecting an offer, avoid saying a blunt "no" and instead find a polite, indirect way to express your thoughts. Similarly, when dealing with someone older or higher in rank, avoid direct confrontation even if they are clearly in the wrong – pointing out mistakes in private will be much more appreciated.

It's also important to allow elders to lead decision-making and honor their opinions when possible. For instance, if a senior insists on picking up the tab after a meal, letting them do so helps them "save face" because Korean society operates on unwritten rules of hierarchy, and letting a senior fulfill these expectations maintains harmony and respect.

JEONG 정

IS PROBABLY THE MOST MYSTERIOUS WORD IN KOREAN DRAMAS

KOREAN EMOTIONS EXPLAINED

Jeong 정 is probably the most mysterious word in Korean dramas because it gets translated differently every time it appears: "affection," "intimacy," "sharing," "generosity," "love," "emotional bond"… you name it. Because it spans such a wide spectrum of meanings, even advanced Korean language experts find it difficult to define, let alone explain to foreigners who may not fully understand the cultural context. As a result, jeong is often labeled a "cultural idiosyncrasy," introduced as something unique to Korea that can't be grasped unless you are Korean.

But is it really that mysterious? Let's follow the journey of Maria, an exchange student from Texas, as she experiences Korean *jeong* firsthand.

Day 1 in Korea – "I arrived at the boarding house in Seoul. The landlady, *ajumma* 아줌마, seemed very caring but also a little nosy. She asked personal questions like if I have a boyfriend, my birthday, blood type (creepy!), age, height, weight… things I would normally share only with a doctor. But I decided to look on the bright side and believe she was genuinely interested in me! She even told me to call her my 'Korean mom,' which I thought was an incredibly kind gesture. I almost cried. This must be the Korean *jeong* they're talking about."

Day 5 in Korea - I came home from school and opened the fridge… and what the heck? There were a bunch of Tupperware containers inside with different types of kimchi and other Korean foods, none of which were mine. I immediately thought someone broke into my room and considered calling the police. Then I reached out to the landlady, and she said, 'Oh, I put them in there for you! I make extra for everyone here. You should try them all!' Wait… so she just arbitrarily went into my room without my permission and put food in my fridge? I didn't know what to say, so I just thanked her. I spoke to another exchange student from Brazil, and she said, 'That's Korean jeong! You'll get used to it.' Alright… when in Seoul, do as the Seoulites do!"

Day 8 in Korea - "I stopped by my favorite *tteokbokki* 떡볶이 place for a quick lunch. The owner, *ajusshi* 아저씨, greeted me with a huge smile, as always. I ordered tteokbokki, and he also gave me a roll of *kimbap* 김밥, saying it was a 'service' (complimentary/on the house)! This must be the awesome Korean *jeong* again."

Day 9 in Korea - "I went to an evening class and sat next to my favorite Korean friend, Min-su. During the break, I took out a bag of BBQ-flavored potato chips and an energy bar I brought for dinner. I asked Min-su if he had already eaten, but he said he wasn't hungry. I finished my snacks just before the break ended, crinkled up the wrappers, and tossed them into the trash can. When I got back, Min-su exclaimed, 'Oh my god… you absolutely have no jeong! You didn't even offer me a bite…!' I was like… What? Sir, you said you weren't hungry…? Was I supposed to insist on sharing with him? This jeong thing really confuses me…!

After a long day of culture shock, I finally got home to chill and watch Netflix. I tuned into a Korean family drama that's all the rage these days. In the drama, an old couple constantly quarrels over the smallest things. The wife leaves the house in a huff, and her worried daughter runs after her. On a park bench, the daughter asks, 'Mom, why don't you just divorce him then? Don't worry about me, I just want you to be happy!' The mom replies, 'It's not because of you, sweetheart! It's because of this damn jeong…' Okay, so there's that jeong again, and this time it really came out of nowhere. I'm just way too tired to process all this… so I'm going to call it a night and go to sleep!"

Day 98 in Korea – "It's my birthday! I woke up to a call from the landlady *ajumma*, inviting me to breakfast with the other housemates. I went down in my jammies and was greeted by everyone shouting, 'Happy birthday, Maria!' Tears flooded my eyes. Natasha from Russia said, 'Ajumma remembers everything about us—for us! She's our Korean mom!' I remembered the first day I arrived, all the personal questions she asked… and she still remembered my birthday. She said, 'Don't cry, Maria, and have your birthday *miyeokguk* 미역국! This is what we eat on our birthday to celebrate and honor your mom.' I lifted my spoon and had my first miyeokguk in Korea, and this is something I had never experienced before. This… must be what Korean jeong tastes like."

That was quite a journey Maria had, wasn't it? I believe her experiences with jeong can help you grasp the concept. In the beginning, we briefly mentioned that some popular translations for jeong include "affection," "emotional attachment," "bond," and "generosity," and we can see that they all point in the same direction: humanistic values. But the real question is – are these uniquely Korean? Of course not. They are universal emotions that all humans possess, regardless of race or culture. What differs is how they are expressed – the style that's uniquely Korean, and that's called jeong. It's similar to how different cultures can create remarkably distinct dishes using the same universally available ingredients, but mixing them with their own cultural touch. Jeong is no different – it's the Korean interpretation of universal emotional "ingredients," blended with cultural elements like yugyo values, social hierarchy, collectivism, and the coexistence of traditionalism and modernism. And just like any ethnic dish, it can feel unusual at first. Jeong can be surprising – even off-putting – for many, especially those from highly individualistic cultures, due to the invasion of privacy, blurred boundaries, or perceived over-familiarity. But like an acquired taste, many come to appreciate it once they understand and choose to embrace the concept.

This jeong has been the glue that has kept the Korean people together throughout history, looking after each other and helping each other, often without being asked – *dure* 두레, a farmer's cooperative group during the Joseon Dynasty, is a prime example. The key idea here is acting proactively on one's own initiative to care for others, while expecting the same in return. A popular chocolate pie commercial catchphrase, "*malhaji anado alayo* 말하지 않아도 알아요 ("You don't have to say it for me to know it")," perfectly captures the essence of this ideology.

It's comforting to know that someone is looking out for you like family, but there is a downside – excessive attention and concern for others can feel burdensome, and many Koreans today find it less compatible with the modern emphasis on individualism rather than the agriculture-based, family-oriented society of the past. Reflecting this shift in sentiment, terms like *ojirap* 오지랖 ("nosy," "meddlesome," "intrusive") and the more recent *kkondae* 꼰대 ("fogey" or "Boomer," as in "OK, Boomer!") have become widely used.

So… what do you think? Showing love is important, but how you show it is even more important. Jeong can be something everyone enjoys if a proper balance is achieved – much like using *gochugaru* 고추가루 ("chili powder"), which adds a unique flavor to Korean dishes.

" HAN 한

ANOTHER TERM THAT GETS MENTIONED OFTEN AS A UNIQUELY-KOREAN EMOTION IS 한 HAN. "

Like *jeong*, it's difficult to find a perfect word-for-word translation, but it's usually described as "pent-up emotions" – a combination of resentment, regret, grief, longing, and sorrow that often arises from feeling powerless in one's struggles and suffering. (Some say the Portuguese *saudade* and the Russian тоска come close in meaning.) Note that han is different from *wonhan* 원한 ("grudge"), which focuses on revenge and retaliation.

While Korean pop culture and literature often portray *han* as a national trait embedded in the Korean people's DNA, some historians trace its roots to modern Korean history. Sandra So Hee Chi Kim writes, "[H]an did not exist in ancient Korea but was an idea anachronistically imposed on Koreans during the Japanese colonial period." Added to this was the fratricidal tragedy of the Korean War, and the shared suffering and struggle of the Korean people helped shape the notion of han.

In Korean dramas and literature, han is often associated with "not being able to achieve or obtain something one earnestly longed for or desired." For instance, older people who had to work to support their families and couldn't attend school may say that it's been their han all their life that they never had the chance to get an education.

On the other hand, critics of the idea that han defines Koreans argue that Koreans are actually the people of *heung* 흥 ("fun/joy"). Koreans are known for bringing energy, joy, and excitement wherever they go. Want to experience heung firsthand? Attend any sporting event, and you'll find yourself in what feels like a giant karaoke: everyone sings the cheering anthem and chants the players' names non-stop. With such overflowing energy, you might even start doubting whether "resentment, regret, grief, longing, and sorrow" truly exist in the Korean dictionary.

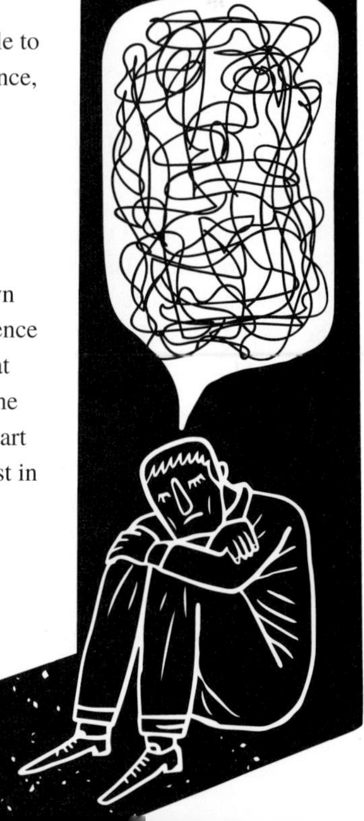

HANSIK

TRADITIONAL KOREAN CUISINE

WHY DO KOREAN RESTAURANTS GIVE YOU FREE SIDE DISHES?

"Hm, I don't think I ordered these…" If you take someone to a Korean restaurant for the first time, this is a common reaction. The assortment of colorful small side dishes is called **banchan 반찬**, and they are served along with the basic Korean table set-up, which includes rice, soup, kimchi, and *jang* (sauce), to complement the main dishes like **galbi 갈비**, **bulgogi 불고기**, or a stew. The banchan are complimentary (yay!) and are presented in the middle so they can be shared by everyone at the table. As for the origin, it's believed to have been influenced by Buddhism (as far back as the Three Kingdoms Era, 57 BC), which strictly encouraged vegetarianism. This gave birth to the vegetable side dishes that complement rice and soup. Depending on the number of banchan offered, the table setting with side dishes – or **bansang 반상** – is named accordingly: 3 (**sam cheop 첩**), 5 (**oh cheop**), 7 (**chil cheop**), 9 (**gu cheop**), or 12 (**shibi cheop**). According to history, Korean kings had five meals a day, two of which were 12-cheop **bansang**, given a special name: **surasang 수라상**, meaning "royal meal."

If you want to taste the essence of Korean banchan culture and feel like a Korean king, visit a **hanjeongsik 한정식** (Korean Table d'hôte) restaurant!

POPULAR KOREAN DISHES

YOU MUST TRY

Naengmyeon 냉면

Chilled Buckwheat Noodle

Yukgaejang 육개장

Spicy Beef Soup

Galbi Gui 갈비 구이

Grilled Beef Ribs

Tteokbokki 떡볶이

Stir-fried Rice Cake

Bibimbap 비빔밥

Rice Bowl With Meat & Veggies

Samgyetang 삼계탕

Ginseng Chicken Soup

Kimbap 김밥

Seaweed Rice Roll

Sundubu Jjigae 순두부찌개

Silky Tofu Stew

Samgyeopsal Gui 삼겹살 구이

Grilled Pork Belly Slices

Sundae 순대

Stir-fried Korean Sausage

Bulgogi Gui 불고기 구이

Grilled Marinated Beef With Vegetables

Pajeon 파전

Green Onion Pancake

Japchae 잡채

Stir-fried Glass Noodles & Vegetables

Bossam 보쌈

Boiled Pork Wrap

Jeyukbokkeum 제육볶음

Stir-fried Marinated Pork

How do you beat the heat of a scorching summer day? A can of ice-cold beer or a scoop of ice cream (with a brain freeze!) might sound like the obvious choice, but Koreans have a very different strategy. Instead of taking the "cool road," they choose to fight heat with heat — by eating *samgyetang* 삼계탕, a simmering hot ginseng chicken soup. Samgyetang is a type of *boyangsik* 보양식, meaning "restorative food" or "health food," that Koreans eat to boost stamina and energy. And they enjoy it on the hottest days of the year, known as *boknal* 복날 — the "dog days of summer."

WHAT IS BOKNAL?
THE "KOREAN DOG DAYS OF SUMMER"

Boknal consists of three distinct days, called *sambok* 삼복 ("three bok days"): *chobok* 초복 ("first bok day"), *jungbok* 중복 ("middle bok day"), and *malbok* 말복 ("last bok day"). These days fall between mid-July and mid-August, spaced roughly ten and twenty days apart. Interestingly, the term fits perfectly with "dog days," because the Chinese character for *bok* 伏 depicts a dog lying on its stomach — perhaps exhausted from the summer heat!

Iyeol Chiyeol - "Fighting Fire with Fire"

The logic behind this seemingly counterintuitive tradition, called *iyeolchiyeol* 이열치열 ("control heat with heat," or "fight fire with fire"), lies in the philosophy of maintaining balance within the body. According to traditional Korean medicine (*haneuihak* 한의학), the body's heat during summer is concentrated near the skin, leaving the internal organs relatively cool. Eating cold food may bring temporary relief but ultimately worsens this imbalance. Instead, a steaming bowl of samgyetang restores equilibrium and replenishes the body with essential nutrients.By the time you finish your soup — drenched in sweat — you'll know you've truly conquered the Korean summer!

보양식 BOYANGSIK "HEALTH FOOD"

Chueotang 추어탕
Loach Soup

Jeonbokjuk 전복죽
Abalone Rice Porridge

Nakji Bokkeum 낙지볶음
Stir-fried Octopus

Jangeo Gui 장어 구이
Grilled Eel

Dakjuk 닭죽
Chicken Rice Porridge

JANG - KOREAN SAUCE AND SOUP BASE

Jang 장, the Korean sauce and paste (and a popular last name) is the staple of Korean cuisine. As a sauce, it nicely compliments other food such as vegetables and raw fish, and as a paste, it becomes the base of numerous Korean soups and casseroles, including *doenjangguk* 된장국 ("bean paste soup") and *kimchijjigae* 김치찌개 ("*kimchi* casserole"). Traditionally, this versatile ingredient comes in 4 different types.

Ganjang 간장 - soy sauce

Makganjang 막간장- Common soy sauce made by dipping *meju* 메주, bricks of fermented soybeans.

Gyeopjang 겹장 – Thick, aged soy sauce made by mixing soy sauce with *meju.*

Eoganjang 어간장 - Soy sauce made from fish which is fermented for more than a year with salt.

Doenjang 된장 - bean paste

Tojang 토장 - Made by mashing the *meju* that's not been used for making *ganjang.*

Makdoenjang 막된장 – Made by mixing *meju* after using it for making soy sauce with salt, barley rice, and chili powder.

Cheonggukjang 청국장 - fermented bean paste

Cheonggukjang 청국장 - Made by crushing the salted boiled beans that were fermented for 2-3 days.

Dambukjang 담북장 – Made by adding minced radish and ginger to *cheonggukjang.*

- The fundamental difference between *cheonggukjang* and soybean paste lies in the fermentation period and the salt content.

Gochujang 고추장 - made with red pepper powder, glutinous rice, meju powder, malt, and salt

Chogochujang 초고추장 – Made by mixing *gochujang* with vinegar. Popularly used as a dressing for *hoedeopbap* 회덮밥 ("rice bowl with raw fish") and a dipping sauce for raw fish.

Ssamjang 쌈장 – Spicy paste made by mixing *gochujang* and *doenjang*, along with sesame oil, garlic, scallions, and onion. Used when eating *ssam* 쌈 – food wrapped in a leaf.

Meju 메주 - A brick of dried fermented soybeans that serve as the basis of Korean *jang*. It's made by crushing, pounding, and kneading the cooked soybeans into a brick shape, which then goes through the fermentation process. Colloquially, maybe because of its bumpy and rough texture, meju is used as a metaphor for an ugly person.

WHY DO KOREANS EAT DOGS?

It wasn't until quite recently that *samgyetang* 삼계탕 became synonymous with "health food." For centuries, there had been an undisputed king of stamina-boosting dishes — *boshintang* 보신탕. This soup, made with dog meat as its main ingredient, was long believed to provide rich nutrients to heat-weary Koreans and promote stamina — as its name literally means "invigorating soup." The original name, *gaejangguk* 개장국 ("dog soup"), was later replaced by boshintang, a more euphemistic term. In flavor and preparation, it closely resembles *yukgaejang* 육개장, a spicy beef soup made with shredded meat, scallions, fernbrake, onions, and *gochugaru* 고춧가루 (chili powder).

However, with the arrival of global attention during events like the 1988 Seoul Summer Olympics, growing voices urged Korea to align its food culture with "global standards," spurred largely by criticism from Western media. In response, boshintang restaurants faced public pressure, government crackdowns, and city-wide bans on serving dog meat. To survive, some adopted new names such as *yeongyangtang* 영양탕 ("nutrition soup") or *sacheoltang* 사철탕 ("four-season soup") to stay under the radar. It was around this time that samgyetang found its opportunity to rise — offering a similarly hearty, stamina-boosting alternative that posed no ethical controversy. Once the substitute, samgyetang soon became the new symbol of Korean *boyangsik* 보양식 ("health food").

Today, boshintang still exists, especially in rural areas, but opposition to dog meat consumption has grown louder than ever. The criticism centers not only on concerns about unsanitary conditions and inhumane slaughter practices, but also on the profound cultural shift in how dogs are perceived — from livestock to beloved family members. With over ten million pet owners in Korea, this change seems natural. Many observers predict that boshintang will likely disappear from the Korean food scene in the near future.

HISTORY OF DOG MEAT

Although Korea has often been singled out internationally for consuming dog meat (perhaps it needs a better PR team!), it is by no means the only country that has done so. Throughout history — and even today — dog meat has been eaten in various regions around the world. In mainland China, it's estimated that over 20 million dogs are slaughtered for meat each year. In Taiwan, the practice was legal until 2001 and was fully banned in 2017. In parts of Vietnam and the Philippines, dog meat remains available as a regional delicacy.

Even in Europe, which now strongly opposes the practice, there are historical records of dog meat consumption — typically during times of famine or war when other food sources were scarce. Whatever the historical or cultural context, most of these countries have long since banned the sale and consumption of dog meat and have joined global efforts to improve animal welfare. Advocates of dog meat consumption argue that Western criticism represents cultural imperialism — an imposition of foreign values on local traditions. However, this argument is losing strength as ethical standards and perceptions of animals evolve worldwide.

During the Siege of Paris (1870–1871), food shortages caused by the German blockade of the city caused the citizens of Paris to turn to alternative sources for food, including dog meat. There were lines at butchers' shops of people waiting to purchase dog meat. Dog meat was also reported as being sold by some butchers in Paris in 1910.

Dog meat has been eaten in every major German crisis since, at least, the time of Frederick the Great, and was commonly referred to as "blockade mutton". In the early 20th century, high meat prices led to widespread consumption of horse and dog meat in Germany. In the latter part of World War I, dog meat was being eaten in Saxony by the poorer classes because of famine conditions.

The consumption of dog meat continued in the 1920s. In 1937, a meat inspection law targeted against trichinella was introduced for pigs, dogs, boars, foxes, badgers, and other carnivores. Dog meat has been prohibited in Germany since 1986.

In 2012, the Swiss newspaper Tages-Anzeiger reported that dogs, as well as cats, are eaten regularly by a few farmers in rural areas. Commercial slaughter and sale of dog meat is illegal, and farmers are allowed to slaughter dogs for personal consumption. The favorite type of meat comes from a dog related to the Rottweiler and consumed as Mostbröckli, a form of marinated meat. Animals are slaughtered by butchers and either shot or bludgeoned.

In his 1979 book Unmentionable Cuisine, Calvin Schwabe described a Swiss dog meat recipe, gedörrtes Hundefleisch, served as paper-thin slices, as well as smoked dog ham, Hundeschinken, which is prepared by salting and drying raw dog meat. It is illegal in Switzerland to commercially produce food made from dog meat.

SO, WHY?

To understand why dog meat became a popular ingredient in Korea and elsewhere, it helps to look back at the realities of premodern, agricultural societies. In the past, cows were the most valuable assets for farmers — essential for plowing fields and transporting goods — so slaughtering them was restricted by law. While beef consumption existed, it was typically reserved for special occasions such as birthdays, weddings, or ancestral rites. Pigs weren't a practical alternative either. They ate the same food as humans and consumed a large amount of it, effectively doubling household food expenses. They also served no role in farming, making them inefficient to raise for everyday consumption.

That left chickens and dogs as the only realistic options for meat. However, chickens were small and provided a steady supply of eggs, which made them far more valuable alive than as a one-time meal. Naturally, this made dogs a more available source of protein.

If it's any consolation, most dogs consumed as meat were not pets but a distinct breed raised specifically for that purpose — the yellow mongrel known as **hwanggu 황구** or **nureonggi 누렁이** ("the yellow one"). Today, with the abundance of other meat options, improved living standards, and growing awareness of animal rights, dog meat consumption in Korea is rapidly declining and may soon vanish altogether.

why do Koreans drink MAGGOT JUICE?

The Internet went wild when a foreign couple traveling in Korea posted a picture of a milky-looking drink on social media with the caption, "Koreans drink maggot juice." The post went viral before they later admitted it was a prank and issued an apology — but the damage was already done.

The so-called "maggot juice" was in fact *sikhye* 식혜, a traditional sweet Korean rice punch made from malt water and cooked rice grains. Those little white "maggots" floating on top? They're just bits of rice! Sikhye has a mild, honey-like sweetness and is often enjoyed after meals as a refreshing dessert drink, especially during holidays or at public bathhouses (*jjimjilbang* 찜질방).

In Park Chan-wook's thriller **Oldboy (2003)**, what shocked audiences even more than the film's twisted plot was the grotesque scene where the vengeful protagonist, Oh Dae-su, stuffs a wriggling live octopus —*sannakji*—into his mouth, chewing it mercilessly as the tentacles cling to his face in a desperate bid to escape. But is that really how Koreans eat octopus? Well, Koreans do enjoy sannakji, usually as an **anju** 안주 (dishes to accompany alcohol), but not in such a life-or-death struggle. The octopus is chopped into bite-sized pieces and drizzled with sesame oil. Even then, the tentacles continue to squirm—not because they're seeking revenge, but due to residual nerve reflexes. That's also why eating sannakji can be risky; choking incidents are not uncommon. A delicacy, yes—but one to be eaten with utmost caution!

Imagine this: It's the year 2310, Earth has been devastated by nuclear war, and humanity survives on silkworm pupae. Sounds like the plot of a dystopian sci-fi movie — but in Korea, beondegi is already a real snack. These boiled or steamed silkworm pupae are sold by street vendors in paper cups with toothpicks, releasing a distinct nutty aroma that can divide opinions. While its insect-like appearance makes some recoil, it's actually packed with protein, amino acids, and vitamins, making it a surprisingly nutritious bite. Canned versions are also available in supermarkets — perfect if you want to prepare for the next apocalypse or just brag that you've eaten "Korea's most futuristic food."

it's just a BIG MISUNDERSTANDING!

CHICKEN ANUS (X) – CHICKEN GIZZARD (O)

Dakttongjip 닭똥집 refers to the chicken gizzard but is often erroneously translated as "chicken's poop pocket/house" because **dak** means "chicken" and **ttongjip** means "poop house," which is a vernacular for "stomach" or "big intestine."

KNIFE NOODLES (X) – KNIFE-CUT NOODLES (O)

Kalguksu 칼국수 refers to the type of noodle that is cut with a knife, but is often erroneously translated as "knife noodle" because **kal** means "knife" and **guksu** means "noodle."

BEAR SOUP (X) – BEEF-BONE SOUP (O)

Gomtang 곰탕 to the type of soup that's boiled for a long time, but is often erroneously translated as "bear soup" because **gom** meaning "well-boiled" happens to be a homonym with the animal "bear."

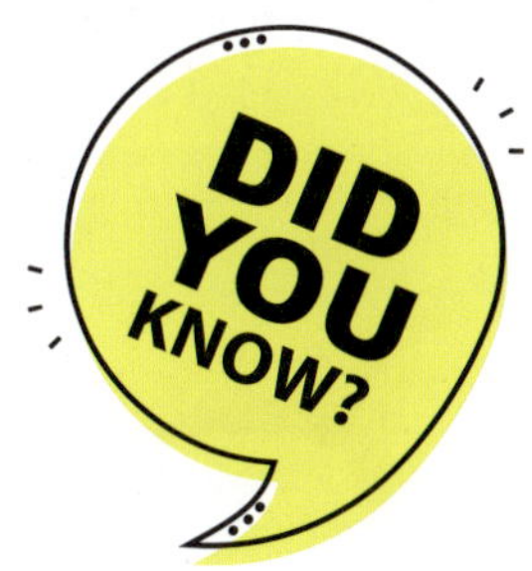

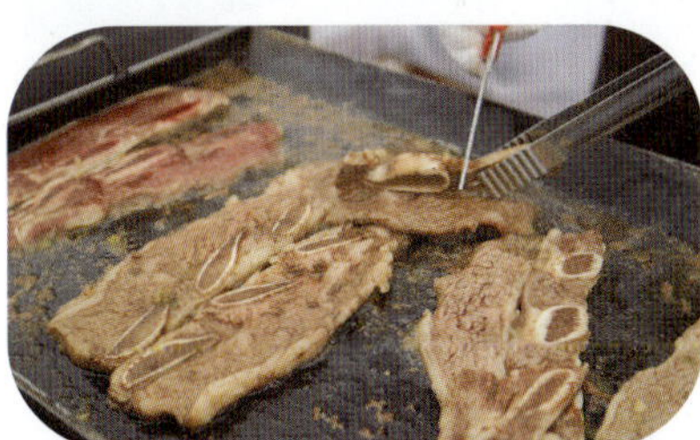

'L.A. GALBI' IS *NOT* FROM LOS ANGELES

L.A *galbi* (above) is a delicious **Korean BBQ** that's mistakenly thought of having originated from Los Angeles due to its name, but the abbreviation actually refers to "lateral," because that's the way the meat and bone are sliced. So it's not "Los Angeles-style *galbi*," but "laterally sliced *galbi*," compared with the regular *galbi* (below).

WHAT ARE THE TYPES OF TTEOK (RICE CAKES) AND THEIR MEANINGS?

MADE BY STEAMING IN A SHIRU 시루 – A LARGE EARTHENWARE STEAMER

Baekseolgi 백설기

Meaning "white snow rice cake," made of white rice. It's considered a "sacred food" as the word **baek 백** means both the color white and number 100, symbolic of "purity" and "completeness," respectively. Used for children's first 100-day celebration, **baekil 백일**, and traditional rituals.

Patshirutteok 팥시루떡

Made of rice, glutinous rice, and topped with red bean. Popularly used for business opening events, and passed around to neighbors after moving to a new place as the red color of the red beans are believed to chase away evil spirits.

Sultteok 술떡

Made with *makgeolli* 막걸리, unfiltered rice wine. The flavor of rice wine stays after steaming, but the alcohol content is almost non-existent.

MADE BY POUNDING RICE OR GLUTINOUS RICE IN A MORTAR OR POUNDING BOARD

Injeolmi 인절미

Made with glutinous rice and coated with bean powder.

Why Do Koreans Eat Tteokguk On New Year's Day? P. 148

Garaetteok 가래떡

A long white cylindrical (traditionally by hand-rolling) rice cake made with white rice, often cut into smaller portions. The long shape symbolizes "longevity" while the sliced pieces symbolize "prosperity" because of their similarity to the traditional Korean coins.

Songpyeon 송편

Gyeongdan 경단

Hwajeon 화전

Half-moon shaped rice cake that contains sweet fillings such as red beans, soybeans, chestnuts, or honey. They are steamed in a steamer over a layer of pine needles. Traditionally, families would gather around to make them during **Chuseok 추석** (Fall Harvest Festival). There's a belief that if a single woman makes a pretty *songpyeon*, she will find a great husband, and if a pregnant woman makes a pretty *songpyeon*, she will have a pretty daughter.

Small ball-shaped rice cakes filled with red bean or sesame paste, coated with black sesame or bean powders.

Thin, mini pan-cake like rice cakes made of glutinous rice, decorated with flower petals.

SHINTO BURI
신토불이

PRODUCES FROM KOREAN SOIL ARE BEST FOR KOREAN BODIES!

Similar to the concept of "locavore," which encourages consuming locally grown food, *shintoburi* 신토불이 literally means "the body and the land (soil) cannot be separated." Though often mistaken as an age-old Korean philosophy, the term actually originated in the 1980s as a government campaign slogan to revive the domestic agricultural industry. It promoted the idea of eating locally produced food at a time when imported goods were flooding the market due to lowered tariffs. The slogan struck a cultural chord and remains familiar today, partly thanks to the popular song of the same name by singer **Bae Il-ho 배일호**.

"Shito Buri" by Bae Il-ho!

RAMYUN

Enjoyed by presidents and beggars alike, *ramyun* 라면 (instant noodles in Korean) is one of the most versatile comfort foods ever created—equally satisfying as a quick snack or a full meal. The best thing about these curly noodles that come in shiny polypropylene packaging is their simplicity: just bring about two and a half cups of water to a boil, add the soup base (nowadays often available in liquid form) and the dried vegetable mix. After a minute or two, gently drop in the noodles—purists insist they must never be broken in half! Submerge them with a utensil, cover the pot, and let them waltz for about three minutes—any longer, and they'll turn soggy. Many people like to crack in an egg for extra protein in what is otherwise a mostly carb-based dish. Voilà! You've just made yourself a perfect bowl of ramyun.

As for eating it, no Korean would consider the experience complete without kimchi on the side. And when the noodles are gone but the soup remains, many can't resist adding a bowl of rice to soak up every last drop (low-carb dieters may want to skip this part).

Now, for a few fun facts while you slurp: the first instant cup noodles produced in Korea were **Samyang Cup Ramen**, inspired by Japan's **Nissin Cup Noodles**, first launched in 1971 (Nissin also invented the world's first instant noodles in 1958). Initially, Korean cup noodles didn't receive much love—too pricey for the time and contrary to traditional Korean dining etiquette, which insists that all food should remain on the table, not lifted to one's mouth. But over time, they won people over, especially when Nongshim introduced **Yukgaejang Sabalmyeon 육개장 사발면**, whose rich, spicy beef flavor and bowl-shaped container perfectly suited Korean tastes.

In 1988 during the Summer Olympics in Seoul, it received worldwide fame when NBC introduced it as Korea's favorite fast food. Today, Korean instant cup noodles are available all over the globe, including the least expected places like the summit of the Jungfrau and Golf Resorts in Brazil. It was also served by international airlines such as American Airline, Air France, and British Airways. Paldo's **Dosirac 도시락** has been one of the most sold cup noodles in Russia for quite some time.

So, how much ramyun do Koreans actually eat? According to a 2024 survey by the World Instant Noodles Association (instantnoodles.org), the average Korean consumes **79 packs of ramyun per year**—the second-highest in the world. Vietnam takes the top spot with 81 packs, while Nepal follows in third with 53. But here's the twist: Vietnamese instant noodles are roughly half the size of their Korean counterparts. So, if you think about it… doesn't that make Korea the real champion of ramyun lovers?

WHY DO KOREANS LOVE FRIED CHICKEN SO MUCH?

Fried chicken — a dish Koreans love so much that they even call it **chineunim** 치느님, meaning "Chicken God" — is more than just food; it's practically a religion. **Korean Fried Chicken** ("KFC") has become a worldwide sensation, adored by locals and foreigners alike.

When Cheon Song-yi famously said, "*Chimaek* 치맥 *(chicken and beer) on snowy days…*" in the mega-hit K-drama **My Love from the Star** (SBS, 2013), the reaction from Chinese viewers was nothing short of explosive. People lined up in front of Korean fried chicken restaurants in Shanghai, and the *Chimaek Festival* in Ningbo, China, drew over 460,000 visitors in just four days. Back in Korea, there's even a tourist hotspot called "Chicken Camp," where visitors can sample Korean fried chicken in every imaginable flavor.

Korean fried chicken has also won over American taste buds, thanks to its thin, crispy coating and distinctive flavors like soy sauce, garlic, and *gochujang*. But what exactly makes fried chicken so special in Korea? Many say it's because chicken is a "community food," meant to be shared with friends, coworkers, or family. Yet, it also perfectly fits Korea's growing solo-dining culture—as the new phrase "one person, one chicken (**1인 1닭**)" humorously suggests. In the end, the popularity of Korean fried chicken comes down to the perfect blend of tradition and modernity, sharing and solitude, and of course, the magic of delivery and a can of ice-cold beer—because, really, what doesn't taste better with beer?

PAJEON AND MAKGEOLLI ON RAINY DAYS?

If it were a rainy day, Cheon Song-yi would have said, "***pajeon*** 파전 *(pancake) and* ***makgeolli*** 막걸리 *(rice wine) on rainy days…*" While the chimaek and snowy days are more of a marketing catch phrase to promote the fried chicken consumption, the pajeon and makgeolli combo has been a long time Korean favorite. As to the origin, there are many theories because it's not clearly recorded in the history book, but these are some of the most plausible ones. The first theory is that it's the result of the "**effect of association**." The sound of the rain is similar to the sizzling sound of a pancake making, so when it rains, pajeon automatically comes to your mind. The second theory has to do with traditional agricultural culture. When the farmers were not able to work due to the rain, especially during the rainy season of Summer, they made pajeon to soothe their hunger and accompanied it with makgeolli, a farmer's favorite drink. Naturally, it became a seasonal food, and the tradition must have been passed down to this day.

Why So Many Retired Korean Ajusshis Run Fried Chicken Restaurants? P. 93

WHY DO KOREANS BELIEVE KOREAN GINSENG GIVES MYSTERIOUS POWER?

The genus name for ginseng, or *insam* 인삼 in Korean, is Panax ginseng, with "Panax" derived from the Greek word meaning "panacea." As the term implies, ginseng has long been considered to possess mysterious healing properties, even in the West. Just like wine, whose flavor differs by its terroir, the nutritional and medicinal quality of ginseng varies depending on soil, climate, cultivation methods, and other environmental factors. Compared to ginseng grown in China, Canada, or the U.S., **Goryeo 고려** ginseng—from the **old Korean kingdom (918–1392)**—is famed for its superior medicinal properties. While American ginseng contains 13 types of ginsenoside, a vegetable saponin and major antioxidant, Goryeo ginseng boasts 36 types, making it one of the highest-quality ginsengs in the world. During the **Joseon Dynasty**, ginseng exports to Japan were so highly valued that payment was often made in silver, and at peak prices, even gold. Its popularity was undeniable. In China and Vietnam, emperors were said to use it as an aphrodisiac. A *shimmani* 심마니 ("ginseng digger") is a person who hunts for *sansam* 산삼 ("wild ginseng"), believed to have more potent medicinal effects than cultivated ginseng. Discovering rare wild ginseng could fetch a staggering sum of money, akin to winning the lottery!

HONGSAM (RED GINSENG) THE SUPER IMMUNE BOOSTER

Hongsam 홍삼 ("red ginseng") is made by steaming and drying ginseng. This process is said to have originated to meet the demands of Chinese consumers in the past, helping to preserve the ginseng so it wouldn't spoil. As a result, the ginseng gradually turns red, and the concentration of its beneficial properties is believed to increase. Hongsam is often credited with boosting the immune system, although the medicinal differences between regular ginseng and red ginseng have not been conclusively proven. The steaming process also reduces the bitter taste, making it easier to consume. Today, hongsam comes in many forms, from traditional teas to candies, gummies, and other modern varieties.

DONGUIBOGAM
THE KOREAN MEDICINAL BIBLE

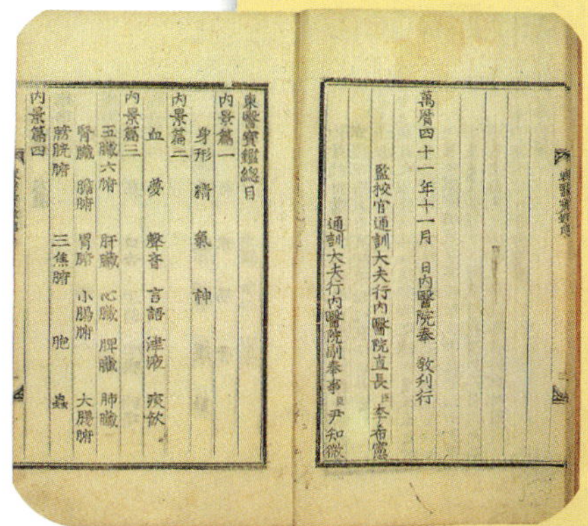

***Donguibogam* 동의보감: Principles and Practice of Eastern Medicine** is a Joseon-era medical compendium compiled by the royal physician **Heo Jun 허준** under the royal order of **King Gwanghaegun** in **1610**. The work involved extensive research and editing of both Chinese and Korean medical texts, resulting in 25 volumes published using woodblock printing in 1613. It serves as a systematic training and prescription guide, tailored to the ingredients and resources available on the Korean Peninsula, while also considering the physical, cultural, and dietary characteristics of Koreans. Today, it is recognized as National Treasure No. 319 and listed in the **UNESCO Memory of the World**, widely regarded as one of the finest medical books in the world. For those curious about Heo Jun's journey and achievements, you can retrace his epic story in the hit TV drama *Hur Jun* 허준 (*The Legendary Doctor*, 1999, MBC).

Hur Jun 허준 (*The Legendary Doctor*, 1999, MBC)

WHAT ARE THE LITTLE GOLD BALLS KOREANS TAKE WHEN THEY FEEL LIKE FAINTING?

In Korean dramas, the main character is at an interview and about to faint. But don't worry – he's got an ace up his sleeve. He quickly whips out a small golden ball wrapped in paper, unwraps it to reveal a shiny sphere that looks like a Ferrero Rocher, pops it into his mouth, and munches it. Within a minute, he's calm as a cucumber, ready to ace the interview as if nothing happened. In another scene, an elderly father faints when he hears that his daughter wants to marry the son of his sworn enemy. The panicked family quickly unwraps the golden ball, puts it in his mouth with a sip of water, and moments later, he magically rises to his feet, continuing to scold his daughter with full energy. So, what's this miracle ball?

Named *woohwangcheongshimwon* 우황청심원, meaning "a ball made with *woohwang* (cow bezoar) that clears the mind and spirit", it is a traditional Korean medicine for emergencies like stroke, paralysis, speech impairment, coma, high blood pressure, mental anxiety, and acute or chronic palsy. Now, about woohwang (cow bezoar) – it's literally a hardened stone found in a cow's gallbladder. Sounds gross? Maybe a little. But in traditional medicine, it's believed to have powerful detoxifying and calming properties, which is why it's been treasured for centuries. Think of it as the ultimate "first-aid candy for your nerves" – a tiny golden miracle that makes people magically composed, at least in K-Dramas!

KOREAN FOLK REMEDIES

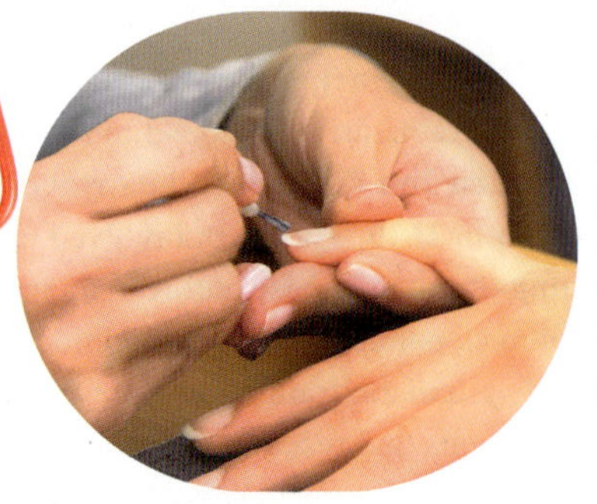

Pricking Fingers

For severe indigestion, Koreans sometimes prick the skin just above the root of the fingernail with a sanitized needle and squeeze out a little blood. If the discomfort persists, they may do it on all ten fingers. The idea is that it boosts blood circulation and stimulates the digestive muscles, like jump-starting a car.

Doenjang on Bee Stings

Surprisingly, *doenjang* 된장 (fermented soybean paste) has historically been used as a first-aid remedy for bee stings in Korea. While it's not common today and its effectiveness hasn't been scientifically proven, it's an interesting glimpse into traditional practices—but don't try this at home!

Rubbing Stomach for Stomachache

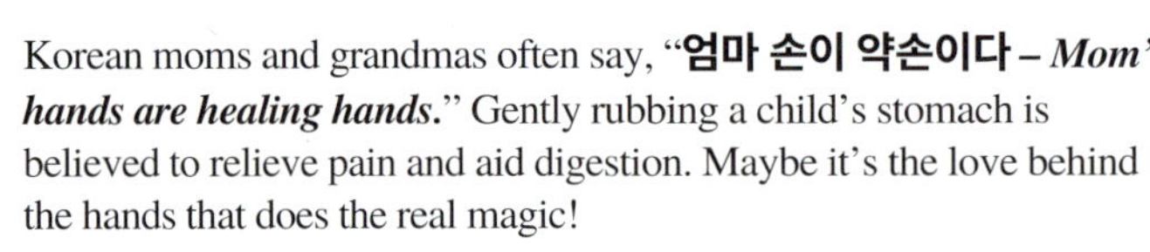

Korean moms and grandmas often say, "**엄마 손이 약손이다** – *Mom's hands are healing hands.*" Gently rubbing a child's stomach is believed to relieve pain and aid digestion. Maybe it's the love behind the hands that does the real magic!

Soju + Chili Powder for a Cold!?

Some Koreans mix *soju* (Korean distilled liquor) with *gochugaru* 고춧가루 (chili powder) when they catch a cold. This isn't really a medical treatment— it's more of a folk remedy, like a "mental boost therapy" or a "sweating cure," meant to warm up the body quickly and sweat out the cold. Alcohol in soju can make you feel temporarily warm, and adding chili powder makes you sweat from the spiciness. It can also give a sensation of clear sinuses and make the cold symptoms feel slightly relieved. In fact, chili contains capsaicin, which can promote blood circulation and cause temporary heat and sweating.

That said, this is very much an old-fashioned practice. Drinking alcohol while sick can lower your immunity and slow recovery. Alcohol also dehydrates the body easily and may interact with cold medicine, causing side effects. The safest way to treat a cold is to drink warm water and get plenty of rest!

Korean Dining Etiquette

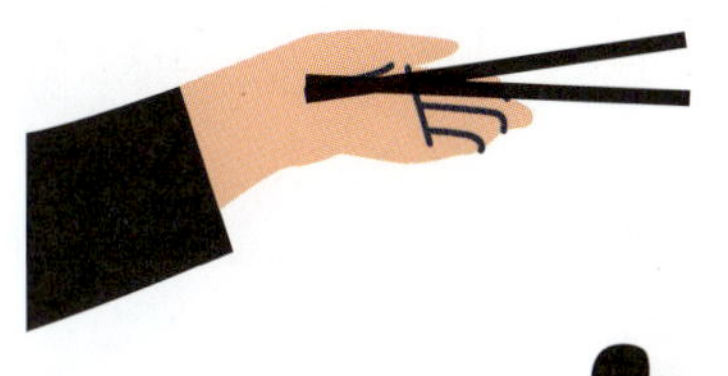

When starting a meal, **the elders always pick up their chopsticks or spoon first**, and everyone else follows. (By the way, during the Joseon Dynasty, there was a practice where a court lady called *gimisanggung* 기미상궁 would taste the king's food first to check for poison, but that's a story for another time!) In Korea, the culture of showing respect to one's elders is deeply ingrained.

Don't leave the table before the eldest does.

Blowing your nose at the table is considered rude, while burping is generally excused —but try to avoid loud or intentional burping in front of elders.

who picks up the tab?

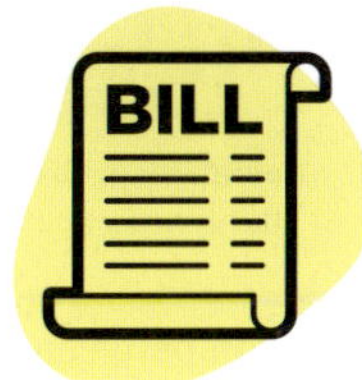

Usually, the senior in the group insists on paying. While it's polite to offer to contribute, pushing too hard can make them feel like they've "lost face."

how young people split the bill nowadays

- Taking turns – Each person pays in rotation.
- Dutch pay / **엔빵** (*en bbang*) – The total is divided evenly among everyone ("1/n").
- Mobile banking / account transfer – Paying instantly through apps.

WHY DO KOREANS EAT OUT OF THE SAME POT?

One peculiarity found on the Korean dining table is people eating out of the same pot when sharing things like *kimchi jjigae* 김치찌개 (kimchi stew) or *doenjang jjigae* 된장찌개 (bean paste stew), using their own spoon rather than a communal ladle! The proponents of this practice say that it creates an emotional bond, but the naysayers try to avoid it at all costs and demand separate bowls for each, for hygienic reasons. As a matter of fact, Koreans have an extremely high infection rate of Helicobacter pylori disease, which can cause stomach cancer, and the food-sharing culture is suspected as the main culprit.

Then, where did it all begin? During the **Joseon Dynasty** and up until the **Japanese Occupation** period, Korea maintained the tradition where everybody dined on a separate mini table, known as *doksang* 독상 ("solo table").

Doksang ("solo table")

외상을질대폐지
가족이한식탁에
영양을취하고분량은적게
同德女高普 宋今璇氏談

Newspaper published in 1936 featuring a column that promotes the *gyeomsang* ("dining together on the same table") culture

It was in line with the *yugyo* philosophy, where the strict distinction between the old and the young and between men and women was clearly defined (they could, however, dine in the same place, though). But things changed during the Japanese Occupation. The Japanese Government-General of Korea encouraged the practice of eating together on the same table, known as *gyeomsang* 겸상, because Japan needed a lot of materials, including tableware, for their military fighting in World War II. As a result, Korean families adopted the practice of putting dishes together on the same table, sharing soups, casseroles, and side dishes with each other. It's an artificial habit rather than a tradition — one that was forced upon the Korean people during difficult times. With modernization and the abundance of products everywhere, this habit has persisted, but it's also something that many people today wish they could unlearn.

WHY DO ONLY KOREANS USE METAL CHOPSTICKS?

"Excuse me! Do all Asian chopsticks look the same to you?" Well, while these thin, long sticks that have carried 5,000 years of Asian culinary history may look similar at first glance, they're actually quite different once you look closely. The culture of using chopsticks exists not only in Korea but across Asia, including Japan, China, and Vietnam. Yet despite their shared origins, there are surprisingly distinct differences in shape, material, and use between countries. The Chinese version is typically made of bamboo or plastic and is the longest among them, as it's ideal for picking up food from large communal dishes placed in the middle of the table. The tips are hexagonal, which are said to symbolize "attracting wealth."

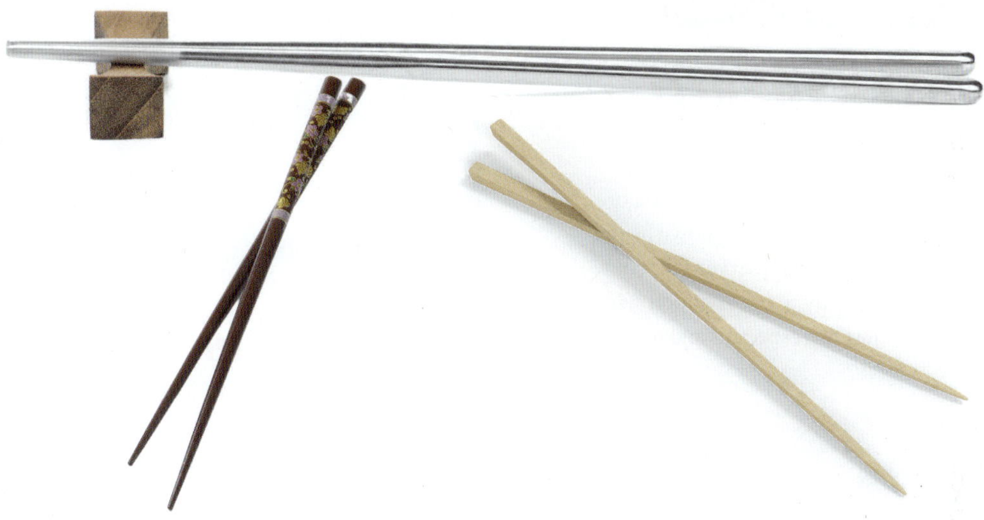

Meanwhile, the Japanese prefer wood as their main material. Their chopsticks are the shortest and have pointed tips, perfect for removing fish bones or handling delicate foods. Wooden chopsticks are the norm, and the custom of owning one's own pair has led to many beautiful and ornate designs. So, what about Korean chopsticks? In fact, Korea is the only country in the world that routinely uses metal chopsticks in daily life. In terms of size, they're shorter than Chinese chopsticks but longer than Japanese ones, and feature flat, rectangular tips. Their history goes back to ancient times—metal chopsticks were unearthed from the tombs of **Baekje 백제** royalty dating back to the **Three Kingdoms Period (18 BC–660 AD)**. At that time, royalty and the upper class used silver spoons and chopsticks to detect poison in their food, while commoners began using cheaper metal versions to mimic the elegant dining culture of the nobility.

Functionally, metal chopsticks are highly hygienic. Germs and bacteria can't survive on them, and they don't absorb odors or flavors like wooden ones. They're also exceptionally durable—artifacts found centuries later remain undamaged and rust-free. Particularly in Korea, where grilling meat at the table is common, metal chopsticks are far more practical than flammable wooden ones. Of course, they do have their downsides. They're heavier and more slippery than wood, making them tricky to use until one gets used to them. But perhaps because of this, some Koreans jokingly claim, *"We honed our dexterity with metal chopsticks—that's why Koreans are so good at crafting precision electronics today!"* In short, Korean chopsticks are not just dining tools—they're a symbol of practicality, endurance, and cultural identity, embodying Korea's balance between tradition and innovation.

WHY IS THERE A ROLL OF TOILET PAPER ON A RESTAURANT TABLE?

A little out of place? Don't panic when you find a roll of toilet paper on the table. Despite the psychological association with the toilet, Koreans treat it as just another type of "tissue," like Kleenex and paper napkins. Just try not to overthink it and focus on enjoying your meal instead.

WHY DO KOREANS USE SCISSORS AT RESTAURANTS?

In many casual Korean restaurants that serve BBQ and **naengmyeon** 냉면, it's common for servers to use scissors to cut meat and noodles for convenience. Rest assured, though — they're used exclusively for food. In fact, kitchen shears are now finding their way into homes and professional kitchens around the world as a versatile cooking tool.

WHAT'S THE BELL ON THE TABLE FOR?

Many restaurants in Korea have a small button or pager affixed to the table, commonly known as the *call button*. Simply press it, and a server will come right over! It's a brilliant way to get attention without raising your voice — just be respectful and avoid overusing it.

WATER IS "SELF"?

You might spot a sign at a casual Korean restaurant that says, *"Water is self."* Don't worry — it doesn't mean you've suddenly become H_2O! It's a classic bit of Konglish that simply means "Water is self-service." In other words, grab a cup and help yourself at the water station.

THE SELF-SERVING RITUAL

At many no-frills Korean restaurants, you might notice that no one comes to set up your utensils — no matter how long you wait. Don't panic! It doesn't mean they're ignoring you; they're simply letting you do the honors. Usually, you'll find a wooden case containing spoons and chopsticks right on the table. If not, check underneath or along the side — there's often a hidden drawer. Just grab your utensils and set them up yourself. And if you happen to be sitting next to the utensil box, you can show off your Korean dining manners by setting the table for your elders or others at the table. A small act, but one that earns big respect.

WHEN CALLING A SERVER

In many Korean mom-and-pop restaurants, the servers are often **ajummas** 아줌마 (middle-aged women). But instead of calling them ajumma—which can sound a bit blunt or unfriendly—people usually say **imonim** 이모님, which literally means "Ms. Auntie" (imo = aunt, nim = honorific suffix). It sounds much warmer and more respectful. If you want to be completely gender-neutral, you can simply call out **yeogiyo** 여기요 ("over here") or **jeogiyo** 저기요 ("over there") to get a server's attention without using any specific title. And here's a tip: if you add a little **aegyo** (애교, a cute tone or gesture), you might just get some service—that's Korean-English for "something complimentary or on the house"!

WHY DO KOREANS LOVE SOJU SO MUCH?

When a survey by Euromonitor was released in 2014, crowning South Koreans as the **world's heaviest hard liquor drinkers**—consuming 13.7 shots per week of any spirit, twice as much as Russians (6.3 shots/week) and four times more than Americans (3.3 shots/week)—everyone was surprised… except the South Koreans themselves. They weren't shocked at all. Even considering that a large portion of Korean consumption comes from *soju* (소주), a Korean spirit with 16–21% alcohol by volume, whereas many other spirits range from 35–42%, Korea still topped the list when adjusted fairly—halving the Korean stats gives 6.85 shots/week.

According to a 2017 study, Koreans consumed 3.4 billion bottles of soju. Divided by the population of legal drinking age, that's 85 bottles per person per year, or about one and a half bottles per week per person. While heavy drinking isn't exactly something to brag about—unless you're at a college frat party—it illustrates just how much Koreans love soju among all available alcoholic beverages.

One major reason is the price: at just 1,800 Korean Won (~$1.50 USD) per bottle in convenience stores, soju has been a loyal companion for ordinary people through thick and thin, overflowing with *jeong* 정 (the Korean sense of deep affection and connection).

In popular culture, the iconic green bottle symbolizes the joys and sorrows of everyday life, magically helping people vent, bond, and even do foolish things like falling in love.

Put simply, soju is at the heart of all the drama around us. Speaking of which, here are some of the most overused Korean drama clichés featuring soju.

KOREAN DRAMA CLICHÉS FEAT. SOJU

DRUNK "LOVE CONFESSION" AT POJANGMACHA

A boy and a girl—let's say Junho and Youngmi, both of legal drinking age—are sitting across from each other at a *pojangmacha* (포장마차, tent-style street bar). Youngmi has a secret crush on Junho. The unsuspecting Junho starts talking about other girls.

Youngmi, a lightweight and drinking with Junho for the first time, fills her shot glass with soju and downs it in one go. Startled, Junho blurts out, "What's wrong with you?" and grabs her wrist to stop her from drinking more. Youngmi yanks her hand away and snaps, "Since when do you care?"

An hour later, completely inebriated and slurring her words, Youngmi manages to blurt out that she likes him—then promptly passes out on the table. Junho tries to help her up, but she's out cold. As a last resort, he gives her a piggyback ride home.

On the way, Youngmi keeps mumbling under her breath, "You little b@stard… I like you so much… and I hate you…"

The next morning, Junho is in the kitchen, busy making breakfast for two. Youngmi finally comes to her senses, slowly opens her eyes, and looks around in confusion. Shocked, she nearly jumps out of bed—only to realize she's wearing Junho's oversized T-shirt. At that moment, Junho turns around, smiles, and says,

"Good morning, my beautiful girlfriend!"

BOSS & SUBORDINATE FACE-OFF AT POJANGMACHA

"Just do as I say! I'm your superior!" shouts Director Kim. Seho, his subordinate, keeps his head down, enduring his boss's angry voice. Back in his cubicle, Seho simmers quietly — burning with a low, blue flame.

It's a classic scene straight out of a Korean drama: a rigid, hierarchical workplace full of unspoken rules. Subordinates are expected to obey without question, and giving honest opinions or showing raw emotion to a superior can easily be seen as disrespect.

Cut to a pojangmacha later that night. Both men sit across from each other, surrounded by empty soju bottles. Director Kim, now softened by alcohol, opens up first.

"Hey, are you still upset about that order I gave? I'm sorry, man. I did it for the good of the team."

Seho, eyes half-closed, mutters, "You know what, sir? If you really cared about the company, you shouldn't have done that… You… You…" He trails off and collapses face-first onto the table. Director Kim sighs, hails a cab, and gently helps Seho into the back seat, paying the driver in advance.

The next morning, Seho stumbles into the office just on time. As he sits down, Director Kim walks by silently and leaves a hangover-cure drink on Seho's desk.

Minsoo, 58, has just been laid off. He sits alone at a pojangmacha (street tent bar), drinking soju with his favorite side dish, *golbaengi muchim* 골뱅이무침 (spicy sea snail salad). Fed up with life, he downs shot after shot and calls for another bottle. But the owner ajumma steps in. "*Aigoo*! You've had enough! Go home to your wife and kids!"

Minsoo slams the table. "I can't, and I won't! They don't respect me — they wouldn't even care if I came home or not. I'd rather just pass out here!" Both funny and heartbreaking, scenes like this capture something deeply Korean — how people cope with frustration, loneliness, and the pressure of societal expectations. In Korea, hierarchy based on age, rank, and social status often makes it hard to express honest feelings openly.

But at places like pojangmacha, alcohol loosens tongues and hearts. Soju acts as a kind of social lubricant, helping the wheels of daily life keep turning — at least in moderation. And Koreans tend to be forgiving of words spoken under the influence. After all, if no one remembers it the next morning, it's as if it never happened. Maybe that's why those little green bottles hold such a big place in Korean hearts.

WHY DO KOREANS LOVE DRINKING IN TENT BARS (POJANGMACHA)?

Pojangmacha (포장마차) — often shortened to *pocha* — literally means "covered wagon." These no-frills, tented outdoor bars are optimized for efficiency and charm. Expect plastic chairs, metal tables, and an ajumma (middle-aged woman) owner-chef who can single-handedly whip up a stunning variety of *anju* 안주 — dishes made to pair with alcohol. From *sundae* 순대, (Korean blood sausage) and *dakkochi* 닭꼬치 (grilled chicken skewers) to *haemul pajeon* 해물파전 (seafood pancake), *kimbap* 김밥 (Korean rolls), *tteokbokki* 떡볶이 (spicy rice cakes), and *golbaengi muchim*, the food is hearty, flavorful, and served fast. Prices are usually cheaper than at regular restaurants, making pojangmacha the perfect refuge for tired office workers seeking a quick bite and a bottle of soju after work. Many are clustered around officedistricts, glowing with neon lights, laughter, and sizzling pans late into the night. But pojangmacha isn't just for workers. It's also a popular dating spot — cozy, unpretentious, and romantic, especially at sunset when the lights flicker on beneath the orange tarp. In recent years, the number of traditional pojangmacha has dwindled due to sanitary and taxation regulations. Yet their spirit lives on in the form of "indoor pojangmacha," modern bars that replicate the nostalgic vibe — minus the cold wind and flapping tent walls.

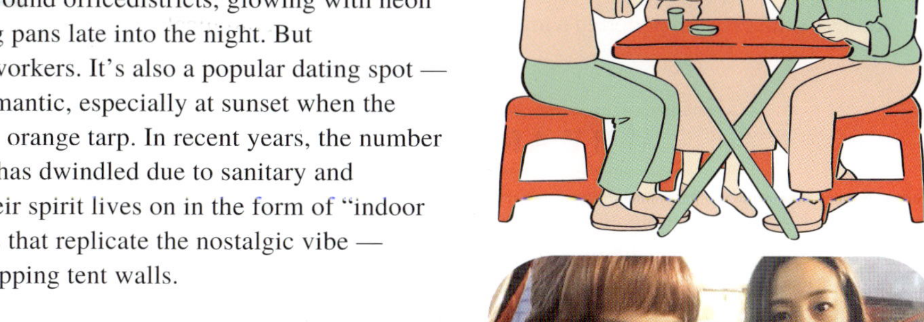

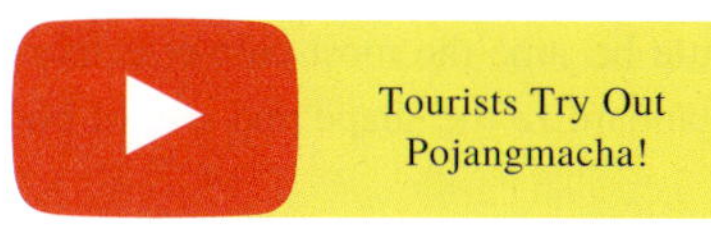

DISTILLED   DILUTED

SOJU – THE WORLD'S BEST SELLING LIQUOR 11 YEARS IN A ROW

The name soju means "burned liquor" because it's made through distillation. It's colorless and has just a hint of sweetness, which varies depending on the sweeteners chosen by each manufacturer — common ones include saccharin, aspartame, and stevia. The first version of soju appeared during the 13th-century **Goryeo Dynasty**, when the distilling technique was introduced amid the Mongol invasions. Today, **Andong 안동** soju is considered the direct ancestor of the modern soju we drink today. Originally, soju was made by distilling alcohol from fermented grains such as rice, wheat, or barley. However, during the 1960s, the traditional distillation method was prohibited to address nationwide rice shortages. As a result, manufacturers began diluting highly distilled ethanol made from alternative starches such as potatoes, sweet potatoes, and tapioca. This shift gave birth to cheaper versions of soju, which still dominate the market today. When the ban was eventually lifted, many companies began reviving traditional distillation techniques. These "premium" soju brands have gradually gained popularity in recent years. How fiery is soju? Diluted versions range between 16% and 21% alcohol by volume (ABV), while distilled ones can range anywhere from 17% up to 53% ABV. In 2015, fruit-flavored soju with a lower alcohol content (around 13%) swept the market among younger drinkers who preferred a milder, sweeter taste.

WHY ARE ALL SOJU BOTTLES GREEN?

Almost all (diluted) soju products come in green bottles, regardless of the manufacturer — and there are both marketing and practical reasons behind this. When mass-produced soju first appeared on the market, bottles were originally clear. This remained the norm until the 1990s, when a new brand called "Green Soju" made its debut. Promoting itself with an "eco-friendly" image and a milder taste than regular soju, it became an instant hit. Naturally, other companies followed suit, packaging their own soju in green bottles. On the practical side, newly manufactured bottles already come in green, which eliminates the need for additional coloring or processing — making them cheaper and immediately ready for use. Because of this, the green bottle became the most cost-effective and widely available design. In 2010, soju manufacturers signed an agreement to standardize the shape and size of bottles so they could be easily shared and recycled among different brands.

WHY DO KOREANS SHAKE AND HIT THE SOJU BOTTLE'S NECK WHEN OPENING IT?

One of the many things that makes drinking soju with Korean friends extra fun is that you get to watch them perform what looks like a mini flair bartending show! The technique goes like this:

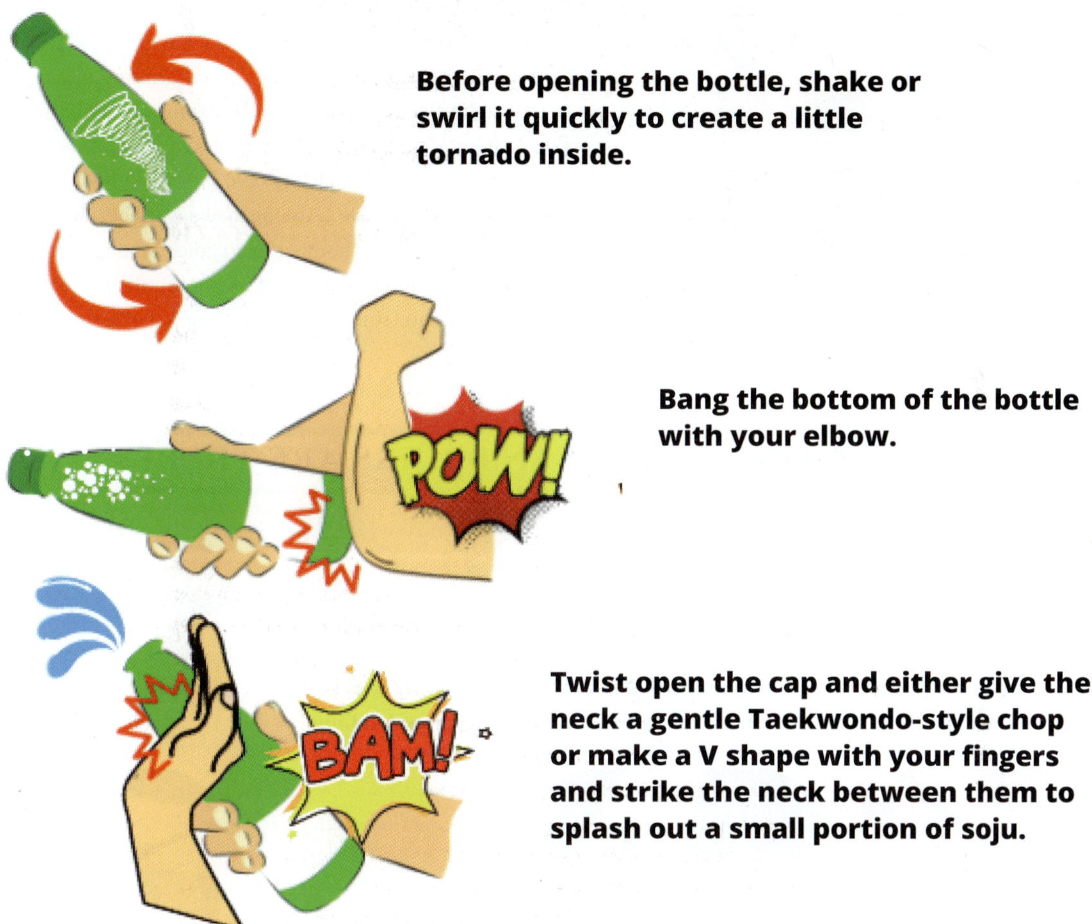

Okay, that's pretty much it for the Korean soju flair show 101 — but have you ever wondered why they do that in the first place? After all, soju doesn't contain mixers or ingredients that need shaking like cocktails do.

Well, there's actually a very practical origin behind this ritual. In the past, soju bottles were sealed with corks rather than screw caps. When corks weren't stored properly, they dried out, crumbled, and sometimes left small pieces floating inside the bottle. To get rid of them, people would shake the bottle to gather the debris in one place, bang the bottom to bring them to the top, then open the bottle and let the top portion splash out — often with a dramatic hand chop for flair.

Now that all soju bottles use screw caps, the ritual is technically pointless — but it's still widely practiced. Even many Koreans don't know the original reason anymore, but the fact that it continues proves one thing: it's just too fun to stop doing!

Poktanju 폭탄주, literally meaning "bomb shot," refers to a cocktail drink made by mixing a high-proof drink, such as whiskey, with a low-proof drink like beer. It is termed so because dropping a shot of whiskey into a glass of beer creates an effect similar to that of a bomb explosion, and also for the fact that it makes you get drunk faster. In the past, only the privileged could afford to drink whiskey, so the ordinary people looked to their friend well within reach, *soju*, as an alternative. Among many variants, *somaek* 소맥 (*soju* + *maekju* 맥주 "beer") is the number one choice among Koreans who lack the time but want to reap the benefits of alcohol in the shortest amount of time possible! The 3:7 ratio (soju:beer) is the most popular formula.

WHAT KIND OF KOREAN DRINKS ARE THERE?

TYPES

Takju 탁주
(unrefined rice wine)

Cheongju 청주
(refined rice wine)

Honseongju 혼성주
(compounded liquor)

Gwasilju 과실주
(fruit wine)

Makgeolli
막걸리
("roughly strained drink")

Beopju
법주
("law liquor")
= liquor made according
to a certain set of rules

Gwahaju
과하주
("summer-passing" wine)

Maesilju
매실주
(plum wine)

PRODUCTS

For those of you over the legal drinking age—do you remember who first introduced you to alcohol? In Korea, drinking isn't just about consuming alcohol; it's a rite of passage. Traditionally, people learned "how to drink" from their elders, as it was considered essential training for surviving in a hierarchical society filled with unspoken rules. It symbolized not only acceptance into adulthood but also acknowledgment as a responsible member of society and family. For the giver, it was a proud moment; for the receiver, a great honor. Many of these customs trace back to *hyangeumjurye* 향음주례, a ceremonial drinking gathering among scholars during the late Joseon Dynasty. It emphasized manners, respect, and intellectual fellowship—values that still echo through modern drinking culture today. Learning these customs will not only help you avoid awkward moments when drinking with Korean friends but also help you better understand those lively drinking scenes in K-dramas!

Using Two Hands

- When receiving or pouring a drink to or from someone older, always use both hands. You can either:
    - Hold the glass or bottle with both hands, or
    - Hold it with your right hand while gently supporting your right wrist with your left hand.

If you're drinking with someone your age, one hand is fine—but if it's your first time meeting or you're still using *jondaetmal* 존댓말 (formal speech), it's safer to stick with two hands until you're closer.

Pouring and Drinking

- Always pour for others first. Never pour your own drink—it's seen as bad manners (and legend says the person you drink with will have bad luck for three years!).
- Wait until glasses are empty before refilling them.
- Turn away when drinking in front of someone older—use two hands and slightly tilt your head to the side.
- If you're seated between two seniors, turn toward the less older one.
- When drinking from shot glasses, it's common to finish the first one in a single gulp—but it's not mandatory. If you can't drink much, no one will fault you for sipping instead.

If You're the Youngest in the Group

Keep an eye out—your role is to help pour drinks for others. If you notice empty glasses, refill them (but only when they're fully empty). Sometimes, the elder or boss might pour the first round and then pass the glass for everyone to drink from the same one—a gesture of unity and trust.

Although this tradition can feel uncomfortable for hygiene reasons, many still go along with it out of respect.

- Don't pour your own drink. If you do, people will say that the person drinking with you will have misfortunes for three years! Of course, it's just an urban legend of unknown origin, believed to have been made up to encourage people to actively participate in drinking by pouring for each other.
- Don't drink before the eldest does. Always wait for the oldest person in the group to propose a toast or raise their glass first.
- Don't drink in three separate sips. It's reminiscent of offering alcohol to ancestors during the *jesa* 제사 ceremony and considered unlucky.
- Don't outright refuse when offered a drink from an older person. "Saving face" is important for elders. Instead, say that although you can't drink it, you would gratefully accept the glass. You can then put it down on the table and even clink glasses to keep pace with others—it's all about keeping harmony and respect.

After a night of heavy drinking comes the inevitable — the hangover.
Koreans, known for their resilience, have long found creative ways to chase
away this unwelcome guest.

TRADITIONAL APPROACH

The word *haejang* 해장 literally means *"to soothe the stomach."* Koreans
firmly believe that a bowl of hearty, nutrient-packed soup can revive their
dehydrated, aching bodies. That's why any soup eaten to cure a hangover is
called *haejangguk* 해장국 — with *guk* 국 meaning "soup," it's commonly
known as "hangover soup." The following are some of the most popular
varieties. Try them all and see which one works best for you! (It's a perfectly
valid excuse to drink… right?)

Kongnamulguk 콩나물국
(bean sprouts soup)

Seolleongtang 설렁탕
(ox bone soup)

Seonjiguk 선지국
(ox blood soup)

Bugeoguk 북어국
(dried pollack soup)

MODERN APPROACH

No time to sit down for a bowl of haejangguk? No worries! Your hung-
over Korean friends have already thought of that and invented a variety
of ready-to-drink hangover cure beverages that you can grab at any
convenience store. These miracle shots often contain ingredients such
as dihydromyricetin (extracted from raisin trees grown in Gangwon
Province), milk thistle, red ginseng, and other medicinal herbs
scientifically proven to help relieve — and even prevent — hangover
symptoms. Try them all and see what works best for you! (Hey, yet
another good excuse to drink!)

Another product that deserves an honorable mention is **Garamandeun Bae 갈아만든 배**,
which literally means "crushed pear (juice)." Among non-Koreans, it's affectionately
nicknamed the "**ldh drink**" because the Korean word "**배**" resembles the English letters
"ldh." This sweet, refreshing pear juice found itself in the global spotlight when GQ
magazine introduced it as a legit potion to prevent hangovers — if taken before drinking.

WHAT ARE 1-CHA, 2-CHA, AND 3-CHA THAT KOREANS COUNT WHEN DRINKING?

When Koreans go out, they *go out-out* — and rarely stay in just one place. Instead, they follow the call of their party spirit, hopping from one venue to another for continued food, drinks, and fun. Each "round" or "stage" is called *cha* (차), which literally means "order," "number," or "turn."

- 1-cha 일차 (*il cha*) — the first round — usually begins at a restaurant for dinner and drinks. The classic combo? *Samgyeopsal* 삼겹살, grilled pork belly) and soju — a pairing as iconic as peanut butter and jelly, at least in Korea.
- 2-cha 이차 (*i cha*) follows once everyone's loosened up. Someone will inevitably shout, "Let's go *i-cha*!" and off they go to a bar or pub for more serious drinking — perhaps with cocktails, beer towers, or another bottle (or three) of soju.
- 3-cha 삼차 (*sam cha*) is where things get musical. Now thoroughly inebriated and ready to meet Apollo, the God of music, everyone heads to a *noraebang* 노래방 (karaoke room). The goal here isn't to sing beautifully — it's to belt out your stress with your friends. And since most noraebangs also serve alcohol, the party energy never really drops (if anything, it hits high notes — literally).

By the end of 3-cha, everyone's laughing, off-key, and best friends for life… until tomorrow morning.

TYPES OF KOREAN DRINKING GAMES

SAM-YUK-GU 삼육구 ("3,6,9")

Players count numbers out loud in order, but must clap instead of saying any number containing 3, 6, or 9. For multiple-digit numbers, clap for each 3, 6, or 9 (e.g., clap twice for 33, three times for 639). The game tests attention and reflexes and is full of laughter.

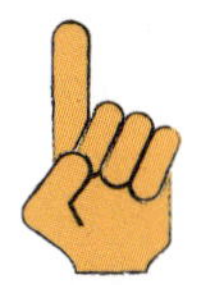

SON BYUNG HO 손병호

Players hold up five fingers and take turns asking statements that might apply to others. If it applies to you, you fold a finger. The player with no fingers left drinks. The game became popular after actor Son Byung-ho showcased it on TV.

IMAGE GAME

Players use a chopstick or finger to point at the person who best fits a given description. For example, someone might ask, "Who here looks like the biggest flirt?" and everyone points accordingly.

NUNCHI GAME 눈치 게임

This game tests quick thinking and reflexes. Everyone starts seated, and players take turns standing up while counting numbers out loud in order. If two people call the same number at the same time, they both take a shot. If everyone survives without a clash, the last person to stand takes a shot.

BASKIN ROBBINS 31

Players take turns counting numbers out loud in ascending order, but each person can say 1, 2, or 3 numbers per turn. The goal is to avoid saying "31," because the player who does loses the game.

HOESIK — THE DREADED COMPANY EVENT EVERYONE WANTS TO AVOID

When partying with friends, 1-cha, 2-cha, 3-cha, or even 4-cha can be fun—but what if it's at work? In the Korean workplace, there is a culture called **hoesik 회식** (literally "eating together"), commonly translated as "company dinner," "company get-together," or "company (un)happy hour." Most employees dread it and try to avoid it whenever possible. At first glance, it sounds harmless—you get to hang out with colleagues over dinner, a mini staff party. And indeed, if done in moderation, hoesik can build team spirit and promote candid exchanges of opinions. But the mandatory nature of attendance and the intertwining of workplace hierarchy make it feel like a boot camp for adults.

First, attendance is expected. Korea is a free country, so technically you can skip it, but the proverb, "an angular stone is bound to be hit by a chisel," warns that opting out marks you as someone who prioritizes themselves over the organization.

Second, hoesik often appears unexpectedly. Your superior might announce it at the last minute, canceling your prior dinner or date plans. In Korean dramas, this is a classic source of relationship drama—but it can also serve as a perfect alibi for someone covering up a little infidelity ("Honey, go to bed first. I'm still at hoesik…").

Third, office hierarchy and politics are ever-present. Where you sit matters: too close to your superior and you seem like an ass-kisser; too far and you risk looking like an outcast. You must laugh at every lame joke your superior makes. If you are the **maknae 막내**—the youngest—you're often in charge of ordering, making somaek (soju and beer mix), filling glasses, and more.

If the gathering ends at 1-*cha* or 2-*cha*, consider yourself lucky. Most hoesik stretch into 3-*cha* or 4-*cha*. You cannot leave before your superiors do. At **noraebang** (karaoke), you are expected to sing to "liven up the mood," preferably choosing songs your superiors enjoy. And once it's all over, you might be tasked with grabbing a taxi for drunk superiors who can barely walk. By the time you get home, only a few hours of sleep remain before returning to your desk. Don't be late!

Why Do Korean People Ask For Your Age At The First Encounter? P. 37

WHY DO KOREANS WORK SO DARN HARD?

For most of you who know Korea as the birthplace of trendy K-pop and home to global giants like Samsung and LG, it might come as a shock to learn that the country was one of the poorest nations not so long ago. And it wasn't an overnight rags-to-riches, Cinderella-style fairy tale.

Here's the real story.

During the first half of the 20th century, Korea endured nothing but hardship and agony. The **Japanese Occupation** exploited the nation in every possible way, reaching its peak during the **Pacific War (1941–1945)** and **World War II (1939–1945)**. The much-needed capital, land, natural resources, and even the lives of Korean men and women were indiscriminately taken to support the Japanese military effort.

The joy of liberation that came with Japan's surrender in 1945 was short-lived. Just five years later, Korea experienced a fratricidal tragedy — the **Korean War (1950–1953)**. This three-year-long all-out war reduced the nation to ashes. U.S. General Douglas MacArthur, the commander of the United Nations forces during the Korean War, lamented the devastation and predicted that it would take a hundred years for the nation to recover. The living conditions of the Korean people at the time were terrible. What was considered a decent meal—if you could get one—was a mere hodgepodge of scavenged or smuggled leftover food from U.S. Army bases. For starving families, dumpster diving was nothing to be ashamed of.

One of those makeshift meals was *kkulkkuli juk* 꿀꿀이죽 ("piggy porridge"), a casserole made from whatever edible scraps could be found near U.S. Army bases. While unwelcome elements like rubber bands, toothpicks, or shoe parts were sometimes discovered, the dish faithfully served its purpose: filling empty stomachs. Although it can no longer be found on restaurant menus, another variation called *budae jjigae* 부대찌개 remains popular today. Meaning "army base stew," budae jjigae is made with spam, ham, sausage, baked beans, kimchi, gochujang, and ramen noodles.

As you can guess from its name and ingredients, its origins lie in the surplus food supplies scrounged and smuggled from the black markets around U.S. Army bases, mixed with Korean seasonings to suit local tastes. It was even nicknamed *jonseun-tang* 존슨탕 ("Johnson soup") after President Lyndon Johnson, who was said to have praised its flavor during his visit to Korea. These days, it's an extremely popular anju (food eaten with alcohol), proof that Koreans don't associate it with the struggles of the past, even though they remain aware of its origins.

Another important term to know is *boritgogae* 보릿고개 ("barley hump"), which refers to the fear and hardship people faced every spring when food supplies ran short — after the previous year's harvest had run out and before the new barley crop ripened. It was called "barley hump" because the struggle felt as difficult as climbing a steep hill.

WHAT IS THE "MIRACLE ON THE HAN RIVER"?

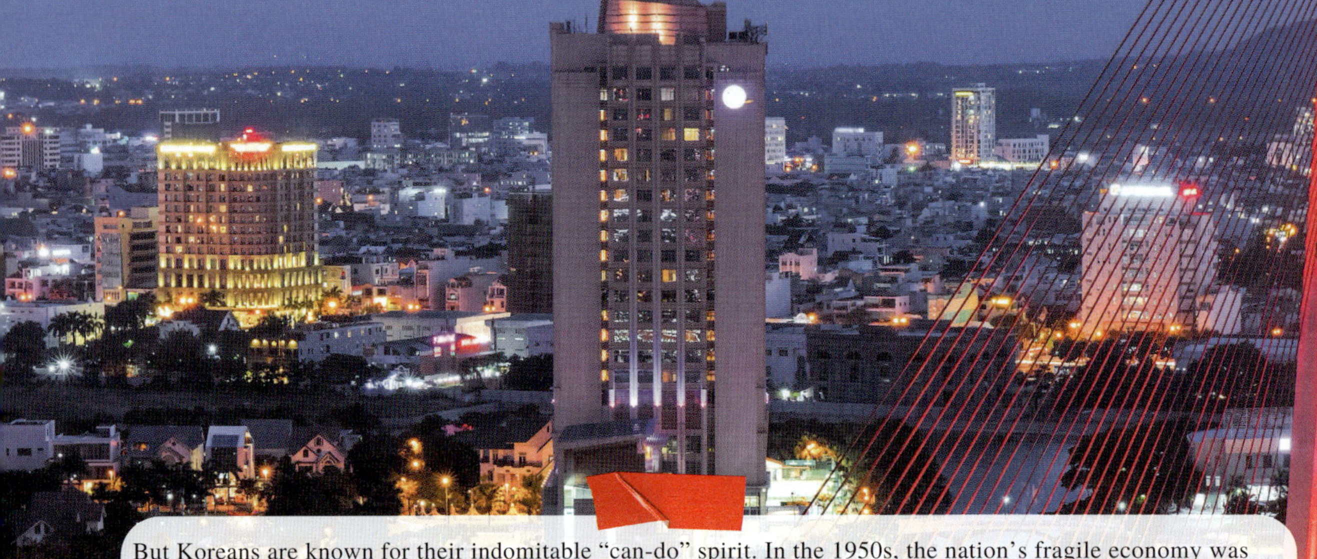

But Koreans are known for their indomitable "can-do" spirit. In the 1950s, the nation's fragile economy was barely sustained by U.S. aid, which began to dwindle toward the end of the decade. To rectify the situation, Korea sought ways to develop its own self-sufficient economy. After the collapse of President **Rhee Syngman**'s 이승만 government following the **April 16 Revolution**, the Second Republic drafted a five-year economic development plan. However, it wasn't implemented until the **Park Chung-hee 박정희** administration came to power through the **May 16 military coup**. The Park government vigorously pushed forward with the plan — a growth policy aimed at transforming Korea into an export-oriented nation.

At the same time, it set "modernization" as a national goal and launched the *saemaul undong* 새마을운동 ("New Village Movement"), which sought to modernize rural communities and reduce the widening gap in living standards between industrialized cities and the impoverished countryside. The campaign's slogan, "*Jal sara bose*" 잘살아보세 ("Let's try to be better-off"), resonated deeply with the Korean people and became the driving force behind the nation's dramatic transformation. Every day, citizens woke up eager to participate in development projects and went to bed proud of their contributions to rebuilding the country. Thanks to the hard work of Korean laborers who provided high-quality labor at low cost, light industries flourished.

Beyond its borders, **Korea's workforce also became a major export**. In the 1960s, **miners and nurses** were dispatched to **Germany**, and in the 1970s, **Korean laborers** worked on large-scale construction projects in the **Middle East**. Around the same time, more than **320,000 Korean soldiers** fought in the **Vietnam War (1964–1973)**, and the subsidies, overseas combat allowances, and U.S. loans earned in return for their participation were reinvested in light industries and national land development projects.

In the 1970s, heavy and chemical industries—such as oil refining, shipbuilding, and fertilizer production—expanded rapidly, while the automobile industry began to take shape. Through the combined efforts of the government and the people, Korea's economy grew at an unprecedented pace in modern world history. The country's per capita income, which stood at just $67 in 1953, surpassed $1,000 in 1977 and $10,000 in 2000. Exports, which were about $22 million in 1957, soared to $10 billion in 1977 and $170 billion by 2000 — representing several hundredfold growth in just three decades.

This period of extraordinary reconstruction, transformation, and economic development became known as *hangang-ui gijeok* **한강의 기적** ("The Miracle on the Han River"). The term was first used by **Prime Minister Chang Myon 장면** of the Second Republic in his 1961 New Year's address, encouraging Koreans to achieve an economic revival similar to West Germany's "Miracle on the Rhine," which symbolized its post–World War II reconstruction. Korea's rapid rise earned it a place among the "**Four Asian Tigers**"—alongside **Hong Kong, Singapore, and Taiwan**. In 1996, Korea reached a symbolic milestone by becoming the 29th member of the OECD (Organisation for Economic Co-operation and Development), joining the ranks of the world's advanced economies.

Korea further demonstrated its global stature by hosting major international events, including the 1988 Seoul Summer Olympic Games, the **2002 FIFA World Cup Korea/Japan**, and the **2018 Pyeongchang Winter Olympics**. As of 2025, South Korea is the 13th largest economy globally by GDP and remains a major exporter, with exports totaling approximately $683.9 billion in 2024. South Korea's gross national income (GNI) per capita reached $36,624 in 2024, ranking sixth among countries with populations greater than 50 million, and surpassing both Japan and Taiwan for the second consecutive year. The country's GDP per capita stood at about $36,129 in 2024.

Ever wonder how North Korea, which chose a vastly different path, has fared? The last time North Korea's GNI per capita surpassed South Korea's was in 1974. By 2024, North Korea's nominal GNI was estimated at 44.4 trillion won (about $32 billion), with a per capita GNI of $1,239—roughly 3.4% the level of South Korea's. **North Korea's entire economy is only around 1.7% the size of South Korea's**, despite recent growth driven by increased trade with Russia and expansions in manufacturing and construction.

"The Miracle on the Han River" remains one of the most remarkable achievements in modern Korean history, making South Korea a model for developing nations aspiring to follow its path of success.

WHY DO KOREANS SAY "BECAUSE OF IMF"?

As the movie *Gukgabudoeui Nal* **국가부도의 날** (*Default*, 2018) accurately portrays, Korea's economic winning streak came to a screeching halt in 1997. The Asian Financial Crisis struck the region violently, causing a cascade of economic collapses. Korea was among the hardest hit — on the verge of default due to a foreign exchange shortage. Countless companies declared bankruptcy, people lost their jobs, and families were forced out onto the streets. Korea managed to avoid total collapse through international rescue—including the **IMF (International Monetary Fund)**—but at a steep cost. The government was forced to implement extensive corporate restructuring and institutional reforms, and ordinary people had to tighten their belts. This era, one of the most difficult and humiliating in modern Korean history, is commonly referred to as the "**IMF Era**," and the phrase "**because of IMF**" became a way for people to explain the drastic changes and sacrifices in their lives.

THE GOLD-COLLECTING CAMPAIGN

Gukgabudoeui Nal 국가부도의 날 (*Default*, 2018)

Remember, Koreans are known for their indomitable "can-do" spirit! In early 1998, following the financial meltdown, the government launched the **Gold-collecting Campaign 금 모으기 운동** *geum moeugi undong*. The idea was to collect gold from the public, export it, and convert it into U.S. dollars to help repay foreign-exchange debt, which exceeded USD 300 billion at the time. About 3.5 million people participated, donating personal items ranging from wedding rings to medals, and in total the campaign collected about 227 tons of gold, roughly double what the Bank of Korea had in its reserves. Thanks to the unified effort of the people and economic restructuring, Korea declared on December 4, 2000 that it had repaid all IMF loans, officially emerging from the crisis three years earlier than scheduled.

WHY DO KOREANS LOVE SPAM?

Gift package consisting of Spam and canola oil by CJ

What would be a good holiday gift in Korea? Surprisingly, one of the most popular gifts during the holidays is **SPAM**. How did SPAM become so popular in Korea when it is considered a "cheap pseudo-food" or "food that reminds you of war" in the U.S.? According to NPR (National Public Radio), South Korea is the second-largest SPAM-consuming country after the U.S. It was during the Korean War that SPAM was first introduced to Korea, at a time when food—especially meat—was scarce. Back then, SPAM was a luxury item that only the wealthy or those connected to U.S. Army bases could afford. For the less fortunate, *budaejjigae* **부대찌개**, made from leftover food from the U.S. Army base, became a beloved dish because it contained SPAM, a precious source of protein. Of course, budaejjigae is not the only reason Koreans love SPAM. Its salty, savory flavor pairs perfectly with rice and kimchi. The growing number of dual-income families and single-person households who prefer convenient meals has also contributed to its popularity. In addition, a series of advertising campaigns promoting SPAM as a "quality processed meat" worked like a charm, firmly establishing it as a beloved staple—and even a luxury gift item—in Korea.

WHO ARE THE CHAEBOLS?

Chaebol 재벌, composed of two Chinese characters — *jae* 재 (財) meaning "wealth" and *beol* 벌 (閥) meaning "clan" or "faction" — refers to the family-owned and controlled large Korean conglomerates with diversified subsidiaries. Occupying a dominant share of the Korean economy, chaebols were heavily fostered by the government's economic development policies in the 1960s and 1970s. During this period, chaebols played a crucial role as a driving force behind Korea's rapid economic growth. However, as they expanded their power through strategic alliances with political and business circles, negative side effects such as monopolization and political collusion also emerged.

Korean dramas like **Royal Family (2011, MBC)** and *Sangsokjadeul* 상속자들 (*The Heirs*, **2013, SBS**) depict the distinctive management culture of chaebols, where the owner family often wields greater power and authority than professional executives. As of 2024–2025, the top Korean chaebols remain Samsung, SK, Hyundai Motor, LG, and Lotte. Together, the top four (Samsung, SK, Hyundai Motor, and LG) reported combined assets of about US$1.04 trillion in 2024. Their combined sales in 2023 were about US$729 billion, accounting for roughly **41% of South Korea's nominal GDP**. The total assets of the five largest chaebols (including Lotte) now exceed **61% of the country's GDP**. The concept of chaebol is so distinctive that it has even been included as a Korean loanword in the **Oxford English Dictionary**.

In Korean pop culture, chaebol has also become a casual term for the "super-rich" and is often featured in Cinderella-type romance dramas. A typical trope involves a cocky, arrogant son from a chaebol family who believes his money can buy anything — including love — until he meets a humble, kindhearted girl who teaches him that sincerity, not wealth, is what truly matters.

SO, WHAT'S IT LIKE TO WORK IN KOREA?

According to the 2022 statistics from the **OECD (Organisation for Economic Co-operation and Development)**, South Korea ranked 5th among the 38 OECD member countries in terms of average annual working hours, with workers clocking in an average of 1,901 hours per year. This is 149 hours more than the OECD average of 1,752 hours. Countries with higher annual working hours than Korea include Colombia (2,405 hours), Mexico (2,226 hours), Costa Rica (2,149 hours), and Chile (1,962 hours).

But does sitting in front of a desk longer necessarily mean higher performance? Not necessarily. Although Koreans work longer hours, their productivity remains relatively low compared to other OECD countries. As of 2023, South Korea's hourly labor productivity stood at $51.1, ranking 24th out of 37 OECD countries. This figure is 61.1% of the United States' productivity ($83.6), 65.3% of Germany's ($78.3), and only about one-third of Ireland's, the top-performing OECD country, which leads with an impressive $154.9 per hour worked. While South Korea's labor productivity has been gradually improving, it still lags behind major economies. Analysts point out that excessive working hours are actually hurting overall productivity.

So, what adds to these long hours? Mostly *yageun* 야근—working overtime at night. While Korea's statutory workweek is 40 hours, with up to 12 hours of paid overtime on weekdays and 16 hours on weekends, many old-fashioned companies still expect employees to work beyond those limits. This stems from the outdated belief that *"working late means working hard."* In some workplaces with poor conditions, employees even pull all-nighters without proper compensation. Adding to this is an unspoken rule that you shouldn't clock out before your boss does.

Fortunately, times are changing. With younger generations demanding a better **work–life balance** and companies increasingly valuing efficiency over face time, working conditions in Korea are gradually improving.

YOUR FIRST DAY AT WORK IN KOREA MIGHT START AT A TRAINING CAMP!

At many large Korean companies, your first day on the job doesn't begin in an office cubicle. Instead, as a new recruit, you're sent to a training camp for an intensive team-building and orientation program! Commonly known as **OT (Orientation Training)** or **OJT (On-the-Job Training)**, new employees spend several weeks together at a dedicated facility learning about the company—its founding philosophy, history, main products and services, core values, and even its company anthem. By the end of the program, you'll have been molded into a seamless part of the corporate system!

WHY SO MANY RETIRED KOREAN AJUSSHIS RUN FRIED CHICKEN RESTAURANTS?

Choegoeui Chikin 최고의 치킨
(*Best Chicken*, MBN, 2019)

**Why Do Koreans Love
Fried Chicken So Much? P. 69**

In the romantic comedy Korean drama, ***Choegoeui Chikin*** 최고의 치킨 (***Best Chicken***, MBN, 2019), Park Choi-go's dream is to open his own fried chicken restaurant. He pompously quits his job at a large corporation to pursue his dream. Although the idea of going from typing away at a keyboard in an office cubicle to frying chicken in a kitchen may seem like an extraordinary transition, it's actually one of the most popular post-career choices among Koreans after retirement.

Why? Knowing how much Koreans love the fried chicken and beer combo *chimaek*, it shouldn't come as a surprise from a pure business perspective—but there's more to it. Koreans tend to identify themselves with their jobs, and the workplace is often seen as an extension of their home. For this reason, they have the notion of "**lifelong jobs**," and pursuing a single continuous career is considered a virtue.

With life expectancy increasing every year and the "60 is the new 50" mindset taking hold, Koreans still want and need to remain economically active to support their post-retirement lives (the legal retirement age in Korea is 65). So what do they do? Having pursued only one career their whole lives, trying something new seems risky, so naturally, they're compelled to choose something anyone can do—a franchise fried chicken restaurant.

The biggest merit is that it's supposedly a turnkey business: the franchise headquarters sets everything up for you—from selecting the location to marketing to interior design. You can just focus on frying chicken and enjoy a stable stream of income. What's not to love?

In reality, it's not as rosy as it sounds. Competition is fierce—there are over 409 fried chicken franchise brands and more than 87,000 stores nationwide, 14,509 of which are in Seoul alone. For comparison, there are 1,350 Lotteria burger stores, 436 McDonald's stores, and 442 Domino's Pizza outlets in Korea. As a result, it has truly become a "game of chicken," and more stores close than open. Once you factor in franchise fees and royalties, it's usually the franchiser who makes the real money.

In that sense, the abundance of fried chicken restaurants reflects the harsh reality of the limited post-retirement options Koreans have.

하이스쿨: 러브온
(*Hi! School-Love On*, KBS, 2014)

스카이캐슬
(*SKY Castle*, JTBC, 2018)

WHAT'S IT LIKE TO STUDY AS A STUDENT IN KOREA?

Your God offered you the opportunity to start your life all over again—but here's the fine print: as a student in Korea, would you take it? Well, the answer would sharply diverge depending on what type of drama you've watched. If a bubbly, lovey-dovey teenage romance like ***Hi! School – Love On* 하이스쿨: 러브온** (KBS, 2014) was your cup of tea, you'd sign the contract in a heartbeat. On the other hand, you'd definitely turn down the offer and walk away from the table if you'd recently watched ***SKY Castle* 스카이캐슬** (JTBC, 2018)—where parents go as far as blackmailing, intimidating, and pulling all sorts of hanky-panky just to push their kids ahead of others and get them into prestigious universities, mostly to keep their egos inflated at the expense of their children's freedom.

It was a shock to viewers around the world who had long believed that all Korean high school boys and girls did was exchange candies and love letters. SKY Castle isn't about puppy love but a reflection of the appallingly grim side of the Korean education system. While it's best to watch the whole series to truly understand what it's like, let me quickly walk you through an abridged version of a day in the life of a typical Korean high school student. Take a deep breath and hang tight!

The first class starts at 9 a.m., five days a week—but you'd better get there early, because you have to go through a rigorous screening process that might add a few extra minutes. When you arrive at the main entrance, teachers on duty and members of the student council check your hair length (if it's over the limit, you'll get a "free haircut" on the spot), and whether it's dyed or permed (both are prohibited). They also check the dress code—whether you're wearing your school uniform according to the official standards. (The rules on hair have changed since ***dubal jayuhwa* 두발자유화**, the "**Prohibition of Haircut Restrictions**," went into effect in 2018.)

"Such intolerance!" you mutter to yourself as you head to the classroom. Okay, you're now in the classroom, and class promptly starts at 9 a.m. A school day consists of seven sessions, each with 50 minutes of lessons and 10 minutes of break time in between. Lunch is from 1 p.m. to 2 p.m. and is served either in the classroom or in the student dining hall. The last session ends at 4:50 p.m. Yes! Free at last? Not so fast! You have to attend extracurricular activities for another hour.

Then it's feeding time again! After an hour for dinner, it's already 7 p.m. It's been such a long day! So… that means you can finally pack up and go home, right? Not so fast! After dinner comes a three-hour-long late-night self-study session, which used to require mandatory attendance until very recently (most schools nowadays have made it voluntary). Okay then, what do you do now with those precious extra three hours? Most students go to *hagwon* 학원 (after-school tutoring academies) or get private tutoring at home. If you don't want to fall behind (so much peer pressure!), you might want to consider one of the two—or both—options, right? Oh wait… don't forget to do your homework! Ugh!

And that's how Korean high school students spend their day. Multiply that by five, and you get their week. The weekends aren't off days either—studying continues at hagwons or at home with private tutors. But the worst comes when you reach *gosam* 고삼 (short for "third-year high schooler," or graduating class), when everything intensifies. How bad is it? A famous Korean saying, *sam dang sa rak* 삼당사락 ("three hours of sleep and you pass; four hours of sleep and you fail"), gives you a pretty good idea.

So… what do you think? Does starting your life over again as a student in Korea still sound like fun? I'll leave it up to you to decide. And while you weigh the pros and cons of each scenario, let's dig into why Koreans are so obsessed with education in the first place!

WHY DO KOREANS STUDY SO DARN HARD?

Does every profession deserve equal respect? Koreans in the past certainly didn't think so. The traditional yugyo ideology called *sa nong gong sang* 사농공상, or "the four categories of occupations" — scholars, peasant farmers, artisans and craftsmen, and merchants, listed in order of social status — dominated Korean society and led it to favor scholars, giving them higher prestige and social standing over those in other categories, who were often looked down upon, even with contempt.

For the noble class, the gateway to success and prestige was passing the state civil service examination called *gwageo* 과거 to become a government official. It was of such importance that unsuccessful applicants would keep trying year after year, and many died without ever bearing fruit. These national traits still remain intact in modern Korean society, but the fervor for education today is far greater than it was in the past. As we've seen, Koreans devote countless hours to studying so they can do well on the modern-day equivalent of the gwageo — the *suneung* 수능, or national college entrance exam. Like in the past, passing the exam with a competitive score will get you into a top university (the three most prestigious being **S**eoul National University, **K**orea University, and **Y**onsei University — hence the name **SKY** Castle). As in the drama, parents use every conceivable means to get their kids into one of these schools because it opens the door to prestigious careers and access to influential alumni networks.

It's of such importance that many students keep trying year after year until they get into their dream university. For the guaranteed success and all the perks that come with it, parents invest massive amounts of money into education, hoping their investment will one day pay off.

SUNEUNG - THE BIG DAY FOR STUDENTS

The second or third Thursday in November every year, when the regular school curriculum is completed, is the big day every graduating gosam student anxiously waits for. *Suneung* 수능, short for *daehak suhak neungryeok siheom* 대학수학능력시험 ("College Scholastic Ability Test," or CSAT), is a national exam that tests the academic ability required for college education. Subjects include Korean Language, Korean History, English, Math, Second Foreign Language/Hanja (Chinese Characters and Classics), Social Studies, Science, and Vocational Education. The test results play a crucial role in determining the likelihood of college admission.

The event receives national attention—because everyone has taken the test at some point—and the entire country seems to walk on eggshells, which often doesn't make much sense to foreign eyes. For example, on test day, airplanes stay grounded or circle around airports to avoid making noise during the listening test session. The stock markets open late, while public transportation increases its frequency to prevent traffic jams and ensure students arrive at the test sites on time.

In rare cases (but it happens every year), police cars come to the rescue of a student running late, providing an emergency ride. Outside the testing sites, parents stick *chapssaltteok* 찹쌀떡 ("glutinous rice cake") and *yeot* 엿 ("taffy") to the gates, both symbolizing the wish for success in passing the exam.

While this day marks the finish line for many students, those dissatisfied with their scores start the race again in hopes of achieving the score needed to enter their desired college. Some decide to go for *jaesu* 재수 ("second try") *samsu* 삼수 ("third try"), or even *sasu* 사수 ("fourth try"). For some, the pressure is so immense that they go as far as taking their own lives for feeling they've let their parents down.

"FREEDOM FOR OUR HAIRSTYLES!" HAIRCUT REGULATIONS

If you're used to seeing the hot and flashy hairstyles of K-Pop idols, you might assume that's what typical Korean teenagers look like in real life. But for decades, Korean schools enforced a strict haircut code. Considered one of the last remnants of the Japanese Occupation—whose education system was modeled after a military academy—it was often criticized for depersonalizing students. The rule was finally lifted in 2018, and since then, each school has adopted its own, more relaxed version of the regulations.

WHY DO KOREAN STUDENTS STUDY ABROAD SO MUCH?

Have you ever had a Korean student studying in your country? They're not exactly a rarity—because, as you can see from the chart, Korean students are one of the things Korea exports a lot of!

We all know that studying abroad costs a fortune—tuition, living expenses, and everything in between—but why do so many Korean parents still send their children overseas at such an early age?

- To escape the limitations of Korea's cramming-style education system, which is heavily focused on college entrance exams and filled with intense competition.
- To take advantage of advanced educational infrastructure abroad and gain the prestige of earning a degree from a top university—an advantage that carries significant weight when job hunting back in Korea.

On the financial side, studying abroad has traditionally been a privilege reserved for the wealthy. For families below the middle class, it often required enormous sacrifices from parents who hoped to secure a better future for their children.

WHO ARE THE KOREAN "WILD-GOOSE DADDIES"?

Known as *gireogi appa* 기러기 아빠 in Korean, "Wild-Goose Daddies" are fathers who remain in Korea to work while sending money to support their wives and children living abroad for the kids' education. The term comes from the image of migratory geese that travel great distances—just like these fathers, who must take long flights to visit their families across oceans.

WHERE KOREAN STUDENTS GO TO STUDY ABROAD

As of 2023, the number of Korean students studying abroad has reached approximately 123,000.
(Source: Ministry of Education, Republic of Korea)

North America – 52,302 students (42.5%)
United States: 40,755 students ╱ Canada: 11,480 students

Asia – 37,052 (30.1%)
China: 15,857 ╱ Japan: 13,701

Europe – 22,495 (18.3%)
Germany: 6,998 ╱ United Kingdom: 4,974 ╱ France: 4,464

Oceania – 10,313 people (8.4%)
Australia: 9,309 people ╱ New Zealand: (Details undisclosed)

Africa – 673 people (0.5%)
South Africa: (Details undisclosed)

Latin America – 346 people (0.3%)
Mexico: (Details undisclosed)

EATING A BLOCK OF TOFU AFTER GETTING RELEASED FROM JAIL

In *Chinjeolhan Geumjassi* 친절한 금자씨 (*Lady Vengeance*, **2005**), the vengeful heroine Geum-ja, who took the fall for a crime she didn't commit and served 13 years in prison, is offered a block of tofu by a pastor upon release. Eating tofu after being released from jail is one of the most frequently seen Korean movie and drama clichés—but as with most customs, there's a story behind it. Practically speaking, this tradition is said to have begun during the Japanese Occupation (1910–1945), when countless Korean independence activists suffered from malnutrition in prison. Upon release, they needed to recover their health quickly and economically—and tofu, rich in protein, healthy fats, carbs, and essential amino acids, was the perfect choice.

Symbolically, tofu's white color represents purity and peace, so eating it is a kind of cleansing ritual—wishing the ex-convict a fresh start and a life free from crime. (Except, of course, in Lady Vengeance, where Geum-ja smashes the tofu to the ground—she wasn't quite in the mood for symbolic purity. After all, tofu and revenge are both dishes best served cold.)

YEOT (KOREAN TAFFY) WILL MAKE YOU PASS THE NEXT BIG EXAM

What's the hottest good-luck charm among Korean students before an exam? *Yeot* 엿, a sticky Korean taffy made from steamed grains like rice, sorghum, or sweet potatoes. The superstition stems from the Korean verb *butda* 붙다, which means both "to stick" and "to pass (an exam)." By the same logic, *tteok* 떡, rice cake made from glutinous rice is also popular thanks to its stickiness. These days, a modern twist on the superstition has emerged—friends often give forks as gifts, since "picking (the right answer)" has become the new exam-day wish.

AVOID EATING *MIYEOKGUK* (SEA WEED SOUP) BEFORE BIG EXAMS

On the other hand, students steer clear of *miyeokguk* 미역국 (seaweed soup) before big tests. Its slippery texture is thought to symbolize "slipping" or "falling" in rank—definitely not the kind of omen you want on exam day. Because of this, the idiomatic expression *"ate seaweed soup"* (**미역국 먹었다** *miyeokguk meogeotda*) has come to mean "failed the exam."

BUT DO EAT *MIYEOKGUK* ON BIRTHDAYS

Miyokguk is a nutritious soup made with seaweed, rich in iodine and calcium—nutrients considered essential for pregnant women and postpartum mothers in Korea. This led to the long-standing tradition of eating miyokguk after childbirth to quickly replenish lost nutrients and improve blood circulation. Interestingly, the custom's origin can be traced back to a **Tang Dynasty text** titled *chohakgi* 초학기 ("Record of First Learning") written by Xu Jian (659–729). According to this record, the people of **Goguryeo** observed that after a year-long pregnancy, **whales** would eat seaweed following childbirth to heal their wounds. Inspired by this observation, they began feeding seaweed to women who had just given birth, believing it would aid recovery.

Over time, this postpartum practice evolved into the tradition of eating miyokguk on one's birthday. Eating the soup is more than just celebrating the day you were born—it's a symbolic act of gratitude and respect for the mother who gave you life. That's why in Korea, when it's someone's birthday, people often ask, *"Did you eat miyokguk today?"* But what if your birthday falls on the day of an important exam? Should you eat miyokguk or skip it to avoid bad luck? When in doubt, go ahead and enjoy the soup—but maybe pair it with some *chapssaltteok* 찹쌀떡 (sticky glutinous rice cake) or sweet *yeot* 엿 (taffy) to balance out the superstition!

WHO OR WHAT DO KOREANS BELIEVE BRINGS BABIES?

While storks are busy delivering babies in other parts of the world—mostly in Europe and North America, thanks to a 19th-century fairy tale by Hans Christian Andersen—there's someone else hard at work in Korea. Known as *samshin halmoni* 삼신 할머니 (grandmother goddess/spirit), where samshin means "triple god/goddess or spirits," she is

Samshin Halmoni
(National Museum of Korea,
© KOGL Type 1 (kogl.or.kr)

believed to embody three divine roles: the one who makes the blood, the one who shapes the bones, and the one who aids during labor and delivery. Combined with halmoni (grandmother), she represents the benevolent goddess of conception and childbirth who appears in the form of a loving grandmother. Unlike the stork, whose only job is to deliver babies, the Korean grandmother goddess has a far more complex job description. Her duties include:

1. Listening to the prayers of couples hoping for a child,
2. Blessing them with a baby,
3. Watching over unborn babies in the womb,
4. Ensuring a safe and smooth delivery for both mother and child, and
5. Protecting the baby from illness until the age of seven (after which protection is taken over by the God of the Seven Stars).

To show gratitude to Samshin Halmoni for her love and protection, families prepare a special offering table for her after childbirth. The table traditionally includes seaweed, rice, and freshly drawn water, and in some regions, scissors, thread, and money are also added. From this offering, the first meal for the mother after childbirth is prepared.

MONGOLIAN BIRTHMARKS? – THE WORKS OF *SAMSHIN HALMONI*

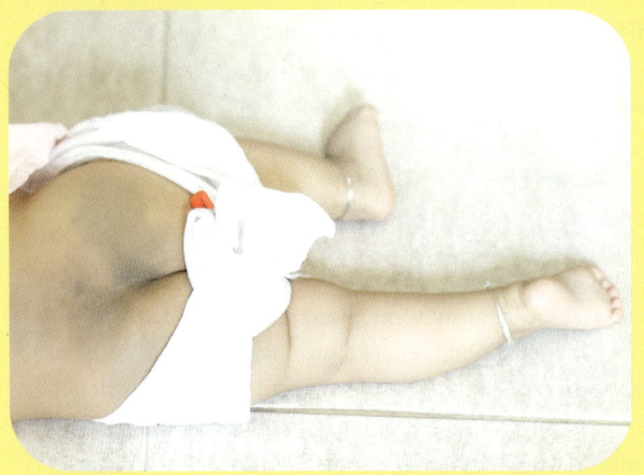

And our beloved samshin halmoni is clever enough to trademark her work through the process of branding! Almost every Korean infant—about 97%, according to research—is born with a bluish mark somewhere on their body: most commonly on the buttocks and torso (97.3%), followed by the arms (1%), legs (0.8%), chest and back (0.7%), and head and neck (0.2%). These marks usually fade as the child grows. According to a Korean folk tale, once there was a woman who struggled through a long and painful labor. Samshin halmoni came to her aid, gently rubbed her belly, and—voilà!—the baby was born. But there was a problem: the newborn wouldn't cry or breathe! Even the experienced goddess of childbirth was momentarily startled. As a last resort, she gave the baby a firm slap on the buttocks, and at last, the baby began to cry and breathe. Her divine slap was so powerful that it left a bluish mark where it landed! For this reason, Koreans believe that these bluish spots—called *mongo banjeom* **몽고반점** or **Mongolian spots**—are the result of samshin halmoni's divine touch, a heavenly seal of quality assurance, signifying that she personally checked the baby's health and blessed it at birth. In reality, these marks are medically known as **dermal melanocytosis**, and they appear not only among Korean babies but also among other Asian groups (China 86.3%, Japan 81.5%), as well as Native Americans (62.2%), Latin Americans (46%), and even Caucasians (5–10%). It seems samshin halmoni has been very busy traveling around the world!

However, in countries where these birthmarks are less common, misunderstandings can occur. Some foreign nurses or teachers unfamiliar with Mongolian spots have mistakenly thought the bluish marks were bruises caused by **child abuse,** leading to Korean parents being reported to the police. Fortunately, increased medical awareness is helping to prevent such incidents—but it's still a reminder of how easily cultural knowledge (or the lack thereof) can lead to serious confusion.

IPDEOT – KOREAN WAY OF SAYING "THERE'S A BUN IN THE OVEN"

At a breakfast table with the whole family gathered, just as the man of the house lifts his spoon, a young woman suddenly jumps out of her seat and dashes to the bathroom, covering her mouth. Moments later, the unmistakable sound of retching echoes through the house. The camera zooms in on the puzzled faces left behind at the table — and then comes the collective realization: "Wait a minute… Is she…?" The medical condition known as *ipdeot* **입덧** — or "morning sickness" in English — is one of the most classic Korean drama clichés used to hint at pregnancy. While in reality it's just one of many symptoms that pregnant women may experience early on, it's become the go-to storytelling shortcut for the big reveal. So if you see this scene in a Korean drama, you know what's coming — it's a sure sign that someone's expecting!

TAEMONG – THE DREAMS THAT FORETELL THE CONCEPTION OF A CHILD

From seeing a majestic dragon soaring into the sky (symbolizing success and prestige) to encountering a worried-looking ancestor (a warning of misfortune), Koreans have long loved interpreting dreams by identifying symbols and assigning meaning to them. Among these, *taemong* 태몽 — or conception dreams — hold a special place. They are believed to foretell the conception of a child and even reveal the baby's gender through symbolic imagery. Interestingly, it's not always the mother who dreams it — fathers, grandparents, or other close relatives may also experience a taemong connected to the unborn baby. The timing varies as well: some people have such dreams before realizing they're pregnant, while others have them during pregnancy. As for interpretation, the symbols often reflect gender associations — For instance, **corn**, **eggplant**, **chili peppers**, **the sun**, **tiger**, **dragon**, **carp**, or **rooster** are thought to signify a **boy**, while **flowers**, **chestnut burrs**, **eggs**, **the crescent moon**, **clam**, or **bird** are linked to a girl.

WHY DO KOREAN BABIES CELEBRATE THE 100TH DAY?

Baekil janchi 백일잔치, literally meaning "100 days party" (*baekil* "100 days" + *janchi* "party"), is a festive event where family members and close relatives celebrate a baby's 100th day since birth. Because **infant mortality rates** were high in the past, making it through the first 100 days was considered a remarkable achievement. As the number 100 symbolizes, it marked an important milestone—showing that the baby had passed the critical stage and was expected to live a long and healthy life. Guests are offered various types of *tteok* 떡, such as *baekseolgi* 백설기, *susugyeongdan* 수수경단, and *songpyeon* 송편, and share words of blessing for the baby. So if you're fond of tteok, it's an event you wouldn't want to miss!

WHY DO KOREAN COUPLES CELEBRATE THE 100TH DAY?

Given the explanation above, it's easy to understand why Korean couples make such a big deal out of their 100th day mark—it symbolizes having persevered through the most critical first 100 days of a relationship. It's also a celebration and a promise of more happy days to come. Couples usually dine out at a nice restaurant and exchange gifts. For your information, here are the gifts to avoid!

WHY DO KOREANS CELEBRATE THEIR 60TH BIRTHDAY SO HUGELY?

Just as we throw parties for babies on their 100th day and first birthday, our parents also deserve a celebration when they reach a major milestone in life—their 60th birthday, or *hwangap* 환갑. According to research, the average lifespan during the Joseon Dynasty (1392–1897) was less than half of what it is today (78 for men / 85 for women, though the high infant mortality rate contributed to lowering the average). The situation wasn't much different even for the privileged—the average age at death among the dynasty's 27 kings was 46.1, although there were outliers like **King Yeongjo 영조**, who lived a long 81.5 years. Therefore, reaching the age of 60 was truly something to celebrate, and children would organize lavish feasts and parties, inviting family friends and neighbors to share blessings and wisdom.

With advances in medical science and improved living conditions, however, the average life expectancy has dramatically increased, and the 60th birthday has become less momentous ("60 is the new 30, y'all!"). Instead of hosting big banquets, families often opt for dining out at a fine restaurant or taking a family trip. But don't think the party's over just yet—those big celebrations are simply saved for the 70th birthday *chilsun* 칠순 and the 80th birthday *palsun* 팔순.

**Technically, the word hwangap 환갑 represents the completion of a 60-year cycle in the East Asian zodiac system used to calculate time in China and across the East Asian cultural sphere, marking the beginning of a new cycle.*

DOLJABI – WHAT YOUR BABY GRABS DETERMINES THEIR FUTURE!

If *baekil janchi* 백일잔치 is a small-scale private event involving only family members and relatives, *doljanchi* 돌잔치, or "first birthday party" (*dol* "first birthday/anniversary" + *janchi* "party"), is a village-wide celebration that includes family friends and neighbors as well. And the highlight of the event is *doljabi* 돌잡이 – the "first birthday grabbing" ceremony (*dol* "first birthday/anniversary" + *jabi* 잡이 "to grab"). It's a traditional ritual held with the belief that the item the baby picks up from the birthday table predicts their future or fortune!

THERE IS A SPECIAL PLACE WHERE
KOREAN MOMS GO AFTER GIVING BIRTH

Who are the VVIPs in Korea? You might have a few names in mind, but new mothers definitely top the list. In Korea, the period between childbirth and recovery is considered crucial for a mother's long-term health, as it's difficult to naturally return to pre-pregnancy condition without proper care.

For this reason, there are service facilities called *sanhujoriwon* 산후조리원, often translated as "postpartum care centers," though the name hardly captures the range of services they offer. These centers provide nutritious daily meals for mothers, assist with newborn care such as diaper changes and baths, and have nurses on staff as well as medical facilities for emergencies.

Of course, this isn't a vacation resort for new moms—they still have to breastfeed every few hours and learn how to care for their babies. In short, sanhujoriwon are support institutions that help share the burden of exhausted mothers, enabling a faster and healthier recovery. In Korea, where paternity leave for men is still limited, such facilities have become an essential service.

SAJU PALJA – KOREANS BELIEVE THEIR FUTURE IS PREDETERMINED!

"Should I quit my job?" "Am I going to meet someone new?" "Is this business plan going to make me rich?" Or, to be more culture-specific, "Will this double-eyelid surgery bring me good luck?" Regardless of culture, we've always been curious about what the future has in store for us. But alas, even in the age of smartphones and quantum physics, we still don't have a future-seeing crystal ball. So what do we do? We turn to people like oracles, messiahs, and shamans—those who claim to possess the ability or knowledge to predict the future—and practice various methods of divination, ranging from bibliomancy (used by ancient Greeks and Romans, who would ask a question, open a book at random, and take the first passage they saw as the answer) to oinomancy, the art of reading the colors and patterns in wine. Meanwhile, in Korea, people have been using a rather sophisticated method of predicting one's fate and destiny!

On New Year's Day, it's common to see people flocking to *saju* 사주 shops with a list of questions prepared in advance. Thought to have originated from ancient Chinese philosophy, the literal meaning of saju is "**the four pillars of destiny**," referring to the year, month, day, and hour of one's birth. Each "pillar" is represented by two characters—one from the **12 Earthly Branches** and one from the **10 Heavenly Stems**—forming a total of eight characters. That's why it's also called *saju palja* 사주팔자, meaning "**four pillars and eight characters.**" These eight characters are drawn from a pool of 60, and each has either *yin* or *yang* energy. They're further categorized into the five primary elements, or *ohaeng* 오행: **wood, fire, earth, metal**, and **water**. Because each element's traits can strengthen or weaken different aspects of a person's personality, it takes a skilled saju reader to accurately interpret and explain one's fate and destiny.

A saju reader will then lay out the interpreted meaning of your chart on paper, and you can ask questions about specific areas of life (e.g., marriage, career, health) or over different time frames (e.g., one year, ten years, or after your 50s). So, next time you visit Korea, stop by a saju shop and have yours read—but don't get too excited if it turns out to be identical to Bill Gates's! Having the same saju doesn't mean you'll live the same life; outcomes also depend on factors like your parents' saju, personal relationships, circumstances, and environment (and, of course, saju readers like to leave some wiggle room for that reason). Oh, and don't get the impression that Koreans blindly believe in saju—though some definitely swear by it. Most people take it lightly, as a fun cultural experience or a way to gain some life advice from ancient wisdom. Nowadays, many would rather turn to Google (or Naver, for that matter) to find answers to their life questions—or at least, how to get kimchi stains out of their favorite shirt.

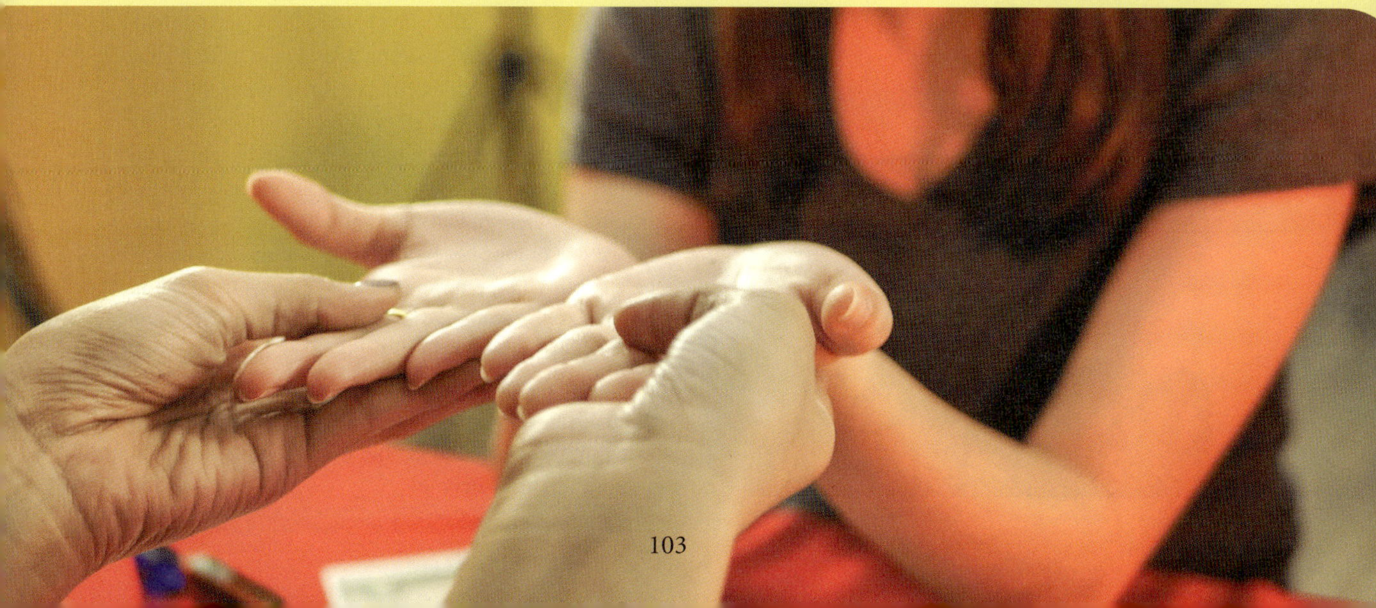

ARE WE A MATCH?
GUNGHAP – THE MARRIAGE COMPATIBILITY OF A COUPLE

Gunghap 궁합, "marital compatibility" is the analysis and interpretation of the complex interaction between the two sajus of a couple, and an attempt to take a peek at what their future would look like. Korean couples, new and old alike, also love visiting a saju shop to have their gunghap assessed and to foreshadow anything to come in the relationship — both good and bad. A saju reader's role is to provide an accurate measure of how well each side complements or conflicts with one another. Quite often, some traditional Korean families give it the utmost importance as a deciding factor of marriage, and it's not rare to hear breakup stories because of their incompatibility. For this reason, some would go as far as fabricating their birth certificates or even buying off a saju reader beforehand to have their story tailor-made to make it look like a perfect match. Such situations are frequently portrayed in Korean dramas. On the contrary, *chaltteok gunghap* 찰떡 궁합 means **"a match made in heaven,"** because *chaltteok* means **"glutinous rice cake**," and its stickiness represents perfect compatibility and harmony. Whether you believe it or not is entirely up to you, but it's a fascinating piece of Korean culture that represents the Korean people's attempt at unlocking the mysterious codes of our fate and destiny.

COUPLES BEWARE! WALKING DOWN ALONG THE DEOKSUGUNG STONE WALL PATH WILL MAKE COUPLES BREAK UP!

There's one place in Seoul that you should avoid visiting with your significant other — the *Deoksugung doldam-gil* 덕수궁 돌담길 ("stone wall path"). On the outside, it's a lovely trail along the stone wall surrounding the **Deoksugung Royal Palace**, but there's an urban legend that says walking down the path together will make couples break up. Although the origin of this belief is unclear, the trail leads directly to the Seoul Family Court nearby, so many couples who decided to part ways had to walk down this path to get there — hence the myth.

GIFTING SHOES TO YOUR SIGNIFICANT OTHER WILL MAKE THEM RUN AWAY!

Korean couples have a strong aversion to gifting shoes to each other because they believe it will make the other person run away — based on the superstition that new shoes will lead them to a better place and to someone better! Another related expression is "putting on rubber shoes the other way around," an idiom used to describe how a girl dumps her boyfriend or cheats on him while he's serving in the military. Rubber shoes were the most popular type of shoe girls used to wear back in the old days, and wearing them the other way around symbolizes a change of heart. So… if your significant other is trying to talk you into buying those fancy Gucci shoes, you can bring up this story and get out of the dangerous situation safely. You're welcome!

GWANSANG – PREDICTING ONE'S FORTUNE BY "READING THE FACE"

"Freeze! You're under arrest for a crime you are predicted to commit in the next 36 hours!" Sounds like something Tom Cruise would say in the cyberpunk movie Minority Report (2002), doesn't it? Set in the year 2054, the movie imagines what our future society might look like — the Washington D.C. Police Department comes up with an amazing new technology called PreCrime, which assesses the likelihood of an individual committing a crime and apprehends them in advance. Kudos to us, we've shortened the expected time to make sci-fi technology a reality by a whopping 30 years. In China, real-time facial-recognition technology capable of tracking down a suspect is already in use. Armed with information obtained from "big data," stopping the bad guys beforehand is becoming a reality.

Centuries before the emergence of computer technology, Korean people had their own facial-recognition system. In the movie *Gwansang* 관상 (*The Face Reader*, **2013**), gwansang (physiognomy) expert Nae-gyeong is a famed face reader known for his ability to assess a person's personality, mental state, and the good luck or misfortunes one is born with, in order to predict their destiny. He finds himself in the middle of a Royal Court murder investigation, where he's asked to use his skills to identify the murderer. After that, he assists the king — who, ironically, had asked him if he had the "face of a king" before ascending the throne — to weed out potential rebels and nip them in the bud.

Not as high-tech as computers, gwansang, believed to have originated in ancient China, embodies the essence of East Asian philosophy. The central idea of gwansang is that our face is a small universe with a yin and yang balance. It is divided into three parts, each part foretelling the fortune for a given period of life:

- Forehead : *sangjeong* **상정** (up until the age of 30)
- Area between the eyebrows to cheekbones : *jungjeong* **중정** (up until the age of 40)
- Philtrum to chin : *hajeong* **하정** (age 50 and beyond)

The characteristics of facial features, such as their form and shape, have different meanings, and their relationships determine one's overall fortune. Some of the major reading points are:

- **Forehead**: Reputation, Parents
- **Eyebrows**: Interpersonal Skills, Siblings
- **Eyes**: Love, Children
- **Cheekbones**: Ambition, Power
- **Nose**: Wealth, Liquid Assets
- **Mouth**: Aspiration, Talents
- **Chin**: Realty Assets, Employees

What A Small Face / Small Head You Got! I Envy You! P. 115

Why Do Koreans Get So Much Plastic Surgery? P. 237

Like saju, the gwansang reader's role is to analyze and interpret the complexities of one's facial features to predict the future. While it's not scientific, it's a common practice in Korea enjoyed by people of all ages, similar to tarot card reading and palm reading. Some swear by it, and some big companies even hire face readers when interviewing new candidates! According to face-reading experts, plastic surgeries won't alter destiny, and race, culture, or ethnicity are irrelevant in the technique. So ditch your crystal ball and look in the mirror — your future is already written on your face.

HAVING A PIG DREAM = GOOD LUCK COMING YOUR WAY

Across many cultures around the world, pigs are a symbol of prosperity, abundance, and fertility. But Koreans arguably have the strongest faith in this chubby animal; if they see a pig in their dream, 10 out of 10 will jump right out of bed and make a beeline for a lottery store. This belief is further strengthened by countless incidents where lottery winners claim the reason they bought a ticket was because of a pig dream!

Still not convinced? In Korean, the Chinese character 豚 (pig) is pronounced *don* 돈, which is the Korean word for "money." So **pig = money**! For that reason, people sometimes "buy" someone else's dream in exchange for money, believing that the ownership of the auspicious dream and its associated good omen are transferred to the purchaser.

WHY DO KOREANS GIFT TOILET PAPER AND LAUNDRY DETERGENT FOR HOUSEWARMING PARTIES?

TOILET PAPER – "MAY YOUR FUTURE BE WITHOUT ANY ISSUES"
because Korean word *pulida* 풀리다 means "to unfold (a roll of toilet paper)," but also means "to resolve (an issue)."

LAUNDRY DETERGENTS – "MAY HAPPINESS BUBBLE UP"

SPOOKY KOREAN SUPERSTITIONS & BELIEFS

WHERE YOUR ANCESTORS ARE BURIED CAN EITHER BRING GOOD LUCK OR MISFORTUNE TO THE DESCENDANTS!

Which direction should my couch face? Furniture arrangement is something we don't usually give too much thought to—but for some Koreans, it requires careful planning, as many still follow the idea of *pungsujiri* 풍수지리 ("wind-water-earth-principles-theory"), the Korean term for the Asian art of divinatory geomancy, more commonly known by its Chinese name *feng shui* ("wind-water"). In a nutshell, it's the study of topography based on the belief that one's destiny is shaped by their natural surroundings. Pungsujiri analysts are believed to determine whether a particular site is auspicious by interpreting the relationship between life-force energy and its environment, claiming that bad energy responsible for misfortune can be blocked or neutralized through the strategic placement of various elements.

According to historical records, it was a Buddhist monk of the **Silla Dynasty 신라** (57 BC – 935 AD) who introduced the philosophy of feng shui from China and adapted it to fit Korean culture. Since then, many Koreans have held the strong belief that a propitious tomb site for one's ancestors can bring good luck and prosperity to their descendants. Some families even go as far as digging up old graves and relocating them to more "favorable" spots when a streak of misfortune is attributed to an ancestor's ill-fated burial site. This reflects Korea's Confucian culture, where honoring and respecting elders—even after death—is of utmost importance. Notably, **General Kim Yu-sin 김유신** (595–673), who led the **unification of the Three Kingdoms of Korea**, and **King Taejong Muyeol 태종 무열왕** (604–661) both incorporated pungsujiri principles in selecting their burial sites. During the same period, noble families often delayed burials for months to find the most auspicious location. A modern portrayal of this belief can be seen in the period film *Myeongdang* 명당 ("*Feng Shui,*" 2018), which tells the story of people competing for the ideal burial ground for their ancestors. The tradition still lives on today—major Korean conglomerates have hired renowned pungsujiri consultants to plan the layout of their new buildings, and even the government has brought in experts before selecting the site for a new administrative complex.

So next time you pick up your futon from IKEA, maybe study a bit of pungsujiri beforehand—because where you place it might just shape your future.

WHAT IS THE KOREAN SHAMANISM - MUSOK & MUDANG?

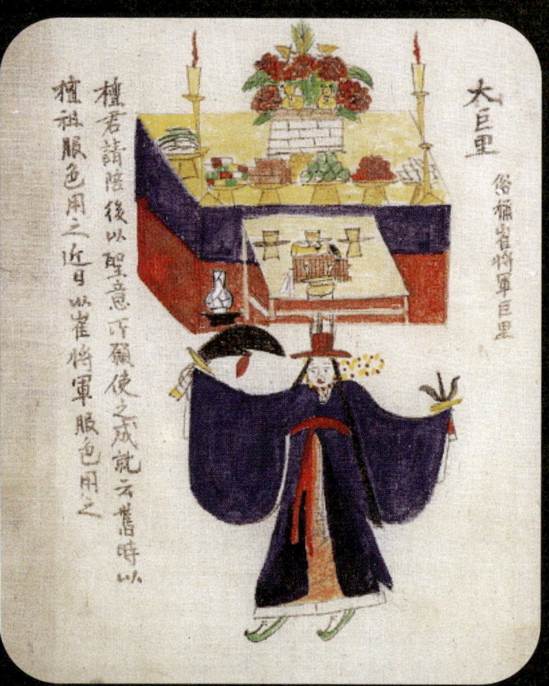

An illustration from *mudangnaeryeok* 무당내력, a compilation of the traditional Korean shaman exorcism methods in the late Joseon Dynasty (1800s). It is currently housed in Gyujanggak, Seoul National University.

"The power of Christ compels you!" In the Hollywood movie *The Exorcist* (**1973**), fearless Fathers Lankester Merrin and Damien Karras join forces in Georgetown, Washington D.C., to desperately cast out the evil spirit from Regan, a little girl believed to be possessed. They fight off the evil using various means—hanging the Holy Rosary, sprinkling holy water on the possessed, and reciting prayers to invoke God and angels to intervene. Now, in the Korean horror movie *Gokseong* 곡성 (*The Wailing*, **2016**), a series of horrifying murders occur in a rural village. The suspects all show strange symptoms— skin rashes and incoherent speech. A young girl named Hyojin begins to display the same signs, but her condition worsens as she screams obscenities and eats uncontrollably for no apparent reason.

Convinced she's possessed, her grandmother summons Ilgwang, a shaman, to perform an exorcism. Ilgwang, dressed in a ritual black garment with colorful sleeves striped in red, green, blue, and yellow, is a *mudang* 무당, or **Korean shaman** (technically, a male shaman is called *baksu mudang* 박수무당). Mudangs are key figures in Korean folk shamanism called *musok* 무속.

Typically, most mudangs are compelled to become one rather than choosing to. They often experience a supernatural phenomenon called *shinbyeong* 신병 ("spirit sickness")—a state described by scientists as "a temporary acute psychotic manic episode." It involves seeing ghosts and suffering from mysterious illnesses that vanish only after being possessed by local deities or ancestral spirits through a ritual called *naerimgut* 내림굿, an initiation rite conducted by another shaman.

A mudang's job is vast. They are invited to perform ceremonies called *gut* 굿, rituals that involve offerings and sacrifices to local deities and ancestor spirits. Most of the time, these are village-wide events because they are quite a spectacle—featuring rhythmic dances, dazzling costumes, powerful songs, mysterious oracles, and prayers. Believed to have the ability to communicate between spiritual beings and mankind, mudangs don't just perform exorcisms—they ask the deities and ancestors to intervene in human fortune: curing illness, bringing good luck, warding off evil, and ensuring a good harvest. After someone's death, shamans also help the soul of the departed leave the earthly life without regrets and find its way to heaven.

MUDANG PROVIDES FORTUNE-TELLING SERVICES TOO

And a popular service provided by a mudang to anyone who wishes is *jeom* 점, or fortune-telling by communicating with the spiritual beings. It's fundamentally different from saju because it solely relies on the messages allegedly obtained from the otherworldly beings, as well as various divination methods such as analyzing the pattern of rice grains sprinkled on the table, and interpreting the meaning of a randomly drawn stick, whereas saju tries to have a more systematic and deductive approach to interpreting one's fate using objective information such as birth date, time, and year.

Like saju, mudang's fortune-telling services are very popular and some people vouch for its accuracy – but use the service at your own risk, because there are many civil cases of a (fake) mudang talking a victim into paying a huge service fee on the pretext of a tribute to appease the local deities or ancestral spirits. It's a situation often appearing in Korean dramas where a naive character gives away all his or her hard-earned money to a (fake) mudang. So, in a nutshell, a mudang is a multi-purpose Korean character who serves the purposes of an oracle, counselor, medium, and shaman.

WHY DO KOREANS PUT A BOILED PIG HEAD AT A BUSINESS OPENING CEREMONY?

Tossing a few coins onto the floor mat of a newly purchased car (known as "coining") or carrying around a rabbit's foot are just some examples of the various rituals and lucky charms people rely on for good luck and divine protection around the world.

Korean people also perform a blessing ritual called *gosa* 고사, which can be done with or without the help of a mudang. People perform gosa for all kinds of occasions – from taking a brand-new car on the road for the first time and opening a new business, to beginning a new TV production season, or even launching a cutting-edge satellite into the sky! At the center of the ritual table, you'll find a smiling pig head because it's a symbol of fertility, prosperity, and good luck. (The Chinese character 豚 [pig] is pronounced *don* 돈 in Korean, which also means "money.") Nothing says "lucky" quite like a pig head in Korean culture. The severed and boiled pig head serves as a sacrificial offering to local deities and ancestral spirits. It's accompanied by many other typical shamanistic elements such as incense, food, and alcohol. Participants in the ritual often stuff wads of cash into the mouth, ears, and even the nose of the pig head as a token of offering and contribution. The money collected usually goes to the host of the ceremony. These days, the gosa tradition still lives on, but many people feel uncomfortable using a real pig head due to its grotesque appearance and concerns about animal cruelty. Instead, they substitute it with a silicone replica or even a cake shaped like a pig head.

WRITING SOMEONE'S NAME IN RED IS A BIG NO-NO!

WRITING SOMEONE'S NAME IN RED IS A BIG NO-NO!

Of all the colors available, there's one you should always avoid when writing someone's name in Korea — **red**. This belief is especially strong among the older generation, and several theories explain why. First, red symbolizes death, as it's the color of blood. Second, the origin may trace back to Korean history — when **Grand Prince Suyang 수양대군**, the second son of King Sejong the Great of the Joseon Dynasty (1392–1897), plotted a coup, he allegedly wrote his enemies' names in red ink to mark them for death. A third theory points to the Korean War, when red ink was used to cross out the names of civilians and soldiers killed in action. Whatever the case, it's best to play it safe — never write someone's name in red!

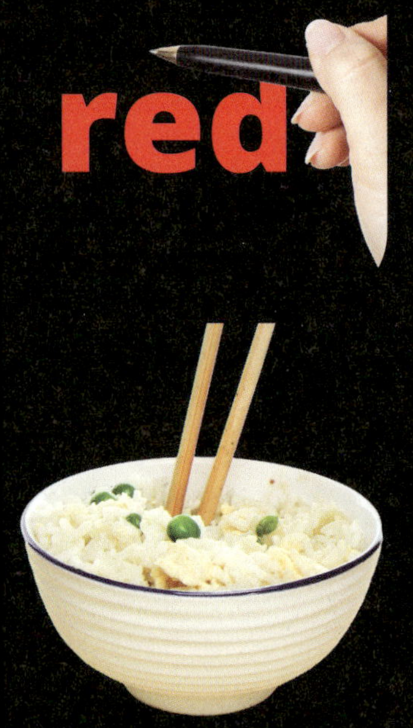

STICKING CHOPSTICKS STRAIGHT INTO A BOWL OF RICE IS ALSO A NO-NO!

This is also a big no-no in Korean culture because it resembles a Korean funeral ceremony and *jesa* **제사**, a memorial ceremony held on the anniversary of the ancestor's death. During the ceremony, incense burners are usually filled with rice to act as the holder, and spoons are stuck directly into the bowl of rice (some families choose to place them next to the bowl instead). To avoid inadvertently offering the person sitting next to you a memorial service (Um… I'm not dead yet!), keep your chopsticks somewhere else, usually on top of the bowl or on the table. Often, a small ceramic rest is provided on the table.

WHY DO KOREANS RUB THEIR CHOPSTICKS BEFORE EATING?

You might have wondered when you dined with your Korean friend – why do they rub their chopsticks before eating? Is it some kind of ritual? Are they trying to start a fire? The quick answer is to get rid of the possible splinters, and for that reason, such practice only applies to wooden chopsticks, mostly the cheap break-apart type that has those itty bitty splinters sticking out. Because Koreans were the only people in the world who have been using metal chopsticks, it can be said with confidence that it's a habit acquired recently. Rubbing chopsticks isn't something that's frowned upon, but you might want to be careful when you are invited to dinner because doing so could send a wrong signal that you think the chopsticks are of subpar quality, offending the host.

DON'T WHISTLE AT NIGHT

No matter how happy you are, whistling at night is something Korean parents would stop you from doing because it's believed to attract snakes (but if you like reptiles, try it by all means)! The logic behind the idea is that in the past, snake hunters used whistling, which is similar to the hissing sound of snakes, to lure and control them. And it's the adults who spread the rumor to elicit behavior (be quiet at night!), such as the case with Santa Claus. With most Korean families now living in concrete apartments and probably never getting a chance to see a snake throughout their life, the idea is pretty obsolete.

There are two surefire ways to get a good smack from mom at the dinner table in Korea: shaking your legs and placing your spoon upside down, or belly up. Both are believed to bring bad luck. Like many other superstitions, it's difficult to track down who holds the copyright to these tales, but we can make an educated guess. In Korea's highly Confucian society, decorum and orderliness are of high importance, and anything that falls outside that realm is frowned upon and discouraged. Shaking legs, considered rude especially in front of older people, checks every single box. Similarly, placing a spoon belly up raises the flag because Korean people have long considered eating one of the most important parts of life. Scooping a hefty amount of rice is symbolic of health and wealth! Thus, to Korean eyes accustomed to seeing spoons neatly placed with the inside bowl facing up—meaning "scooping up" good luck—doing the opposite symbolizes "scooping away" good luck.

WHY IS THERE NO 4TH FLOOR?

The Korean word for the number four, *sa* 사, is pronounced the same as the Chinese word for "death" (死). For this reason, the number 4 is often replaced with the English letter "F" in elevators, or skipped entirely in places like hospitals. This superstitious practice of avoiding the number 4—similar to the Western fear of number 13—is called *tetraphobia* (from the ancient Greek tetrás meaning "four," and phobia meaning "fear"). It's common in East Asian countries that use Chinese characters as part of their written language. For example, Korea's national railroad, Korail, deliberately left out train number 4444 when assigning numbers from 4401 upward. Some Koreans might even jump out of their skin if they receive a phone call from a number ending in 4444 —especially at 4:44 AM!

NEVER CLIP YOUR NAILS AT NIGHT

And if you thought snakes were creepy, this one's even worse. There's an old belief that if you cut your nails at night, rats will sneak into your home, eat the clippings off the floor, and then transform into a human—taking your form! As strange as it sounds, this superstition likely originated before the invention of electricity and nail clippers. Cutting nails at night by candlelight or lamplight was risky, and cleaning up properly was difficult. Over time, that practical warning evolved into a spooky folktale. Now we know that every superstition has a story behind it—and most of the time, it's our parents and grandparents who came up with these tales with the best intentions at heart, just like the story of Santa Claus. And it's fun to know the hidden meanings behind them, because they give us a snapshot of what society looked like at the time.

FAN DEATH — THE SILENT KILLER

WHY DO KOREANS BELIEVE LEAVING THE FAN ON WHILE SLEEPING WILL KILL YOU?

Can you guess the leading cause of death in the summer in Korea? Naturally, you'd think of things like heat stroke, dehydration, or drowning from drunk-swimming at pool parties when the mercury can climb above 40°C (104°F) during the dog days. But Koreans would put something entirely different at the top of the list—something you probably never expected: **Fan Death**. First and foremost, this refers to electric fans, not the lethal hand-held fans made of sharp sheet metal wielded by lady Kung Fu masters. Secondly, it's not the blades of the electric fans that cause direct physical harm. The way those "evil" electric fans kill people is much sneakier than that. Fan death is the belief that sleeping with an electric fan running in a closed room, with no windows open, can kill a person. The proposed causes are **hypothermia** (body temperature abnormally lowered by the fan), **asphyxiation** (suffocation due to oxygen depletion and carbon dioxide intoxication), and even **facial paralysis**. Back in 2006, the Korea Consumer Protection Board issued an official safety alert, stating that "asphyxiation from electric fans and air conditioners" was among the five leading causes of death in Korea. Over the years, scientists and medical experts have repeatedly tried to debunk this urban legend, arguing that such deaths were coincidences and cases of false attribution bias—people died of other natural causes, but the running fan in the room took the blame. Yet the belief remains deeply rooted. So much so that Korean news channels still report fan death cases every summer, keeping the superstition alive year after year.

MOVING? PICK THESE DAYS TO KEEP EVIL SPIRITS AT BAY

Congratulations! You just signed the lease contract for your new apartment in Seoul, and now it's time to pick the best moving date! Upon calling multiple moving companies for a quote, you quickly notice that prices fluctuate—sometimes as high as double or triple compared to other days—but you can't quite figure out why. Sometimes it's the weekend, and sometimes it just falls on the "hump day" of the week. Befuddled, you call your go-to Korean buddy, and he explains: "In Korea, people believe that evil spirits will get in your way on moving day, and may even follow you to your new home! According to folklore, this evil spirit, called *son* 손, roams the four points of the compass depending on the day of the week and takes delight in bothering humans. Luckily, these spirits keep regular hours during their workdays. Every month on the lunar calendar:

• They are active in the East on the 1st and 2nd,
• In the South on the 3rd and 4th,
• In the West on the 5th and 6th,
• And in the North on the 7th and 8th.

They go up into the heavens and are "off work" on the 9th, 10th, 19th, 20th, 29th, and 30th. These are the days to aim for—they're called *son eopneunnal* 손 없는날 ("a day without evil spirits"). People will even pay a premium to reserve these days, which explains why moving prices spike." Now you know the whole story, and the decision is yours. Will you shell out a few extra bucks to make sure no evil spirits follow you to your new place? Or will you keep the money for a home party instead? Whatever you choose, just don't put Mr. Son on the guest list if

Odd Questions and Compliments

WHAT IS YOUR BLOOD TYPE?
IT DETERMINES YOUR PERSONALITY

Many Korean people—a whopping 75%!—strongly believe that blood type is closely related to personality traits, and they often stereotype people according to their blood type. If you go on a blind date, chances are very high that you'll be asked what your blood type is, so make sure you know it beforehand. While many will just laugh it off and say it's "for fun," some take it quite seriously. So, where did this idea come from? It is believed to have started when a **Japanese professor** named **Takeji Furukawa** published his work titled "**The Study of Temperament Through Blood Type**" in 1927. Although his research was largely regarded as non-scientific due to lack of credentials, the idea was intriguing enough to quickly gain popularity. In the 1970s, a Japanese journalist who advocated Furukawa's idea further amplified it, and the belief eventually made its way to Korea. Another factor contributing to its spread is that all elementary school students in Korea have a mandatory annual health examination—which included blood type testing until 2016—making children more familiar and sensitive to the idea than kids in countries where blood type is rarely discussed. All right, that's enough background—now for the fun part! Below are the descriptions commonly used to illustrate the characteristics of each blood type. Take a good read and compare them with your own self-assessment to see how (in)accurate they are.

A  INTROVERTED PERFECTIONIST

- Conservative / Introverted.
- Find difficulty in expressing emotions or trusting others.
- Often called a fundamentalist and a perfectionist.
- Have a strong sense of responsibility at work, and easily gain the trust of the organization.
- Always make plans with extreme caution, but often seen as lacking flexibility.
- Look like a hard worker, but you can be a party animal in disguise.
- Can be quite adventurous when dating.

B CREATIVE AND (TOO) CURIOUS

- Inquisitive / Full of curiosity.
- Have an endless stock of topics for conversation.
- Full of original ideas.
– Exceptional ability in project planning.
- Have a strong interest in new things and often have trouble focusing.
- Sometimes called inconsistent.
- Prefer working at your own pace than in organizational settings.
- Compassionate and tender-hearted but sometimes seen as too nosy.

O  COMPETITIVE LEADER

- Personality – Warm-hearted / Behavior – Goal-oriented.
- Not bothered by minor obstacles and have the ability to focus on given tasks.
- Strong sense of comradeship, often assuming the leadership role within a group.
- Often seen as a romanticist pursuing dreams, but can be surprisingly cool-headed in pressing situations.
- Hate losing and competitive- can be seen as condescending and self-complacent.

AB MYSTERIOUS AMPHIBIAN

- Unpredictable – different characteristics depending on which side of the A&B combination gets ignited.
- Superb ability to adapt to any given situation.
- Objective in making decisions, thus less prone to making mistakes.
- Often seen as someone who is easily led, but also can be wishy-washy.
- Prefer to keep personal life private and do not care much about those of others, either.

So… how accurate are they? The Korean Society of Hematology officially announced that there is **absolutely no scientific basis for the belief that blood type determines personality**. Personality is actually a byproduct of environmental factors such as family and education. In fact, many experts attribute it to the **Barnum effect**, the tendency to accept vague or general statements as personally meaningful. Examples include character assessment tests, horoscopes, and tarot reading. The similarity between them is that the descriptions provided are so general that they can apply to anyone, leading people to falsely believe they are tailored to their unique circumstances.

Maybe it's because our desire to find explanations for what happens around us is deeply embedded in human nature, and these tools help alleviate our uncertainties. And, of course, there's the entertainment value—they make us feel a little better when our horoscope (or a fortune cookie!) says something hopeful.

A bonus story: There is even a compatibility chart between blood types to show how well people match romantically. As you might guess, a research survey conducted by a matchmaking company concluded it was baseless. They examined 3,000 couples and found that blood type had no significant impact on the likelihood of a couple getting married. Well, there you have it. Do you believe the theory? Then you must be blood type B! (sarcasm)

WHY DO KOREANS ASK IF YOU ATE?

Bap meogosseo? 밥 먹었어? *("Have you eaten?")* might sound like the first thing you hear when visiting your grandma's house. But for Koreans, it's a common greeting, used as frequently as *annyeonghaseyo* 안녕하세요 (*"Are you at peace?"* = *"How are you?"*). Why ask if someone ate? Its origin lies in history. In agricultural Korea, meals were crucial because they not only provided energy but also served as a bonding ritual for laborers and the community. After the Korean War, when food scarcity was common, asking if someone had eaten became a way to check in on one another. Today, its meaning has shifted. It's essentially the same as asking "How are you?" in English, to which you might answer "Fine, thanks," even if you weren't feeling fine.

So when asked as a greeting, just respond with "I ate," or "I haven't, but I will soon." If the person really wants to share a meal, they will usually add something like, "I was going to ask you to have lunch with me," which makes the difference clear.

DON'T EAT ALONE

If you decide to dine alone at a Korean restaurant, don't be surprised if people give you a strange look. In traditional collectivist Korean society, meals were a key bonding ritual meant to be shared with family, friends, or co-workers. Dining alone was unusual and could draw curious glances or questions from the owner *ajumma* out of genuine concern. However, times have changed. Modern Koreans are often pressed for both time and space, and meals have shifted from being social rituals to a practical source of energy and nutrition. Reflecting this change, many restaurants now offer *honbap* 혼밥 ("solo-dining") and *honsul* 혼술 ("solo-drinking") options, catering to the busy lifestyle of contemporary Korea.

Mukbang - You Can Also Make Money Broacasting Your Eating Session! P. 241

THE MBTI BOOM IN SOUTH KOREA

The **Myers-Briggs Type Indicator (MBTI)** is a personality assessment tool that categorizes personalities into 16 distinct types. It classifies how people perceive and make decisions about the world using four indicators: **Extroversion (E)** vs. **Introversion (I)**, **Sensing (S)** vs. **Intuition (N)**, **Thinking (T)** vs. **Feeling (F)**, and **Judging (J)** vs. **Perceiving (P)**. These combinations yield types like INTJ or ESFP. The origins of MBTI lie in the personality typology theory of early 20th-century psychologist Carl Jung. Based on this, Katharine Cook Briggs and her daughter Isabel Briggs Myers developed the MBTI in the 1940s. Their original purpose was to help women during World War II choose occupations suited to their personalities. Since then, it has been applied across diverse fields including education, organizational management, and counseling.

In South Korea, MBTI has transcended being merely a psychological test to become a cultural phenomenon. While once used primarily for job hunting and self-improvement, it has now become a fundamental question in everyday conversation, permeating topics like romance, friendship, and workplace dynamics. Among younger generations especially, the question *"What's your MBTI?"* is an indispensable part of self-introductions and frequently appears in dramas, variety shows, and advertisements. Recently, more people ask about MBTI instead of blood type, solidifying MBTI as a new "personality yardstick." While MBTI has taken root in Korea as a new language for self-expression and understanding others, it faces criticism for lacking sufficient scientific basis. Therefore, it is suggested that MBTI be used more as a lighthearted cultural code for enjoyment rather than as a definitive personality assessment tool.

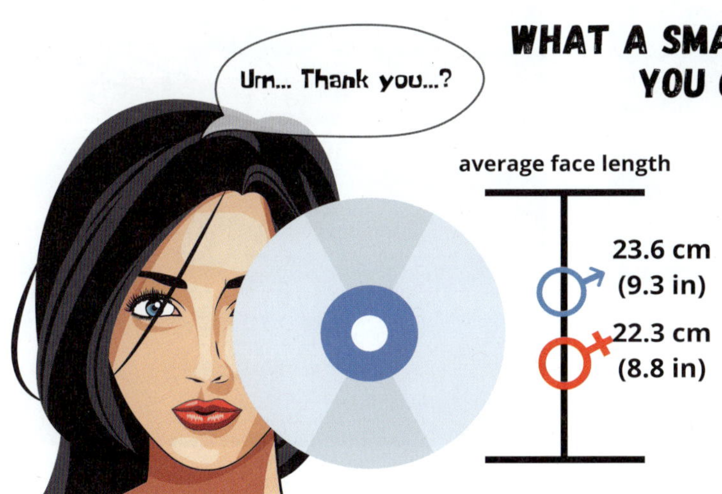

"Wow! Your face is the size of a fist!" If someone says this to you, don't panic—they're not picking a fight. It's actually a genuine compliment. One of the most important standards of Korean beauty is having a nicely proportioned body, with the *pal deung shin* 팔등신 ("eight-head figure") considered ideal. Having a smaller face is admired, especially among the younger generation, because it helps achieve that ideal proportion.

Another belief is that a smaller (slim and thin) face gives a more youthful look and makes facial features appear more well-defined—and thus more photogenic. Koreans' fascination with small faces is evident on TV, where celebrities with unusually small faces are often asked to hold an object next to their face for quick measurement, and sometimes even pull out measuring tools. One of the most convenient and popular ways to measure if your face qualifies as "small" is to hold up a **CD-ROM** above your face. If it completely eclipses or covers most of your face, congratulations—you've got a super small face! But the trend doesn't stop there. There's even a study, The Standard Figure of Korean People, which measures face sizes. According to the study, the average face length of men and women is 23.6 cm (9.3 in) and 22.3 cm (8.8 in), respectively.

So… how do you measure up? Do you fall within the Korean beauty standards? Uh oh… Why the long face?

Gwansang - Predicting One's Fortune By "Reading The Face" P. 105

DEATH & AFTERLIFE

WHAT DO KOREANS BELIEVE ABOUT AFTERLIFE?

Jeonseoleui Gohyang 전설의 고향
*(Korean Ghost Stories / Hometown Legends,
1977~2009, KBS)*

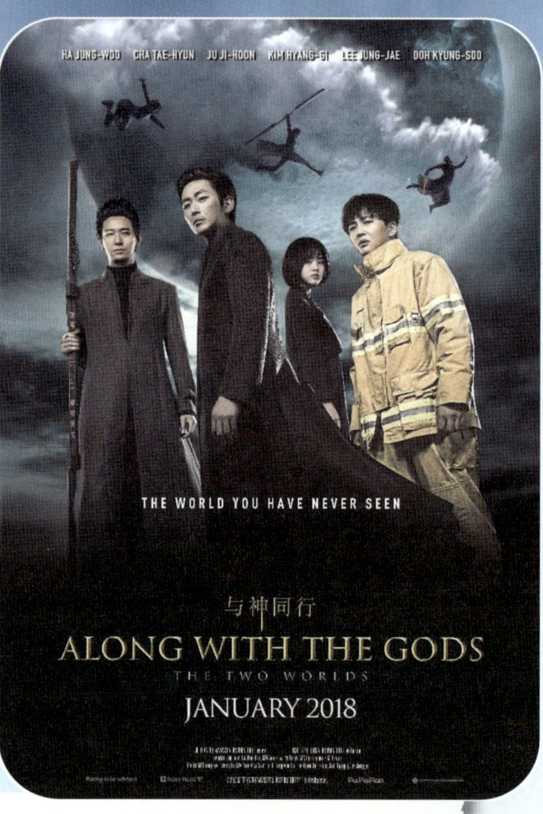

Shingwa Hamkkae 신과함께
(Along With The Gods, 2017)

One of the most popular ways for Koreans to survive the hot summer dog days is by watching a spooky TV series like ***Jeonseoleui Gohyang*** 전설의 고향 (***Korean Ghost Stories / Hometown Legends***, **1977–2009, KBS**). The series is a compilation of traditional Korean folk tales, myths, and legends passed down from generation to generation. Aside from being genuinely scary, it's also a fun way to learn about Korean people's views on the afterlife. If you want a slightly less intense introduction, sampling a few episodes of ***Shingwa Hamkkae*** 신과함께 (***Along With The Gods***, **2017**) can also give you a clear layout of the Korean concept of the afterlife—without scaring you stiff.

Why Do Koreans Eat Simmering Hot *Samgyetang* On The Most Sweltering Days Of Summer? P. 60

JEOSEUNG SAJA -
THE MESSENGER FROM
THE OTHER WORLD

A still from *Gimakhin Yusan* 기막힌 유산
(*Brilliant Heritage*, KBS, 2020)

What happens when you die? Here's what Korean people believe occurs after the last breath. First, immediately upon death, a messenger from the other world, ***Jeoseung Saja* 저승사자** (Yes, the **Saja Boys** from **the K-Pop Demon Hunters** are them), arrives to guide the soul to the afterlife (if seen while one is still alive, it foreshadows imminent death). Usually, they are depicted fully dressed in black (symbolic of death, though the style of attire changes depending on the time period), wearing a ***gat* 갓**, the traditional Korean hat, and a face paler than a living person. To add to the numinous effect, their legs are often depicted as buried in fog, masking their gait, as if they are floating. In traditional paintings, however, they are sometimes portrayed as a prosecutor dressed in colorful yet solemn robes. Their job begins with checking IDs to ensure they are taking the correct soul. Although they are otherworldly beings, Jeoseung Saja are believed to have a "humane" side and can make mistakes, sometimes taking the wrong person. It was precisely because of this belief that the family prepared offerings for the messengers of the afterlife. This ritual involved placing three bowls of rice, soup, namul (seasoned vegetables), three pairs of shoes, and money at the entrance of the house. By doing so, the family sought to guide the messengers, appeal to their human side, and ensure that they would take the correct soul. It was based on the belief that messengers from the underworld arrive in groups of three, and through this ritual, the bereaved family prayed for a safe and hassle-free passage of their loved one to the afterlife. Additionally, in the past, people performed the ritual known as ***gobok* 고복**. Once death was confirmed and wailing arose, one person from outside the house would take the clothes the deceased had worn in life, climb onto the roof on the east side of the house, wave the clothes while reciting the deceased's address and name, and cry out "Return!" three times. This ritual, also called "soul-calling," aimed to call back the soul that had departed and simultaneously notify the neighborhood of the bereavement.

YEOMRA DAEWANG -
THE KING OF HELL

Yeomra Daewang in a Buddhist painting

What makes Jeoseung Saja more relatable is that they also have a boss to report to. Once everyone is on board, they take the soul of the deceased to ***Yeomra Daewang* 염라대왕** (**King Yeomra the Great**), the King of Hell, an almighty ruler (there are 10 rulers in the netherworld, known as ***Shiwang* 시왕**, the "**10 kings**," but he's the most well-known) in charge of judging the sins of the deceased and deciding where they should be sent. Because his main job is preventing bad souls from entering the heavens, he is mostly depicted with a wrathful look and a deafening howl of rage. Yet, while appearing cold-hearted on the outside, he has a soft side as well. In some instances, he magnanimously grants another chance and revives the dead upon hearing their pitiful stories.

MYTHICAL CREATURES & GHOSTLY BEINGS OF KOREA

HELL HATH NO FURY LIKE A WOMAN SCORNED – *CHEONYEO GWISHIN* THE "VIRGIN GHOST"

In the extremely patriarchal times of early Korea, life for women was far from easy. Taught to be subordinate to men and often denied education, their existence revolved around sacrifice — serving their fathers and husbands, raising children, and tending to endless household chores. As a result of this suppressed life, many Korean women carried lifelong **han 한** (a deep, unresolved sorrow) or resentment.) This *han* is believed to intensify if a woman dies unmarried, preventing her soul from leaving the mortal world and turning her into a **cheonyeo gwishin 처녀귀신**, or "virgin ghost." Dressed in traditional white mourning clothes called **sobok 소복** and with long, pitch-black hair hanging over her face like a curtain (only married women could wear their hair up), she roams the earth seeking vengeance, usually targeting the men who wronged her, haunting them until her resentment is finally appeased. The male equivalent is known as **chonggak gwishin 총각귀신**, the "**bachelor ghost**."

MARRIAGE OF THE POOR SOULS

When one or both partners die before tying the knot, a **yeonghon gyeolhonsik 영혼결혼식** — a "wedding ceremony for the soul(s) of the deceased" — is performed. This shamanistic ritual is meant to console the spirits of the dead so they can rest in peace and not become *cheonyeo* or *chonggak gwishin*.

BE CAREFUL WHEN NEAR WATER - *MULGWISHIN* THE "WATER GHOST"

Even if you swim better than Michael Phelps, you should still be extra cautious around water in Korea. *Mulgwishin* **물귀신** ("**water ghosts**") are believed to be the spirits of those who drowned. Condemned to the cold and lonely depths, they seek to drag the living down to their watery graves so they won't be alone. Even the most skilled swimmer is said to be powerless against their grasp...

Inspired by this legend, Korea even has a phrase called "Mulgwishin tactics." The expression comes from the story of the water ghost dragging innocent passersby into the depths, reflecting the mindset of *"If I have to suffer, you're coming with me!"* In modern usage, it refers to someone who, when facing trouble, tries to pull others into the same misfortune.

POOR SOUL LONGING HOME –
GAEKGWI THE "WANDERER GHOST"

Gaekgwi 객귀, or "**wanderer ghost**," is the spirit of someone who met an untimely death far from home before completing their allotted lifespan, or *cheonsu* 천수. Filled with lingering resentment, these souls cannot ascend to the heavens or leave the world of the living. Trapped between two realms, they drift among humans near the place of their death, often causing harm to unsuspecting passersby.

MISCHIEVOUS MONSTERS –
DOKKAEBI THE "KOREAN GOBLIN"

Koby-Koby 꼬비꼬비 (KBS, 1995)

Dokkaebi 도깨비, or Korean goblins (and no, not the handsome Gong Yoo kind), are supernatural beings from Korean folklore often seen as nature spirits or minor deities. Unlike ghosts, which come from human deaths, dokkaebi are born when inanimate objects—like an old wooden poker or worn-out broom—gain a spirit and transform into a human-like form. Mischievous yet oddly compassionate, they love playing tricks on people but also reward the kind-hearted. Their magic club, *dokkaebi bangmang-i* 도깨비 방망이, can summon anything or transform objects at will. Traditionally depicted with horns, sharp fangs, and a wild grin, they can also shapeshift into human form when it suits them. The hit drama *Dokkaebi* (*Goblin: The Lonely and Great God*, 2016, tvN) reimagines these mythical beings with a romantic twist—and, true to K-drama style, plenty of heartbreak and destiny.

GUMIHO - THE "NINE-TAILED FOX" THAT WANTED TO BECOME A WOMAN

If a fox lives a thousand years, it becomes *gumiho* 구미호 ("**nine-tailed fox**"). They often appear in scary stories, but they are said to harbor a strong desire to become a human. Legend has it that it transforms into a beautiful woman and falls in love with a man and marries him because it's believed that if it can live 100 days without having its true form revealed by the husband, it will become a real woman. However, at the end of the legend, gumiho gets its identity exposed with I only one day left, and unable to fulfill its wishes, it ends up leaving its husband. A TV drama titled *Nae Yeoja Chinguneun Gumiho* 내 여자친구는 구미호 (*My Girlfriend Is a Gumiho*, 2010, SBS) is a bubbly romance story with the motif coming from the legend and is definitely worth watching. In other versions of the legend, they are depicted as evil creatures that lure men to death and eat their liver. I don't know about you, but I prefer the first version.

TRADITIONAL VS. MODERN KOREAN FUNERALS

Time-traveling Korean dramas, like *Daleui Yeonin - Bobo Gyeongshim Ryeo* 달의 연인 - 보보경심 려 (*Moon Lovers: Scarlet Heart Ryeo* SBS, 2016) where characters move back and forth through time via a mysterious portal, actually serve as great educational resources. They vividly contrast Korea's traditional and modern ways of life. However, they can also create confusion if you don't understand the cultural details behind what's being shown. Among many examples, the way Koreans deal with the death of a loved one has changed dramatically over time. With that in mind, here's a quick comparison chart to bring you up to speed.

	TRADITIONAL	**MODERN**
DURATION	3 / 5 / 7 / 9 Days	3 Days / 2 Days
PLACE	Home	Hospital Funeral Halls
ORGANIZER	*Sangju* (Chief Mourner)	Funeral Service Provider
MOURNING CLOTHES	Hemp Dress / Hat, Straw Shoes	Black Formal Attire, Cloth Armband
WHO'S INVOLVED	Whole Village	Family / Relatives
GETTING TO THE BURIAL SITE	Village Neighbors Carry The *Sangyeo* Together On Foot	Hearse
GRIEVING	Loudly	Minimal
LEAVING OFF MOURNING PERIOD	3 Years / *Sangju* Lives Next To The Grave	49 Days / 1 Year

<h1 style="text-align:center"><u>HOW LONG ARE KOREAN FUNERALS?</u></h1>

In the past, Korean funerals began immediately upon the passing of a loved one and could last for **3, 5, 7,** or even **9 days**—odd numbers being considered auspicious—depending on the family's social status and traditions.

During this period, families performed an elaborate and physically demanding series of rites rooted in Confucian philosophy, which placed the highest importance on filial piety and family hierarchy. These rituals were believed to help ensure a smooth transition of the departed soul into the afterlife. However, with modernization and the fast pace of contemporary Korean life, traditional funerals have become more simplified and practical. Most funerals today last **3 days**, with **2-day ceremonies** becoming more common as well. Despite these changes, the essential elements of the rites remain and continue to form the foundation of Korean funeral culture today.

Let's take a look at the typical order and roles involved in a modern Korean funeral, especially for one's parent:

◆ *Bugo* 부고 Obituary Notice
◆ *Binso* 빈소 Mortuary / Memorial Hall Set-Up
◆ *Yeomseup* 염습 Clothing the Body of the Deceased
◆ *Ipgwan* 입관 Placing in the Coffin
◆ *Seongbok* 성복 Wearing Mourning Clothes
◆ *Munsang (Jomun)* 문상 (조문) Receiving Guest Mourners

-- takes place on the last day of the funeral --

◆ *Balin* 발인 Carrying Out of the Coffin / Procession
◆ *Anjang* 안장 Burial

<u>WHERE DO KOREAN FUNERALS TAKE PLACE?</u>

In the past, funerals were held in the home of the deceased, a tradition that still continues in some rural areas. In urban settings, however, most people spend their final days in hospitals or care centers. Many large hospitals in Korea even include funeral halls within their complexes, providing convenience for families who wish to hold services there.

<u>WHO ORGANIZES THE FUNERALS?</u>

Traditionally, the ***sangju*** 상주 ("chief mourner", usually the eldest son or grandson of the deceased)—was responsible for organizing and managing the funeral, greeting guests, and finding an appropriate burial site. The sangju was also expected to refrain from washing their hair or shaving during the mourning period as an expression of grief. Today, much of this burden has been eased thanks to professional funeral service providers. Most hospital funeral halls employ advisors who oversee every detail of the ceremony, allowing the family to focus on honoring the deceased and receiving guests.

Bier Belonging to the Goryeongdaek House of the Jeonju Choe Clan, Sancheong, Important Folklore Cultural Heritage of Republic of Korea No. 230
국립민속박물관 (National Folk Museum of Korea) / © KOGL Type 1 (kogl.or.kr)

WHO'S INVOLVED WITH KOREAN FUNERALS?

Traditionally, funerals were community events that involved the entire village. While the bereaved family members were occupied with rituals, food preparation, and guest hospitality—often over the course of several days—neighbors would gather to assist. Today, the communal aspect has largely been replaced by professional funeral staff. As a result, families can concentrate on receiving guests rather than managing the logistics. The traditional *sangyeo* 상여 or the funeral bier which villagers once carried on foot to the burial site, has also been replaced by a modern hearse.

WHAT DO PEOPLE WEAR AT KOREAN FUNERALS?

In the past, mourners wore *sangbok* 상복, traditional mourning attire made of off-white *sambe* 삼베, hemp cloth. This included a hemp robe, a hemp hat called *gulgeon* 굴건, and straw shoes known as *jipshin* 짚신.

According to Professor Lee Cheol-yeong of Eulji University, hemp garments were traditionally associated with **sinners—symbolizing the mourner's sense of guilt for "allowing one's parent to die."** The hat, meanwhile, was meant to conceal one's face from the heavens in shame.

Today, most people wear modern black formal clothing. The sangju still distinguishes themselves by wearing a hemp armband with black stripes—a fusion of traditional and modern mourning symbols, though the origin and meaning of the stripes remain unclear.

OBITUARIES are sent out via Kakaotalk, email, phone calls, and even social media channels like Instagram, detailing who passed away, where the funeral is held, and when the funeral procession and burial is.

3-DAY FUNERAL is most common, but some families do a 2-day funeral. Make sure to attend the funeral within three (two) days of the announcement.

WHAT TO BRING

JOEUIGEUM / BUEUIGEUM
조의금 / 부의금
(CONDOLENCE MONEY)

50,000 KRW-100,000 KRW ($50 - $100) is a safe range but for close friends or special relationships, a larger amount may be prepared depending on the circumstances.

FLOWERS

Individual guests are not required or expected to bring flowers. If you happen to represent a large company, you may send pre-arranged chrysanthemum wreaths through flower delivery shops.

DRESS CODE

STICK WITH DARK COLORS

Black is the color of mourning, if not available, wear dark (i.e., dark gray, navy, brown) clothes, and avoid colorful clothes.

BEING THERE IS MORE IMPORTANT

There are instances where you can't keep the dress code (e.g., became aware of the news last minute while you were out). In this case, it's better to pay a visit than skipping because your presence would be much appreciated, and people will understand.

BLACK TIES AND SOCKS

One thing people often overlook is wearing black ties and socks. Socks are especially important because there are more instances where your socks are exposed than you might expect. So choose the ones that are long enough to cover your ankle.

BE CONSERVATIVE

For females, if wearing a skirt, avoid those that are either too short or too tight.

At A Korean Funeral

1 SIGNING THE GUESTBOOK

Upon entering the funeral hall, you will be asked to sign the guestbook.

Tip: Write down your name vertically. If someone made a mistake and wrote their name horizontally, just write down your name vertically right underneath it.

2 ENTER THE MEMORIAL ROOM (BINSO 빈소)

After signing the guestbook, you'll be guided to the memorial room. You must take off your shoes before entering, just as if you were entering a house. You should expect to stand in line outside the memorial room if you happen to visit at a crowded time.

3 FLOWER OFFERING AND INCENSE BURNING

Upon entrance, give a slight nod to the chief mourner. Proceed to the altar and grab (or you will be given one) a flower from the altar and place it in front of the portrait of the deceased, with the bud facing it, and offer a brief moment of silence. If visiting as a group, the oldest person can do it on behalf of the group.

Once done, kneel before the small table in front of the altar, pick an incense stick (traditionally 3, but 1 is okay these days), and light it up using a candle. DO NOT blow out the flame. Use the other hand (usually the left hand) to wave it out. Then stick it upright in the incense burner.

 **PAY RESPECT TO THE DECEASED**

Step back from the altar, and:

- Do 2 full-bows *keunjeol* 큰절 (for females, *banjeol* 반절 is also acceptable), getting down on both knees, palms touching the floor, with right hand on top of the left for males and left hand on top of the right for females.

- Bowing is skipped if the deceased is a minor.

Turned to face the grieving family, and:

- Do 1 full-bow to the chief mourner (he will reciprocate the full-bow at the same time) and offer words of condolences.

Tip: Even if the chief mourner is your close friend, use *jondaemal* or honorifics.
Don't ask too many details about the deceased or the chief mourner. You can do this at a later point in time.

5 **CONDOLENCE MONEY**

Similar to *chukeuigeum* 축의금 ("congratulatory money") at Korean weddings, the amount to give depends on your relationship with the grieving family, but as a rule of thumb 50,000 - 100,000 Korean Won (50 - 100 USD) is a safe range. But again, you're welcome to contribute more should you feel compelled, as the money will go to the family to cover the funeral expenses. ***In many cases, condolence money can be given immediately after signing the guestbook.**

AMOUNT: GENERAL RULE OF THUMB

DEATH OF A…

Family member of a co-worker – 50,000 KRW
Family member of a friend – 100,000 KRW
Family member of a very close friend – 100,000+ KRW

Tip: Have Cash Beforehand – Cash is the only means expected, so make sure to visit an ATM machine beforehand, or if that's not an option, borrow from someone.

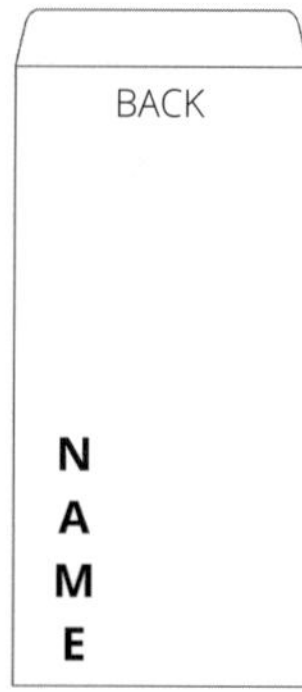

① **Grab an Envelope for** *joeuigeum / bueuigeum* 조의금 / 부의금**("Condolence Money")** - If you haven't prepared an envelope, you can get it from the reception desk.

Don't give the condolence money directly to the chief mourner or grieving family.

② **Write Down Your Name On The Envelope**- On the bottom left corner on the back of the envelope, write your name down.

③ **Put Money In The Envelope and Drop It In The Box** - Make sure not to fold the paper bill and drop it in a box provided. The receptionist will collect it and record your name and the amount to reciprocate at future funeral events (which certainly isn't something we look forward to).

Now you will be guided to the dining area attached to the memorial room. Here, you will be served on disposable plates a set of dishes like rice, *yukaegaejang* 육개장 (spicy beef soup), *jeon* 전 (Korean pancakes), *tteok* 떡 (rice cakes), and various *banchan* 반찬 selections, along with *soju* and other soft drinks.

Don't *clink glasses when you drink with other guests.*

WHY DO KOREAN PEOPLE WAIL SO MUCH AT FUNERALS?

One notable difference about Korean funerals lies in the expression of grief. In the past, female family members of the deceased were expected to openly display their sorrow by continuously weeping and wailing, as it symbolized the deceased person's virtue, social standing, and the depth of the family's love and respect. The louder and more passionate the cries, the greater the perceived value of the departed. In contrast, male family members were expected to suppress their emotions, maintaining composure as a reflection of dignity and strength. Showing tears in public was considered inappropriate for men. Modern Korean funerals, however, have moved away from such overt displays of emotion. While expressions of sadness remain heartfelt, excessive wailing has become less common, replaced by quieter, more restrained mourning in keeping with changing cultural norms.

WHY DID KOREANS LIVE NEXT TO THE PARENT'S GRAVE FOR THREE YEARS?

Lastly, the time required for *talsang* 탈상, or "taking off the mourning clothes" (meaning the end of the mourning period), has changed over time. In the past, to express deep gratitude for the debt owed to one's parents and as repentance for filial shortcomings, the *sangju* 상주 (chief mourner) would build a mud hut next to the parent's gravesite and live there for three years, tending to the grave daily while wearing hemp mourning clothes. Upon completing this period, the mourner would finally remove the mourning clothes in a solemn and reverent ceremony.

Today, this practice has been greatly simplified. The talsang ceremony is usually held immediately after the burial, on the 49th day, or on the one-year anniversary of the passing, often accompanied by **jesa** 제사, a memorial service for the deceased.

Some say that funerals should be lively and boisterous — "the more boisterous, the better the funeral" — because such an atmosphere is considered a way of offering consolation to the bereaved family. For this reason, you may often see people playing card games, chatting, and even laughing loudly. However, it depends on the situation, so use common sense (or **nunchi 눈치**) and take cues from how others behave before doing the same.

Tip: In the event of a co-worker's family member passing away, it is customary for the juniors on the team to offer assistance at the funeral. Their duties can include guiding visitors, cleaning the dining tables, or neatly arranging the guests' shoes at the entrance.

WHY DO KOREANS EAT YUKGAEJANG AT FUNERALS?

Yukgaejang 육개장, or spicy beef stew, is considered a staple dish at Korean funerals. There are two main theories behind this tradition. First, the soup's red color is believed to drive away evil spirits. Second, because funeral meals must serve many guests over several days, a dish that doesn't spoil easily was ideal. Yukgaejang, with its generous use of red chili powder and salt—both natural preservatives —fit the purpose perfectly.

WHAT DO KOREANS PREFER? BURIAL OR CREMATION?

Traditionally, Koreans preferred natural burials in rural areas. However, as land has become scarce and maintaining gravesites more difficult, cremation has become increasingly common. Today, many families choose cremation for both practical and environmental reasons.

WHY DO KOREAN PEOPLE THROW SALT WHEN YOU RETURN FROM A FUNERAL?

Upon returning home from a funeral, it's customary for someone to sprinkle salt on you before you enter the house. This practice is meant to ward off evil spirits that may have followed from the funeral. The belief stems from salt's purifying qualities—just as it prevents food from spoiling, it's thought to protect people and spaces from impurity.

In modern Korean culture, "throwing salt" can also be used figuratively as an expression of rejection or irritation, similar to saying, "Get him out of here—and throw some salt!"

JESA

WHY DO KOREAN PEOPLE OFFER FOOD TO THE PHOTOS OF THE ANCESTORS?

If you enjoy heartwarming Korean family dramas like *Neongkuljjae Gulleo-on Dangshin* 넝쿨째 굴러온 당신 (*My Husband Got a Family*, **KBS 2, 2012**), you may have noticed scenes where multi-generational families gather around a large, low dining table. A wide array of traditional Korean dishes and seasonal fruits is laid out in front of the ancestors' photos, followed by rituals such as burning incense, bowing, offering rice wine, and sticking a spoon upright in a rice bowl. What you just saw is a traditional memorial ceremony for ancestors called *jesa* 제사. Technically, jesa can refer to any memorial ceremony, but they are categorized by when they are held. Here is a list of rituals and their typical dates to keep in mind.

- FOR UP TO YOUR GRANDPARENTS OF THE PATERNAL SIDE.
- IF BOTH HAVE PASSED AWAY, A SINGLE JESA IS HELD FOR BOTH, ON THE DEATH ANNIVERSARY OF THE GRANDFATHER.

◆ *Charye* 차례 – **Seollal** 설날 (Korean Lunar New Year) and **Chuseok** 추석 (Fall Harvest Festival, 15th day of the 8th month of the lunar calendar).

◆ *Gijesa* 기제사 – On the night before or morning of the ancestor's death anniversary

◆ *Sije* 시제 – Every season, for ancestors who are the fifth generation and beyond.

◆ *Myoje* 묘제 – Memorial ceremony held at the gravesite

◆ *Seongmyo* 성묘 – On **Hansik** 한식 (April 5th) and **Chuseok**. It's a memorial ceremony performed at the gravesite of the ancestors. On top of the memorial ceremony, families tidy up the grave by cutting the weeds and mowing the grass.

ORDER OF THE CEREMONY

The rituals can be quite complex, and even the most orthodox Confucian families often struggle to remember every detail—not to mention the average Korean. But getting bogged down in the rules and stressing over them is not what the ancestors want. What they truly wish for is to see everyone gather, enjoy each other's company, and honor those who came before them. That said, for the sake of preserving tradition, here is the typical order of a memorial ceremony.

Kangshin 강신 – "Inviting The Souls Of The Ancestors"

All attendees stand before the altar while the eldest male descendant, *jeju* 제주, kneels down in front of the memorial altar. He burns three incense sticks and bows twice. (Sometimes the bowing is skipped). The jeju kneels again. Another person (usually the wife) gives the jeju an empty cup with a saucer and pours it (about 30% full). The jeju then takes the cup and makes a circle three times over the incense. The liquor is poured into a bowl filled with sand, called *mosa* 모사, in three equal pours. The empty cup and a saucer are returned to the wife.The jeju makes two full bows. It's believed that the incense invites the souls of the ancestors from the above and the liquor invites those from the underground (which the sand is symbolic of).

◆ *Chamshin* 참신 – "Greeting The Souls Of The Ancestors"

All attendees make full bows (twice for men and four times for women).

◆ *Choheon* 초헌 – "First Offering Of Rice Wine"

The jeju makes the first offering of rice wine, followed by his wife. At the conclusion of the first ritual offering, the jeju makes two full bows and the wife makes four.

◆ *Aheon* 아헌 – "Second Offering Of Rice Wine"

The second eldest male descendant within the family (the next eldest sons or sons-in-law) makes an offering of rice wine, following the same procedures.

◆ *Jongheon* 종헌 - "Final Offering"

The offering of rice wine continues until no high-ranking male descendants are left.

◆ *Sapsi* 삽시 - "Food Serving"

The meals are served to the ancestors by the jeju, by sticking a spoon upright in the middle of the rice bowl.

◆ *Yushik* 유식 – "Receiving of the Offerings"

All attendees leave the room or turn away for a few minutes so that the souls of the ancestors can enjoy the offerings.

◆ *Cheolsang* 철상 - "Removal of Table"

The table is cleared by first blowing out the candles and removing the dishes on the table, starting from the innermost. All the attendants make two full bows, sending the spirits off.

◆ *Eumbok* 음복 - "Receiving Blessings"

Attendees share the food offerings removed from the table and partake in the feast, and it symbolizes the receiving of the blessings from the ancestors.

There's no single "correct" answer for what goes on a jesa table—it varies by region and family.
Over time, items that weren't traditionally available, such as non-Korean dishes or fruits like pizza and
bananas, have started to appear. The idea is simple: the memorial ceremony is for the deceased ancestors,
so if they enjoyed something when they were alive, why not serve it to honor them? Of course, Korean
traditionalists might frown upon this modern twist. With that in mind, here's a look at a typical table
setting for a jesa ceremony.

Row 1 - Rice and soup, but on Seollal, *tteokguk* 떡국 (rice cake soup) is served instead. When serving
liquor, it has to be clear (e.g., filtered rice wine). *Songpyeon* (half-moon shaped rice cake) takes the place
of liquor and rice during **Chuseok**.

Row 2 - Various kinds of meat, pancakes, and fish. When you put the fish, keep the head facing east
(right). Place the meat on the left side, and the fish on the right side.

Row 3 - Various soups. Place in the order of meat soup, tofu soup, and fish soup. Place soy sauce
between them.

Row 4 - Vegetables, dried fish, and *shikhye* 식혜 (sweet rice drink). Place the dried fish on the left
(west). *Shikhye* goes on the far right.

Row 5 - Place fruits, cookies, and desserts.

RESTRICTED FOODS

- Peaches because they expel ghosts & spirits.

- No fish ending with "*chi*" such as *kkongchi* 꽁치 (mackerel) and *galchi* 갈치 (cutlass fish) because it's believed that fish without scales are "cheap."

- Red beans, food with *gochugaru* 고추가루 (red pepper powder) or garlic seasoning cannot be served because ghosts and spirits hate red color and garlic.

WHY ARE THE FOODS PLACED IN SPECIFIC ORDER? ARE THERE ANY RULES?

◆ *Banseogaengdong* 반서갱동: Rice on the west, soup on the east (opposite to the living).

◆ *Jeokjeopgeojung* 적접거중: Roast meat in the center.

◆ *Eeodongyukseo* 어동육서: Fish on the east and meat on the west.

◆ *Dongdoseomi* 동두서미: The head facing the east and the tail facing the west.

◆ *Baebokbanghyang* 배복방향: Dried fish with its back upward.

◆ *Sukseosaengdong* 숙서생동: Cooked vegetables on the west and raw *kimchi* on the east.

◆ *Hongdongbaekseo* 홍동백서: Red fruits on the east and white fruits on the west.

◆ *Jwapouhye* 좌포우혜: Dried fish at the left end and *shikhye* at the right end.

◆ *Dongjoseoyul* 동조서율: Dates on the east and the chestnuts on the west.

◆ *Joyulishi* 조율이시: Starting from the left, place dates, chestnuts, pears, and persimmons.

Although their origins are unclear, these rules have been handed down through generations as customs, and some even contradict one another. For example, if you place red dates on the left according to the *joyulishi* rule, you violate the *hongdongbaekseo* rule, which says red should go to the east (right). Not only are they complicated to follow, but they also often cause quarrels among family members.

WHAT ARE THE ANCESTRAL TABLETS?

Shinwi 신위 are objects representing the presence of the deceased, such as portraits or memorial tablets. Traditionally made of wood, most families could not easily build a permanent shrine, so a disposable shinwi, called *jibang* 지방, was used. It included the name and official position of the deceased on paper and was burned after the ceremony. Today, portrait photos are more commonly used.

WHY IS A FOLDING SCREEN SET UP DURING A JESA CEREMONY?

Byeongpung 병풍 is a folding screen with poetic calligraphy that faces north—the direction associated with the dead. It serves to hide household objects like TVs during jesa and symbolically represents the presence of the deceased, as in traditional funerals, the body was placed behind it.

WHY ARE ONLY WOMEN RESPONSIBLE FOR PREPARING FOR JESA?

While many look forward to the long holiday, it's a time many married Korean women dread—the endless kitchen labor, spending the whole day preparing a large feast for jesa and charye held for their husbands' ancestors. In Korea, when a woman marries, she becomes part of her husband's family, and priority is always given to his family matters. For example, visiting the husband's parents' home during holidays is essential, while visiting her own parents' home is not. Naturally, pent-up emotions can surface during these visits—tensions with in-laws and labor inequality are among the factors contributing to the spike in divorces after the holiday season. It's even a Korean drama cliché: couples bickering in the car on the way back to Seoul from the husband's parents' home in the countryside.

HOW DO KOREANS WITH DIFFERENT RELIGIONS HANDLE JESA?

Korea guarantees freedom of religion under the constitution. Regarding jesa, Catholics (recognized as a civil practice by the Pope in 1939) and Buddhists observe the memorial ceremonies, while Protestants typically do not, as it could be seen as "worshipping" deities other than the Lord. Protestant family members are therefore excused from participating.

WEDDINGS IN KOREA

Foreign weddings, with their exotic ceremonies and rituals, can be quite a spectacle, but they can also be confusing if you're not familiar with the cultural background. Traditional Korean weddings, however, are second to none in complexity. Let's explore what Korean weddings were like in the past so that their rituals carry more meaning.

PRE-WEDDING RITUALS

Traditional Korean weddings embody Confucian values centered around *hyo* 효, or "**filial piety**"—respecting one's parents and elders, and honoring the ancestors. Weddings were considered not just the union of two individuals but the joining of two families. Because of this sacred perspective, every step of the process, from the initial discussion to the ceremony itself, involved elaborate procedures.

In the past, most marriages were arranged by the parents. The first step was called *euihon* 의혼, or "**marriage discussion**," where the parents of both families would discuss the possibility of marriage, often facilitated by a well-connected matchmaker. For elite families, marriage was a strategic tool to strengthen social status, so factors like age, family customs, social standing, academic achievements, wealth, and hereditary disorders were carefully considered. If everything checked out, the groom's family would send a marriage proposal letter, and the bride's family would respond with a permission letter.

The next step was *napchae* 납채, the announcement of the intention to marry and beginning of the engagement process. After exchanging intentions through a matchmaker, the groom's family sent the groom's saju—his year, month, day, and hour of birth written according to the sexagenary cycle—and, in some cases, a marriage proposal letter, to the bride's family. The bride's family received the saju respectfully, recorded it at the family shrine, and then sent back a formal reply. Acceptance of the saju signified the engagement, while rejection meant the marriage would not proceed. Following this, the bride's family set the wedding date in a process called *yeonggil* 연길. After receiving the groom's saju, they sent a *taegildan* 택일단 (a date-selection document) back to the groom's family, indicating the auspicious dates for the ceremony. This document typically included the jeonan ilsi, the day to send the wedding gifts, and the *nappye ilsi* 납폐일시, the day for the wedding gifts and the formal ceremony *pyebaek* 폐백 to be presented.

The final step before the ceremony was *nappye* 납폐, or "**sending valuables.**" Once the date was set, the groom's family sent a *ham* 함, a box of wedding gifts for the bride. The ham contained several important items:

- *Honseo* 혼서: marriage documents given to the bride to keep throughout her life; upon her death, they were placed in her coffin.
- *Chaedan* 채단: red and blue cloths representing the traditional Yin/Yang philosophy, used to make the wedding clothes.
- *Yemul* 예물: gifts for the bride's family, including jewelry, clothing, and household items.

Traditional Korean weddings were typically held in the bride's yard or home, and the groom would travel there on horseback. On this special day, ordinary people could wear luxurious clothing traditionally reserved for the upper class. The bride and groom often wore costumes modeled after those of the royal court.

- The groom wore a black hat.
- The bride covered her face with a veil until the midpoint of the ceremony.
- On her head, she wore a *jokduri* 족두리, a beautifully embroidered bridal crown adorned with accessories.
- Her hair bun was secured with a *binyeo* 비녀, an ornamental hairpin.

Traditional Korean Wedding

ORDER OF CEREMONY

◆ *Chinyeongrye* 친영례: **Bride's Family Greets The Groom**

-The groom enters the yard where the wedding is held, led by *gireokabi* 기럭아비, who carries the wedding geese. He hands the geese to the groom.

◆ *Jeonanrye* 전안례: **Presentation of The Geese**

-The groom places the wild geese on a table where his mother-in-law is sitting and bows twice.
-Mother-in-law accepts the wild geese and takes them into the house.

*The wild geese, replaced by wooden ones these days,
represent many virtues a newlywed couple must possess.

- Love and loyalty - They mate for life and do not find another partner even if they lose one.
- Harmony - Even when flying in a group, they maintain hierarchy and order, thus creating harmony.

◆ *Gyobaerye* 교배례: **Bowing to Each Other**

- Helpers wash the hands of the bride and groom.
- Facing each other while standing on the mat in the yard, they make full bows to each other, taking turns.

*Helpers on each side had to assist the bride because she had to sit cross-legged and stand up.
*Surprisingly, this was the first opportunity to see each other's faces because marriages were arranged by the parents, which means they could only hope their parents made the right choice!

◆ *Hapgeunrye* 합근례: **Drinking Together**

- One of the helpers pours rice wine into a small cup for the groom, who then drinks it.
- Another helper pours rice wine for the bride who only pretends to drink it.
- The groom's helpers then pour rice wine into the gourd dipper and the groom drinks it again.
- The bride's helper does the same in her gourd dipper.
- The groom and bride join together and make three separate full bows: one for their parents, one for their ancestors, and one for the guests.

*Drinking in a gourd dipper symbolizes marital harmony because the half-divided gourd has only one perfectly matching counterpart.

◆ *Seonghonrye* 성혼례: **Declaration of Marriage**

- Bride and groom bows to both families and guests.
- The ceremony is concluded.

After the wedding ceremony, the groom takes his wife in a beautifully decorated palanquin called *kkotgama* 꽃가마 to his parents' house to live in.

WHAT ARE THE RED DOTS ON THE BRIDE'S FACE?

Yeonji 연지 refers to red-colored cosmetics traditionally used by women, while *gonji* 곤지 specifically refers to a red dot drawn on the forehead with that pigment. Scholars differ on its origin: Confucian scholars Lee Ik and Lee Gyu-kyung of the late Joseon Dynasty claimed it was a custom of the **Huns** that spread to **China** and then to **Joseon**, while poet Choi Nam-sun argued that it originated from the **Mongols** and was introduced during the **Goryeo Dynasty**. Regardless of its origin, the bride's yeonji/gonji served both as makeup and as part of a shamanistic ritual—meant to protect her from mischief caused by evil spirits. However, not all brides wore this red makeup simply because it was their wedding day; it was a custom reserved only for women marrying for the first time.

WHY WAS PEEPING INTO THE BRIDAL CHAMBER ON THEIR FIRST NIGHT ALLOWED?

What did people do before pay-per-view or adult movies existed? In old Korea, they peeped into the bridal chamber of the newlyweds! After the couple entered their freshly prepared room, neighbors and even relatives (et tu...?) would gather outside the papered doors, poke small holes with their fingers, and peek inside to see what was going on.

While it sounds creepy and perverted today, it was actually done with the couple's best interests in mind. During the Joseon Dynasty, early marriage was common—boys were often around ten, and girls were in their early teens.

Naturally, this led to many problems (after all, they were still kids!). Some brides, frightened on their wedding night, tried to run away, and in rare cases, a secret lover might even sneak in to take her away from the young groom. To prevent such chaos, neighbors and relatives formed an informal "neighborhood watch," keeping an eye on the situation from outside. The peeping, then, was their way of making sure everything went smoothly inside. Their duty was considered complete once the groom blew out the candlelight.

This bizarre yet well-intentioned custom has completely disappeared today—after all, most people live in apartments now, and you can't exactly peek in unless you know the door password!

- Modern -

These days, modern—or Western-style—weddings with a Korean twist are by far the most popular choice among couples, mostly for the sake of simplicity and convenience. Compared to traditional ceremonies, modern weddings take less time to plan and execute, and finding a venue is much easier. Traditional weddings are often held outdoors, making them vulnerable to unpredictable weather.

Let's take a look at what a modern Korean wedding looks like!

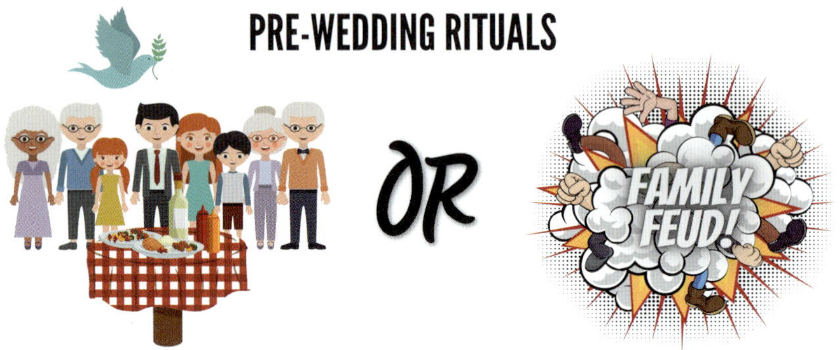

SANGGYEONRYE - THE IN-LAWS FACE-OFF!

If you've watched any Korean dramas, you've probably seen this scene: the soon-to-be-married couple and their parents sitting together at a nice restaurant for dinner. This meeting, known as *sanggyeonrye* 상견례, is a formal introduction between the two families—usually just the couple and their parents, though sometimes extended family members join as well. As Koreans traditionally view marriage as the union of two families (not just two individuals), parental approval remains extremely important. Unsurprisingly, this is where conflicts often begin—both in dramas and in real life. Power struggles between the two sides are common, especially when one family views the other as "inadequate," whether due to financial background, social status, or education level. Since both sets of parents typically contribute financially or materially to the wedding, they naturally want to have a say in major decisions. In some unfortunate cases, these disagreements can even lead to the engagement being called off.

YEDAN, YEMUL, AND HONSU

Even if you passed sanggyeonrye, it's too early to let your guard down, because there's another major hurdle – agreeing on how much to give, receive, and contribute. For Korean weddings, *yemul* 예물 is the wedding gift for the bride, typically matching jewelry sets such as diamond rings, earrings, and necklaces. *Yedan* 예단, originally meaning "silk gift for the groom's family," refers to the wedding gift for the groom's family, which is usually cash or other expensive items such as nice silverware and luxury goods like leather handbags. On top of that, the groom is expected to provide housing, while the bride is expected to provide household items such as the TV and refrigerator, known as *honsu* 혼수, or dowry. Most of the time, when these gifts from the bride fall short of the groom's parents' expectations, things can fall apart, resulting in major quarrels between the couple.

WHERE ARE MODERN KOREAN WEDDINGS HELD?

One good thing about choosing a modern-style Korean wedding is convenience! That's partly because there are dedicated service providers who handle every aspect of the event, but the biggest reason is the Korean people's notion of *bbali bbali* 빨리빨리 ("quick, quick!"), which values speed and efficiency. For this reason, the go-to venues for most weddings are wedding halls. While it's certainly convenient to have everything handled by professionals, it has its drawbacks too. These venues are businesses, after all, and they try to squeeze in as many weddings as possible on a given day. Since most weddings take place on weekends, it's only natural for them to maximize profits by increasing turnover rates. A typical wedding ceremony takes no longer than 90 minutes — meaning that just as your ceremony is wrapping up, staff are already cleaning and preparing for the next couple in line. (Talk about a party pooper!)

DRESS CODE

When it comes to what to wear, keep it conservative and avoid clothing that makes you stand out — especially bright colors like red or yellow. Some people also advise avoiding white, particularly for female guests, since it's the color reserved for the bride. As for style, semi-formal (no jeans) is generally acceptable these days. And regarding *hanbok*, you don't need to wear one — it's typically reserved for the mothers and female relatives of the bride and groom.

CONGRATULATORY MONEY, GUESTBOOK, FOOD VOUCHER, AND PARKING PASS

As with Korean funerals, guests are expected to offer *chukeuigeum* 축의금 ("congratulatory money") as a gift, which helps cover the wedding expenses. Upon arrival, you'll find two reception tables — one for the groom's side and one for the bride's side — where friends or relatives collect the envelopes, have you sign the guestbook, and hand out a parking pass along with a food voucher. There are generally two dining options. One is a sit-down meal, typically offered at upscale hotel weddings, where guests are served a multi-course meal at round tables. The other is a buffet-style setup in a separate dining hall within the same building.

As for gifting money, the same general etiquette applies as at funerals. These days, the minimum is typically ₩50,000 KRW for acquaintances or less-close friends, and you can adjust the amount as you see fit. If you're close to the couple, ₩70,000–₩100,000 KRW is a safe range — and feel free to contribute more if appropriate. One thing to keep in mind: if you're bringing your significant other, it's polite to double the amount, since the extra guest means extra food expense for the newlyweds.

ORDER OF EVENTS

◆ **Opening Ceremony**: The emcee (MC) of the event welcomes and gives thanks to the guests as they announce the beginning of the wedding. In some cases, they crack a joke to create a more lively atmosphere.

◆ **The Entrance of the Mothers**: Mothers of both families enter, holding each other's hands. If one's parents are already deceased, divorced, or not able to enter for any physical reason, it can be omitted.

◆ **Candle Lighting**: Mothers of both families light the candles. Afterward, they greet each other by exchanging bows and greet the guests. Introducing the Officiant: Introduce the officiant who will preside the wedding ceremony. If it is a wedding without an officiant, it is naturally omitted.

◆ **The Entrance of the Groom**: The groom passes the "bridal path" and goes forward to greet the officiant first and then turns back to greet the guests.

◆ **The Entrance of The Bride**: The bride comes in holding her father's hand. If the father of the bride is deceased or unable to enter with the bride, the groom may enter together at the same time.

◆ **Groom/Bride Bow Exchange**: The bride and the groom bow to each other. Sometimes standing too close to each other when bowing causes a head-on collision, and causes some laughs!

◆ **Reading of The Marriage Vow**: The officiant asks the bride and groom if they will swear to love forever. If it's a ceremony without an officiant, the bride and groom can read each other the letter of promises.

◆ **Reading of The Declaration of Marriage**: The officiant reads the declaration following the marriage vows. If without an officiant, the emcee or, in general, the father of either side of the family does it. In the case of international marriages, it's often conducted in two languages.

◆ **The Officiant's Speech**: The officiant gives a speech to the newly-born couple. Popular topics include life lessons, tips on married life, and words of blessing. The father of either side of the family can assume the role in a wedding ceremony without an officiant.

◆ **Chukga Singing (Congratulatory Song / Wedding Song)**: The friends of the couple sing for them. More often than not, it's the most entertaining part of the ceremony. Some choose to sing in a musical-like format and some even dance with the couple. Hiring a choir to sing a congratulatory song is a popular option for those not wanting any surprises.

◆ **Thanking Each Other's Parents**: First, the couple goes to the bride's parents (sitting in a chair) and makes a full bow. Then the parents get up and hug the couple. The couple repeats the same to the groom's parents.

◆ **Thanking the Guests**: The couple stands in the middle of the podium and thank the guests by making a half-bow, but the groom can make a big bow should he wish so. The parents of both families sometimes come to the podium together to thank the guests.

◆ **Groom/Bride Exiting and Flower Shower**: The couple leaves together. Upon approaching the end of the "bridal path," the friends sprinkle the flower petals.

AFTER CEREMONY

GROUP PHOTO TIME!

Memories may fade, but photos last forever. For many guests, group photo time might be the most important part of the event — it's solid proof that you were there! After the ceremony, guests usually hang around waiting for this moment. First, the family members are invited to the podium to take photos with the couple. Then, friends and colleagues take turns joining in. During this time, the photographer often encourages the guests to join in creating dramatic or fun moments — like clapping as the couple kisses or turning on their smartphone flashlights so the background lights up like a sky full of fireflies celebrating together.

PIROYEON 피로연 – AFTER PARTY/RECEPTION

After the wedding, guests are guided to a separate room for the *piroyeon*, or wedding reception. These days, it usually takes place at a banquet hall within the same building. Upon entrance, you'll need to present the food voucher you received earlier in the lobby after signing the guestbook. Two types of meals are typically offered: a sit-down course, where servers bring dishes to your table, or a buffet, where guests help themselves.

In some cases — especially for younger couples — the traditional reception is replaced with a private after-party for close friends. Don't worry, you don't need to offer another cash gift for this part.

WHY DO KOREANS EAT NOODLES AT THE WEDDING?

Janchiguksu 잔치국수 ("party noodles") is a traditional Korean noodle dish commonly served at weddings and birthday parties because the long noodles symbolize longevity. It's also a practical choice for large gatherings — easy to prepare in bulk, needing only a few garnishes and hot broth to serve quickly. From this custom came a fun idiom: when people ask a bachelor *"When are you serving noodles?"*, it's a playful way of asking *"When are you getting married?"*

***PYEBAEK* – DO YOU WANT MANY KIDS? THEN CATCH THE DATES AND CHESTNUTS!**

Gotta catch 'em all! Nope, it's not *Pokémon GO* — it's what you might hear during the ***pyebaek* 폐백** ceremony, a private, family-only ritual that takes place after the *piroyeon*, once all the guests have left. Originally, this was when the bride made her first formal visit to her in-laws, bowing deeply to show respect and symbolically joining the groom's family. (Technically, the ceremony was called ***hyungugorye* 현구고례**, while pyebaek referred to the set of valuables the bride offered to her in-laws — but over time, the entire ceremony came to be known simply as pyebaek.) In this ceremony, the newlyweds bow deeply to the groom's parents, and the bride presents dates and chestnuts, which symbolize fertility. The parents then share words of wisdom for the couple's future together. Then comes the highlight — the date and chestnut toss! The parents throw the fruits toward the couple, who must catch them in the bride's long wedding skirt. The number they catch is said to predict how many children they'll have. Originally, this ceremony served to introduce the bride to her new family, but in modern Korean weddings, the bride's parents often join in as well. The ceremony traditionally ends with the groom giving the bride a piggyback ride, symbolizing his promise to care for her throughout their marriage.

IBAJI FOOD - SHOW OFF THE COOKING SKILLS!

If Michelin inspectors had existed in the Joseon era, they might have given stars for *ibaji eumsik* 이바지 음식 — the "contribution food." This long-standing tradition still remains in modern weddings. Lavish home-cooked meals, prepared with the bride's family recipes using seasonal and regional ingredients, are beautifully arranged and sent to the groom's family. These dishes symbolize the bride's parents' gratitude for accepting their "imperfect daughter" as part of the groom's family — and their promise to show respect and harmony between the two families. At the same time, it's also a chance for the bride's mother to show off her culinary skills with pride. Each dish is wrapped carefully in silk cloth, placed inside bamboo baskets, and delivered to the groom's home on the wedding day — a gesture of warmth, hospitality, and tradition.

WHO'S THE GUY WEARING A SQUID MASK?

Remember the old tradition where the groom sent a *ham* 함 — a box containing wedding gifts — to the bride's family before the wedding? Well, that tradition still survives today, though with a modern twist. In the past, servants were responsible for delivering the ham, but these days, the groom's close friends or relatives take on the role — becoming what's known as *hamjinabi* 함진아비, meaning ham carrier (and no, not the SPAM kind!). Traditionally, the ham carrier wears a dried squid mask — or paints their face with charcoal — to ward off evil spirits. Upon arrival at the bride's home, the hamjinabi shouts three times, "*Ham saseyo!* 함 사세요!" — "Buy the *ham*!" — to summon the bride's family and neighbors. What follows is all part of the fun: a playful haggle over the "price" of the ham. The bride's side tries to bring the box home with minimal effort, while the ham carrier does their best to "maximize profits" by demanding a "payment" for every step they take. Sometimes, they even ask the women on the bride's side to sing in exchange for another "discount." Beyond delivering the gifts, this custom served as a joyful way to announce the upcoming wedding to the community. Though the scene was a familiar one in neighborhoods — and a staple in vintage Korean dramas up until the 1990s — it's now a rare sight due to the rise of apartment living.

HOW DO KOREANS FIND THEIR BETTER HALF?

So, we've learned how Koreans get married — but that must leave you wondering: how do they find their better half in the first place? With the deluge of dating apps these days, your next date is literally at your fingertips, but many still prefer time-tested, traditional methods. They often appear in Korean dramas and movies, so knowing them will help you enjoy the scenes even more.

SOGAETING 소개팅 – BLIND DATE

Sogae 소개 means "introduction," and *-ting* 팅 comes from "meeting," so sogaeting literally means a "meeting through introduction" — in other words, a blind date arranged by someone else, usually a mutual friend. There are two common ways a *sogaeting* happens:

Scenario 1 – Target-specific
Tony spots a girl named Jenna on social media and learns they share a mutual friend, Sarah. He messages Sarah and asks if she can set him up on a sogaeting with Jenna.

Scenario 2 – Broad-approach
Lauren, newly single, is having coffee with her friend Sarah and asks if there are any single guys available for a sogaeting. Sarah remembers Ricky, who also recently broke up, shows Lauren his picture, and Lauren finds him cute.

If both parties agree, Sarah connects them — and then the grown-ups handle the rest themselves.

MEETING – GROUP HANGOUT

Similar to sogaeting but slightly different — meeting involves two groups: male and female participants brought together through mutual friends. It can be as small as four people (2 vs. 2) but can go much larger. You might imagine it as a "battle royale of love," but in reality, it's a casual group hangout meant to get to know each other and expand social circles (though, of course, sparks sometimes fly right away). It's also much less pressure than a one-on-one sogaeting, since there's no need to impress your date the entire time. That's why meetings are often held at pubs — where people can relax, play Korean-style drinking games, and just have fun. (And yes, this might explain why Korea has so many drinking games.)

MATSEON 맞선 – ARRANGED DATE WITH A PROSPECTIVE MARRIAGE PARTNER

If sogaeting and meeting represent free-market dating, *matseon* 맞선 — also called *seon* 선 — is more like a formal business meeting arranged by parents, or professional matchmakers, with one clear goal: marriage.

Unlike casual dating, matseon focuses on practical criteria such as education, occupation, and family background rather than chemistry or ideal type. It's a classic K-drama scene: a mother secretly sets up a matseon for her son to separate him from his "unsuitable" love from a poor family — because, of course, she doesn't meet the family's standards.

SPECIAL DAYS FOR COUPLES IN KOREA

In the bubbly teenage Korean dramas like *Hakgyo 2013* 학교 2013 (*School 2013*, **2013, KBS**), there are many "couple days" and "remembrance days" which the high school kids fuss over. Most of them are considered as marketing gimmicks disguised as a Valentine's Day spin-off, which explains why most of them fall on the 14th day of each month. Whatever the origin is, as long as they help to reconfirm the love of couples and give them happy memories, it seems like a fair trade.

FEB 14TH
VALENTINE'S DAY

In Korea, Valentine's Day is when girls give chocolate to boys — and often confess their feelings first.

MAR 14TH
WHITE DAY

Exactly one month later, boys return the favor by giving candy to the girls who gave them chocolate. If you received chocolate on Valentine's Day, you're expected to reciprocate — or risk being branded a heartless villain.

APR 14TH
BLACK DAY

A tragic day for the singles who didn't receive anything during the previous months. On this day, they dress in black and eat *jjajangmyeon* 짜장면 — black bean noodles — together. It's part self-pity, part humor, and maybe a tiny hope that the "curse of singleness" will finally be lifted.

NOV 11TH
PEPERO DAY

A sweet, stick-shaped day of love. Couples exchange **Pepero** (cookie sticks dipped in chocolate, similar to Pocky), while singles hand them to their crushes as a cute, calorie-filled confession.

WHY DO SAME-SEX PEOPLE HOLD HANDS?

If you stroll around Korea, you might see two men or two women walking hand-in-hand or arm-in-arm — and no one bats an eye. Depending on where you're from, that might raise a few eyebrows (or rainbow flags), but in Korea, it's simply a gesture of friendship, not romance. Korean culture is deeply collective and close-knit, so people are generally more comfortable with smaller personal space. On top of that, because discussions about homosexuality have traditionally been kept out of the public sphere, physical affection between friends of the same sex isn't associated with romantic meaning. So when you see two guys walking arm-in-arm, they're not making a statement — they're just being friends.

WHY DO KOREAN COUPLES WEAR THE SAME CLOTHES?

Want to mark your territory and let the world know your significant other is officially taken? In Korea, there's no better way than wearing matching outfits — couple T-shirts are the classic choice. They can be identical or form a design that only makes sense when you're standing next to each other. But it doesn't stop there. Koreans take couple culture seriously — there are couple phone cases, couple diaries, couple shoes, and even couple rings (which are often worn on the fourth finger of the left hand, just like wedding rings — so don't assume someone's married just because you see one!). Whatever form it takes, it's a loud-and-proud way of saying "We're together!" — though, admittedly, some people do find it a little too cringe-worthy.

WHY DO KOREAN CHILDREN GIVE CARNATIONS TO THEIR PARENTS ON PARENT'S DAY?

Every **May 8th**, Korea celebrates **Parents' Day** — a time to thank moms and dads for their endless love and sacrifice. Children make paper carnations at school and pin them on their parents' chests, while grown-up children send bouquets and gifts (and yes, cash is still the number-one favorite). The tradition of giving carnations actually traces back to the origins of Mother's Day in the U.S. In 1868, three years after the Civil War ended, a woman named Ann Maria Jarvis organized Mothers' Friendship Day to bring together mothers from both sides of the conflict for healing and support. After her passing, her daughter, Anna Jarvis, began holding memorial events to honor mothers — and carnations, her mother's favorite flower, became the symbol of the day.

WHAT ARE KOREA'S OFFICIAL HOLIDAYS?

◆ Shinjeong 신정- *New* Year's Day (Jan 1st of solar calendar)

Like many other countries, Koreans celebrate the first day of the Gregorian calendar. Many people head to the coast or mountains to watch the first sunrise of the year, believing it brings good luck and new beginnings.

◆ Seollal 설날 – Lunar New Year's Day (Jan 1st of lunar calendar)

Seollal is one of the most important traditional holidays in Korea, even more significant than January 1st. Most people travel to their hometowns to spend time with their families. On this day, Koreans wear *hanbok* 한복, bow to their elders, and eat *tteokguk* 떡국 (rice cake soup) and *manduguk* 만두국(dumpling soup). They also play traditional games such as *yutnori* 윷놀이 (a traditional board game), spinning tops, and kite flying.

◆ Samiljeol 3.1절 - Independence Movement Day (Mar 1)

This day commemorates the Declaration of Independence proclaimed on March 1, 1919, during the Japanese occupation. It's one of the key milestones in Korea's modern history of resistance and national pride.

◆ Eorininal 어린이날 - Children's Day (May 5)

The day every Korean kid looks forward to! Families celebrate by wishing for their children's happiness and health — often with trips to amusement parks, zoos, or shopping malls (to buy gifts, of course!).

◆ Seokgatanshinil 석가탄신일 - Buddha's Birthday (8th day of 4th lunar month)

Traditionally a Buddhist country, Korea celebrates Buddha's Birthday with colorful lanterns adorning temples nationwide. The sight of beautifully decorated temples glowing at night creates a serene and festive atmosphere.

◆ Hyeonchungil 현충일 - Memorial Day (June 6)

A solemn day to honor fallen soldiers and civilians who gave their lives for the country, especially during the Korean War. Official ceremonies take place at the National Cemetery in Seoul, with flags flown at half-mast across the nation.

◆ Gwangbokjeol 광복절 - Liberation Day (Aug 15)

This day marks Korea's liberation from Japanese rule in 1945, when Japan surrendered to the Allied Forces, ending World War II. The name Gwangbok means "Restoration of Light," symbolizing the nation's regained independence.

◆ Chuseok 추석 – Fall Harvest Festival (15th day of the 8th lunar month)

Alongside Seollal, Chuseok is one of Korea's two major traditional holidays. Families gather to honor their ancestors through charye (ancestral memorial rites) and to celebrate the year's bountiful harvest. It's also a time to enjoy traditional foods like songpyeon (half-moon rice cakes).

◆ Gaecheonjeol 개천절 - National Foundation Day (Oct 3)

According to legend, **Dangun** 단군, the God-King, founded the first Korean kingdom, **Gojoseon** 고조선, marking the beginning of Korean history. The day, literally meaning "The Opening of Heaven," is celebrated with ceremonies at **Chamseongdan Altar** 참성단 on **Manisan Mountain** 마니산 in **Ganghwado Island** 강화도.

◆ Hangul Day 한글날 (Oct 9)

This day celebrates the proclamation of *hunminjeongeum* 훈민정음 ("The Proper Sounds for the Instruction of the People") in 1446 by **King Sejong the Great**, who created *hangul* 한글, the Korean alphabet. It honors the king's vision to make literacy accessible to all Koreans.

◆ Christmas 크리스마스 (Dec 25)

With a large Christian population, Christmas in Korea is both a religious and festive holiday. Families gather to spend time together, while couples often treat it as a romantic day to celebrate their love — think of it as Korea's version of Valentine's Day with twinkling lights.

WHY ARE THERE TWO NEW YEAR'S DAYS?

Are Koreans crazy about partying? Koreans actually celebrate New Year's Day twice every year — once on January 1 (Solar/Gregorian calendar) and again on January 1 of the Lunar calendar (usually between late January and mid-February).

So, why two New Year's Days?

This unique "two New Year's Days" culture traces back to the Japanese colonial era (1910–1945). When Japan annexed Korea, it renamed the **traditional Lunar New Year, *Seollal* 설날** to *Gujeong* 구정, meaning "**Old New Year**," and called the **Western (Solar) New Year *Shinjeong* 신정**, or "*New New Year*." Japan had already replaced the Lunar New Year with the Solar one under Emperor Meiji in the late 1800s, and during its rule over Korea, it suppressed Korean customs and promoted Japanese traditions. By labeling Seollal as "old," the colonial authorities attempted to make the Korean holiday seem outdated and less significant. They also argued that celebrating two similar holidays was "socially wasteful," and thus declared Shinjeong the only official New Year holiday. As a result, the traditional Lunar New Year was pushed aside and lost its national holiday status. It took 75 years for Seollal to regain official recognition. In 1985, it returned as "**Folklore Day**," and in 1989, the name Seollal was restored — along with a three-day national holiday. If it weren't for the Korean people's determination to preserve their culture despite colonial suppression, Seollal might have disappeared entirely. Even after Seollal's revival, the Solar New Year, Shinjeong, continued as an official holiday — originally three days, then shortened to two in 1991, and finally reduced to a one-day holiday in 1999.

WHY DO KOREANS EAT
TTEOKGUK (RICE CAKE SOUP) ON NEW YEAR'S DAY?

***Tteokguk* 떡국**, or rice cake soup, is the must-have dish for Seollal, the Korean Lunar New Year. According to historical records, it was served instead of rice during charye (차례), the ancestral memorial service held on New Year's Day. But why tteokguk, among all the possible dishes? On New Year's Day, Koreans bid farewell to the old and welcome the new with a clean slate. Because of this, the food served carries symbolic meaning — purity, renewal, and solemnity. The white, cylindrical rice cake called ***garaetteok* 가래떡** was seen as a perfect fit: its color represents cleanliness, and its long shape symbolizes longevity. When sliced into round pieces, they resemble old Korean coins, representing prosperity and wealth.

Although tteokguk was eaten year-round by everyone — from royalty and aristocrats to commoners — it held special significance during Seollal. An old saying from the 1800s Joseon Dynasty humorously noted, *"Your age equals the number of bowls of tteokguk you've eaten."*

But don't worry — even if you have two or three bowls, you still only age by one year!

SEBAE - MAKE THE NEW YEAR'S BOW (AND RECEIVE MONEY!)

On New Year's Day, men and women of all ages change into new clothes called *seolbim* 설빔 early in the morning and gather together to hold a memorial service for the deceased ancestors. Then, they bow to their grandparents first, and then, taking turns, the younger family members bow to the older family members to greet them for the first time in the New Year. This New Year's bow is called *sebae* 세배. People visited the nearby neighbors' houses to give greetings for the New Year. It was customary for adults to serve alcohol and food to those who come to do *sebae*, but children were given a little money or *tteok* and fruits instead of alcohol. Nowadays, kids look forward to Seollal because they can earn pocket money from doing *sebae*, but if you're too young, it will probably go into your mom's pocket, who acts as your "money manager," happily of course. When bowing to the elderly, New Year's greetings such as, "May you be healthier in the New Year," and, "Happy New Year and live a long life," can be said. The elderly would return by giving words of blessings, such as, "I hope you get promoted in the new year," and, "I hope you achieve your wish in the new year."

SEOLBIM - NEW YEAR, NEW YOU, IN NEW DRESS!

New Year's Day is a day to celebrate the new year with a new resolution. This determination was also expressed through a new dress called *seolbim* 설빔 worn on New Year's Day morning. Wearing *seolbim*, which was made by weaving and sewing material by hand, was a must-have ritual even in the days when the family was not well-off. Presenting themselves neat and tidy in new clothing was a way to pay respect to the ancestors as well as praying for the wishes of the New Year. The children's *seolbim* was particularly colorful. The boys wore a five-colored **durumagi** 두루마기, and a traditional Korean overcoat including blue, red, yellow, white, and black, related to the energy of the traditional Five Elements (metal, wood, water, fire, earth). For girls, yellow **jeogori** 저고리, the upper garment of Korean traditional clothes, and a flower-pink **chima** 치마, skirt, were typical.

Traditional Korean Games
1. ***Tuho* 투호** - Throw sticks into a canister to win the match.
2. ***Yutnori* 윷놀이** - Korean board game. Players cast a set of four sticks to receive a set number of moves to bring home all four tokens before the opponent.

Korean Lucky Charms
3. ***Bokjumeoni* 복주머니** - "Fortune Bag"
4. ***Bokjori* 복조리** - "Fortune Strainer"

HWATU - WHAT IS THIS CARD GAME KOREANS PLAY?

Tazza : The High Roller 타짜 (2006)

Swapping cards? Try it at your own risk — you might just lose your hand if you get caught! That's the kind of world depicted in *Tazza: The High Roller* 타짜 (**2006**), a movie about high-stakes gambling where deception, hammers, and even death threats come into play. Anyone familiar with poker or mahjong might follow the tension easily, but the game itself? That's a whole different story.

Often called "**Go-Stop**" 고스톱, the formal name of the game is *hwatu* 화투, literally meaning "battle of flowers." The game originated in Japan, where it's known as Hanafuda, and the Korean version evolved over time with local twists. Technically, hwatu refers to the card set, while Go-Stop is the most popular game played with those cards.

Why "battle of flowers"? Because each card features floral illustrations — 12 sets of 4 cards each — representing the 12 months of the year. While many assume hwatu came from Japan during the colonial period (1910–1945), records suggest it had already arrived in Korea earlier, during the late Joseon Dynasty. In fact, an advertisement for hwatu cards appeared in the 1902 issue of *Hwangseong Shinmun* 황성신문, proving that the game was already well known before Japanese occupation. Today, hwatu remains one of the most popular tabletop games in Korea, though it sometimes carries a negative image due to its association with illegal gambling. The rules vary, but typically 3–4 players compete to reach a certain score first. Once you accumulate enough points, you can either "Go" (continue playing for higher rewards at greater risk) or "Stop" (end the game and secure your winnings). Interestingly, hwatu isn't always about gambling. You'll often see elderly people playing Go-Stop at funerals — not for money, but to help create a lively, noisy atmosphere. In the past, people believed that such chatter and activity would ease the family's sorrow and help them focus on welcoming guests rather than sinking into grief.

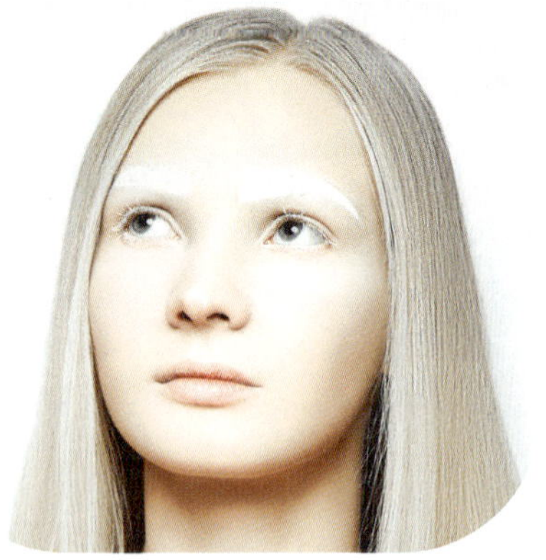

DON'T SLEEP ON NEW YEAR'S EVE OR YOUR EYEBROWS WILL TURN WHITE

In the past, Koreans believed that sleeping on New Year's Eve would cause one's eyebrows to turn white. Parents used to tease children who couldn't stay awake by secretly sprinkling white flour on their eyebrows while they slept. This custom of staying up all night, called *suse* 수세, is said to have originated to encourage people to work hard and prepare for the busy morning of New Year's Day.

WHY WOULD KOREANS HIDE THEIR SHOES ON NEW YEAR'S EVE?

According to old folklore, there was a ghost named *Yagwang* 야광 who would come down to the human world on New Year's Eve, try on children's shoes, and take the ones that fit. It was believed that any child who lost their shoes to Yagwang would suffer bad luck for the entire year, so children would either hide their shoes in their rooms or place them upside down before going to bed.

THE KOREAN NEW YEAR COUNTDOWN - BOSINGAK BELL-RINGING CEREMONY

The **Bosingak Bell-Ringing Ceremony** 제야의 종 타종행사 is Korea's version of the New Year's Eve countdown. Its origin can be traced back to a Buddhist tradition in which a temple bell was struck 108 times to symbolize the cleansing of the 108 defilements of humankind.

However, the modern bell-ringing ceremony as we know it today actually began during the Japanese Occupation. In 1928, the Gyeongseong Broadcasting Station aired a New Year's Day bell-striking program—using a bell borrowed from Dongbonwonsa Temple, a Japanese temple located below Namsan Mountain in Seoul.

After Korea's liberation and the reconstruction of the Bosingak Bell (which had been destroyed during the Korean War), the tradition resumed at the end of 1953. The bell is struck 33 times, symbolizing the opening of the four main city gates at 5 A.M. during the Joseon Dynasty, and representing a prayer for national peace and prosperity. Today, the event is one of Seoul's most popular New Year's celebrations, drawing massive crowds to watch the bell strike at midnight. It's especially popular among couples, though the dense crowd might make it hard to even glimpse the bell.

But don't worry—you can still see the bell-ringing ceremony on other occasions throughout the year if you miss the New Year's one.

WHY DO SO MANY PEOPLE TRAVEL DURING CHUSEOK?

The holiday **Chuseok** 추석, literally meaning "Autumn Eve," and **Hangawi** 한가위, an old native Korean word meaning "the great middle (of autumn)," falls on the 15th day of the 8th lunar month. It is one of the biggest holidays in Korea, along with Seollal (Lunar New Year). Originally, Chuseok was a time to harvest some grain in advance after passing the most critical part of the farming season and to perform ancestral rites praying for a good harvest. Since most summer farming work was already done and the weather was mild, it was also the perfect time to visit ancestral graves and enjoy a bit of rest. For this reason, Chuseok differs from Thanksgiving Day, which is a celebration of gratitude after the harvest. In Korea, it's more of a mid-harvest festival and family reunion. With one or two days left before Chuseok, millions of Koreans travel back to their hometowns, leading to massive traffic jams across the nation. It's one of the few times when downtown Seoul looks almost empty due to the "great migration." Train tickets sell out within minutes, and driving can take three to four times longer than usual. Yet, people willingly endure the long journey just to be with family. After finally arriving late at night, families stay up chatting, and women traditionally spend extra hours preparing food and washing dishes.

On Chuseok morning, everyone wakes up early to prepare breakfast made with that year's harvest and holds the ancestral memorial rite, called **charye** 차례. Afterward, they visit the family graves, where they had previously gone to cut weeds and clean the area. At night, families make wishes upon the bright full moon and often gather to make **songpyeon** 송편 (half-moon-shaped rice cakes) together. Until about a decade ago, this scene was a familiar one in almost every Korean household. But as times change, so do traditions — nowadays, many people spend Chuseok traveling abroad or simply resting at home, rather than visiting relatives in their hometowns.

**Want a beautiful child? Then make a beautiful *songpyeon!*
P. 67**

WHY DO KOREAN PEOPLE BELIEVE THERE IS A RABBIT LIVING ON THE MOON?

On Chuseok night, people make wishes on the bright full moon — but before Apollo 11 ever landed there, what did Koreans believe lived on the moon? Most Koreans imagined a rabbit pounding something with a pestle in a mortar, because the moon's dark spots resemble that image. The story originally came from ancient Chinese folklore and spread throughout East Asia, though the details differ by country. In Korea and Japan, the rabbit is said to be pounding rice cakes (*tteok* and *mochi*), while in China, it's believed to be making the elixir of life.

HANBOK 한복

THE TRADITIONAL KOREAN CLOTHES

DO KOREANS WEAR KIMONO?

It's one of those questions that would make your Korean friends — who take pride in their 5,000 years of rich history and culture — go, "*Oh, no you didn't!*" But to be fair to foreign friends who may not be familiar with Asian culture, kimono, a Japanese word meaning "clothing," has become a kind of catch-all term for "traditional Asian attire" — like Kleenex for tissues or Band-Aid for adhesive bandages. Kimono just happens to have the first mover's advantage in global awareness.

To answer the question clearly: Koreans have their own traditional clothing called *hanbok* 한복, known for its harmonious beauty of straight lines and subtle curves. If you've seen Korean historical dramas, that's likely how you imagine hanbok — and no, those were *not* "Korean kimonos."

Over nearly 5,000 years of history, Korea has seen many kingdoms and diverse cultures, some of which were influenced by neighboring regions. (Even in modern times, the fashion of the 1960s looks completely different from today's trends — though fashion always comes full circle.) So, when you watch historical dramas set in different eras, you might notice the hanbok styles vary quite a bit.

In fact, even Koreans sometimes find it hard to distinguish all the historical variations. As for its origins, hanbok is believed to have descended from the ancient **Scythian-Siberian culture of Northeast Asia**, reflecting the attire of nomadic peoples. While the designs evolved over centuries, the hanbok has consistently followed the *sangyuhago* 상유하고 style — meaning "**the upper garment goes on top, and the pants or skirt go on the bottom.**" This design made it ideal for active lifestyles like **horseback riding and hunting**.

THREE KINGDOMS PERIOD (57 BC ~ 668 AD)

7th century Tang Dynasty painting of envoys from the Three Kingdoms illustrates the different styles of clothes worn by the people of each kingdom.

While there were more ancient kingdoms before this period, we'll start from here due to the lack of historical records and relics from the ancient times. But more importantly the Three Kingdoms period is when the basic standardized style of *hanbok* was established. According to the historical paintings, relics, and records, the basic format for men was *jeogori* 저고리 (upper garment) and *baji* 바지 (trousers), and for women, it was *jeogori* and *chima* 치마 (skirt). They both put on *durumagi/po* 두루마기/포 (outer jacket/coat) on top. Also added were *gwanmo* 관모 (hat/headgear), *dae* 대 (belt), and

various accessories depending on the class and status. One unique aspect of *hanbok* was that it must include pants, which even women wore as innerwear. Another characteristic is that it's worn in many layers, as many as 5-6 layers of tops and bottoms (Don't worry! Lighter and more breathable materials were used for summer *hanbok*, and *hanbok* clothes have easy-to-put-on-and-take-off open-front style). Moreover, *hanbok* is categorized into formal and casual clothes, which are further divided into men and women, adults and children, and seasonal. During the Three Kingdoms Period, textile manufacturing techniques vastly improved, capable of producing various types of silk and woolen fabrics.

야금모행 *Yageummohaeng* "A Secret Night Journey" by Shin Yun-bok depicts the Joseon-era Hanbok.

Another important highlight of this era was class stratification, in which the clothes served as a means to represent different classes. The clothes of the privileged class were different from those of the ordinary people.

Pictures of the scale models from the Lotte World Folk Museum

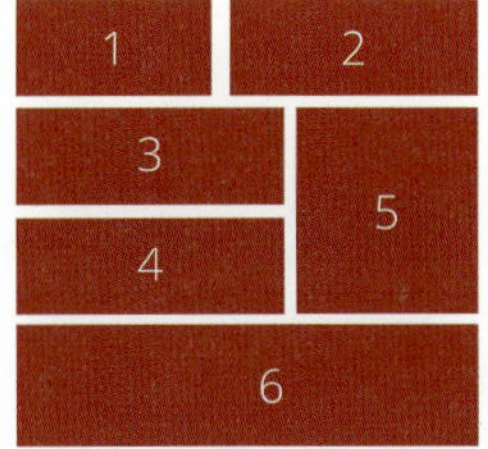

1. A mural from the 5th century CE Muyonchong (tomb) depicting a hunting scene.
2. A miniature scale model of a Goguryeo man hunting.
3. A mural from same tomb depicting several dancers performing "sleeve dance."
4. A mural from the Susanri tomb depicting a parade of women.
5. A miniature scale model reenactment of the procession scene painted on the walls of corridor on No.3 tomb in Anak. Shown in the picture are female servants.
6. From left - the clothes of a female aristocrat, male aristocrat, queen, king, lady-in-waiting, and chamberlain.

The **Goguryeo 고구려** people were located in the cold northern part of the country and always had to stay alert for possible Chinese invasions. This is reflected in the clothes worn by the Goguryeo people. The basic structure of Goguryeo men's clothes is separated into top and bottom, ideal for activities like shooting arrows, and the top *jeogori* had narrow sleeves, pants, and high-necked shoes that were suitable for horse riding. The woman's *jeogori* was long enough to cover the hips that a belt had to be worn and a skirt was worn over the inner pants. Men also wore a hat, *gwanmo*. Both Goguryeo men and women wore *po* **포**, an outer jacket/coat both for ceremonial occasions but also ordinary occasions. The male aristocrat wore a headgear called *jeolpung* **절풍**, which was decorated with feathers, and earrings were worn, too. The female aristocrat wore long skirts and *jeogori*, which had a relaxed look with the sleeves stretched out. The lower-end of *jeogori* with embroidery on the high-end silk and a pleated skirt with various colors of cloth add to the overall refinement. Women wore skirts with a lot of pleats to mark their high status. The married commoner woman's hair was neatly tied, and the man wore a black hood. A belt around the waist was common in the Three Kingdoms Period, usually knotted at the front. Most commoner women wore pleated skirts made of hemp cloth or animal skins.

BAEKJE PERIOD (18 BC ~ 660)

It's not easy to know the style of **Baekje's 백제** costume in detail because there aren't many artifacts or records related to Baekje's costume, but according to the accounts found in the Book of Liang, a Chinese historical text, it's assumed to be almost the same as Goguryeo's. One unique aspect is that Baekje distinguished the ranks of government posts with their official hat, belt, and colors. *Gwanmo* was decorated with silver for high-rank officials, with purple, red, and blue garments that were separately used according to their ranks. The king wore a purple coat with wide sleeves, wide blue silk pants, a leather belt around his waist, black leather shoes, and a

<table>
<tr><td>1</td><td>2</td><td>3</td></tr>
<tr><td colspan="3">4</td></tr>
</table>

1. (From previous page) A scale model of a Baekje male commoner.
2. (From previous page) A scale model of a Baekje female commoner.
3. (From previous page) A scale model of a Baekje female aristocrat.
4. From left - the clothes of a government official, queen, king, and the Secretary of State.

cone-shaped black silk headgear adorned with gold accessories on the sides. The queen wore a similar headgear, a *jeogori* (upper garment), and a *chima* (skirt), and a *durumagi* (outer coat) or a short-sleeved shirt on top of it. The royal family embellished the cloth with gold thread or gold foil and decorated it with high-quality ornaments, enhancing the royal authority. The commoners were not allowed to wear red clothes and used the blue inner bark of kudzu or hemp for cloth.

SILLA PERIOD (57 BC ~ 935)

Silla's 신라 clothing was similar to Goguryeo and Baekje until the unification of the Three Kingdoms. After the unification, the culture became more mature and luxurious (Silla was known as the "Golden Kingdom"). Also, the clothes of the **Tang Dynasty** came in and brought about many changes in style. Silla established a detailed class of status to establish the authority of the ruling class as the country became stronger. At that time, besides silk, woven hemp cloth rose to popularity, and the quality of the cloth was an indication of one's class. Belts, shoes, and even combs were different according to class. Both men and women wore *jeogori* (upper garment), *baji/chima* (pants/skirt), and *po* (outer coat).

The king and the royal family wore a gold crown *gwanmo* which was a symbol of absolute power. On top of a splendid *durumagi*, a gold belt full of ornaments, which was originally created for practical purposes, (such as carrying personal items, tools, and weapons) became a fashion accessory and were worn as such. The queen was sumptuously adorned with earrings and a necklace made of curved jades which show Silla's top-notch quality of workmanship and sophistication. The upper class mainly wore wide sleeves, wide pants, and the common people wore narrow sleeves and narrow pants.

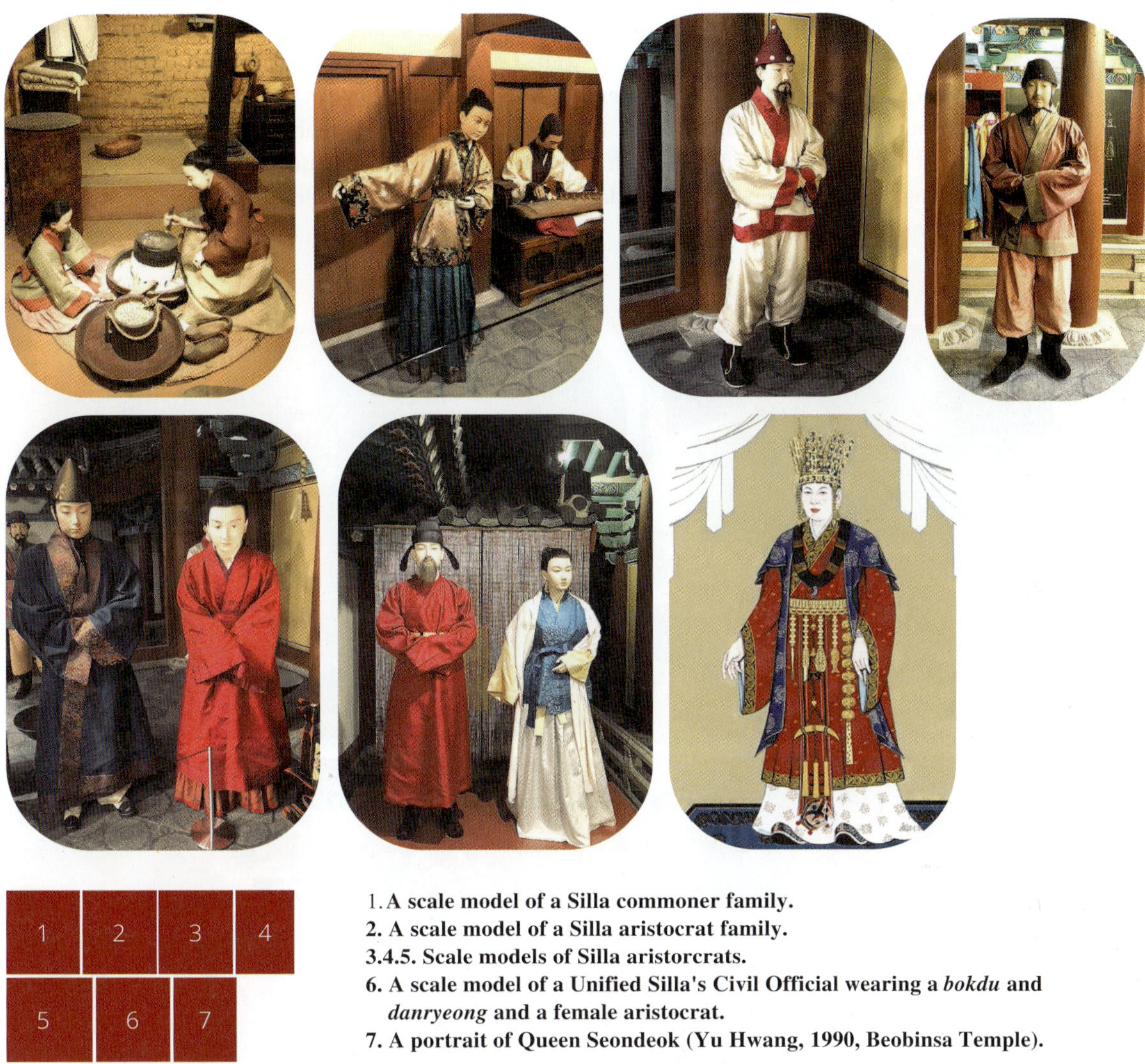

1. A scale model of a Silla commoner family.
2. A scale model of a Silla aristocrat family.
3.4.5. Scale models of Silla aristorcrats.
6. A scale model of a Unified Silla's Civil Official wearing a *bokdu* and *danryeong* and a female aristocrat.
7. A portrait of Queen Seondeok (Yu Hwang, 1990, Beobinsa Temple).

Unified Silla was greatly influenced by the **Tang Dynasty**, and a new style of clothing that didn't exist previously during the Three Kingdoms Period was introduced. Ceremonial dresses such as *hwalot* 활옷, *wonsam* 원삼, and *dangeui* 당의 are such examples. Also, short-sleeved upper garment *banbi* 반비 was introduced. Also, the government adopted the Tang Dynasty's uniform system for officials. Until the Three Kingdoms Period, each had its own official uniforms. During the reign of **Queen Jindeok 진덕여왕** of Silla, **Kim Chun-chu 김춘추** visited the Tang Dynasty of China as an envoy to meet with the Emperor Taizong of Tang and brought the official uniform system, including *bokdu* 복두 headgear and *danryeong* 단령, circular-collar robe, and made it the official uniforms of all government officials. After that, from Goryeo to Joseon Dynasty, Chinese-style ceremonial robes were adopted and worn as a government uniform. According to *Gyeonggukdaejeon* 경국대전, a collection of codes of rules for the government, different colors were used according to one's rank. As a result of the cultural exchange with the Tang Dynasty, a new unique clothing style based on the traditional style was developed.

The clothes of **Goryeo 고려** were inherited from the **Silla Dynasty** while absorbing and developing the styles of the Chinese Dynasties. The farmers and merchants wore white ramie and hemp clothing. Goryeo adopted the royal and official uniform system from the Song, Yuan, and Ming Dynasty (they put on a black hood and a white coat when off duty). The Mongols invaded Goryeo in 1231, and Goryeo later lost part of its territory to the Mongols who exploited, and interfered in domestic affairs (but Goryeo was not conquered nor did lose political independence), including forcing to embrace **Mongolian customs**, including their clothing style. As a result, they are still found in the form of Korean tradition.

Clockwise: Goryeo commoner family, Confucian scholar's clothes,
Queen's ceremonial clothes, King's ceremonial clothes, *jokduri*, *otgoreum*.

Influenced by Mongolian costumes, the length of *jeogori* became shorter and the sleeves narrower, and *otgoreum* 옷고름 (garment strap ribbon) replaced the waist strap. It was also a Mongolian custom for a bride to wear on her head *jokduri* 족두리 (bridal crown) at a wedding. The Mongolian style was popular among the upper classes, while the commoners adhered to traditional costumes. Due to the active human and cultural exchanges between Goryeo and Yuan Dynasty, Mongolian customs were introduced to Goryeo, but Goryeo customs were also introduced to the Yuan Dynasty. Among the customs of Goryeo, clothing, shoes, and hats were popular, and the style was referred to as *goryeoyang* 고려양 (a nascent form of *Hallyu* 한류, the Korean Wave?). During the 31st reign of **King Gongmin 공민왕**, the **Yuan Dynasty** collapsed and the **Ming Dynasty** of the Han tribe reigned over China. As a result, the Mongolian style gradually disappeared.

Hanbok of the Joseon Dynasty is closest to the image of *hanbok* that we have now, because chronologically it was the most recent Dynasty, with most data and records remaining. As a result, there are more Joseon Dynasty-era historical dramas than any other periods, adding to the familiarity. During this time, Confucianism was the governing philosophy, and hierarchical order was clearly shown through clothing.

In the early Joseon Dynasty, **seuran** 스란 skirts (a decorative wrapping skirt with gold leaf patterns), which were almost similar to those of the Ming Dynasty, were popular but only the people with high social status could wear them. Since the mid-Joseon period, the back length on the men and women's clothes were generally long, coming down to the waist, but became shorter over time.

From left: A woman wearing a short, tight-fitting *jeogori* (jacket) and a plump *chima* (skirt) /
A man in *durumagi* (traditional topcoat), A man in male *hanbok* consisting of *jeogori* (jacket) and *baji* (trousers),
A woman wearing a jacket featuring the gorgeous-looking *jogakbo* (Korean traditional patchwork).

In the 18th century, *jeogori* was so short that it hardly covered the chest that the belt had to be worn high. The skirts were long and plentiful throughout the Joseon Dynasty, but they were especially long and wide in the 17th and 18th centuries, leading to a bell-shaped silhouette.In the 19th century, the area around the knees and ankles was expanded to make the overall look a triangular shape, and it's still widely used today.

After the mid-Joseon period, the Confucian ideology was further strengthened and more restrictions were put on women's clothes. Women used a kind of long hood called *jangot* 장옷 or a pair of skirts called *sseugaechima* 쓰개치마 to cover their faces when they went out. The commoners wore a *jeogori/chima/durumagi* combination, the basic style that came down from the Three Kingdoms Period.

Left: *jangot* / Right: *sseugaechima*
From paintings by Shin Yun-bok

Painting by Kim Hong-do illustrating the different clothes worn by different classes.

Painting by Chae Yong-shin

Heungseon Daewongun wearing *magoja*

The *jeogori* was long and relaxed, but after the Japanese Invasion of Korea in 1592, the **hahusangbak** 하후상박 (slip top and puffy bottom) style, with a small, short *jeogori*, a puffy *chima*, appeared. In 1887, Regent **Heungseon Daewongun** 흥선대원군, who was kidnapped by the **Qing Dynasty**, returned from Manchuria wearing **magua**, which was the jacket of the Qing Dynasty, and this became **magoja** 마고자, which was worn over *jeogori* and had buttons. Since the 1880s vests with pockets (influenced by the Western suits) became popular as it compensated for the shortcomings of *hanbok* which lacked them. As Western culture began to flood in, changes were brought about in clothing. People wore both *hanbok* and suits. Women's clothing also changed, and wearing seamless one-piece skirts called **tongchima** 통치마 and white *jeogori* was the beginning of the modernized *hanbok*. As society changed, there was a movement to abolish wearing *jangeui* and *sseugaechima*, which women had to put on to cover their faces when they went out.

After the Korean War, *hanbok* and suits coexisted, but *hanbok* gradually lost its place due to rapid economic development and the influx of Western-style culture through the 1960s and 1970s. *Hanbok* has become special clothing worn only during the holidays, but it is hard to see it even during the holidays today. However, with the Korean Wave, foreign tourists are showing a greater interest in *hanbok*, combined with the efforts of the younger generation to revive and improve the traditional clothes, the future of *hanbok* doesn't look too gloomy.

Oh My Gat 갓!

WHAT ARE THE COOL HATS ANCIENT KOREANS WORE?

"Korea seems to be the land of hats: they are made in all kinds of shapes, and I have nowhere seen a greater variety, from the crown of gilded cardboard for the provincial governor to the modest headband of the peasant."

- Charles Varat, a French explorer charged with an ethnographic mission by the minister of Public Instruction. <Voyage en Corée> *Le Tour du Monde, LXIII*, 1892 Premier Semestre. Paris.

During the Joseon Dynasty, wearing a hat was an important part of the dress code, and a foreigner who visited Joseon described it as "the land of hats" because there were so many kinds of hats worn depending on one's status and situation. So, without further ado, let's take a trip to the world of hats from the Joseon Dynasty!

163

***Chorip* 초립 -** A hat that was usually worn before *heukrip* became popular. Made of bamboo strips. Originally, it was worn by both the scholars and the common people, but in the late Joseon Dynasty, it was mostly worn by boys who weren't yet married but had a coming-of-age ceremony, as people started to wear *heukrip*.

———

***Heukrip* 흑립** – Literally means "black *gat* 갓 (traditional Korean hat made of bamboo strips and horsehair)." It was designated as an official hat during the reign of **King Gongmin 공민왕** of Goryeo to break down the customs of the Yuan Dynasty and establish its own attire system, but it wasn't widely put in place until the late Joseon Dynasty. It was worn by *yangban* 양반 (noblemen) and *seonbi* 선비(scholars).

Painting by Shin Yun-bok

***Paeraengi* 패랭이** – A hat worn by the officials at post stations (they painted it black), and lower-class people like peddlers (they put a large cotton ball on it), and butchers. Made of bamboo strips.

Painting by Kwon Yong-jeong

***Hwiyang/Hwihang* 휘양/휘항** – A winter cap worn by men. It covers the head and shoulders. Made of leather, cloth, or cotton.

Painting by Kim Yang-gi

Sungkyunkwan Scandal 성균관스캔들 (2010, KBS 2)

***Yugeon* 유건 -** Indoor hat of Sungkyunkwan Confucian scholars. Worn during studying or ancestral rites.

WHAT'S THE OLDEST UNIVERSITY IN KOREA?

Sungkyunkwan, founded at the beginning of the Joseon Dynasty in 1398 by royal decree to promote the scholarship in Confucianism, was the highest and foremost national educational institute. The current Sungkyunkwan University succeeded the original Sungkyunkwan, making it the oldest university in East Asia. The original Sungkyunkwan is located at the south end of the Humanities and Social Sciences Campus. Within the original campus, *seokjeon daeje* 석전대제, the ceremonial rite to honor Confucius and the Confucian sages of China and Korea are performed in the **Munmyo Shrine 문묘,** the primary temple of Confucius, twice a year in May and September.

Jeongjagwan, Chungjeonggwan, Dongpagwan 정자관, 충정관, 동파관 – Originally one of the hats of China. It's always worn in the house and is the symbol of **yangban** 양반, the noblemen.

Portraits of Kim Je-deok, Kim Man-jung, Yi Chae wearing *jeongjagwan, chungjeonggwan, dongpagwan*

Tanggeon 탕건 – Originally worn only by government officials, it's more similar to a skullcap/hood than a full hat. It was mainly made of horsehair or leather, but cloth or bamboo was also used.

Painting by Kim Deuk-sin

Portrait of King Yeongjo

Gamtu 감투 – A hat similar to **tanggeon**. Worn by ordinary people who could afford it. Made with horsehair, leather, or cloth, and doesn't have a brim, making it easy to wear. This hat was worn by low-class people since the Goryeo Dynasty. It was used by commoners during the Joseon Dynasty.

Painting by Sung Hyeop

Ikseongwan 익선관 – The king of Joseon wore this hat when he wore his official uniform. It was introduced from the Ming Dynasty.

Neoul 너울 - Worn by the court or upper-class women to cover their faces when they go out.

Part of "The royal procession of King Jeongjo"

Jisatgat 지삿갓 – Made by weaving bamboo into a circle and applying *hanji* (traditional Korean paper) and oiling it. Used to prevent rain and sunshine. It's a hand-held rather than fixed on the hat with a ribbon.

Jeonmo 전모– It was worn by lower-class women such as **gisaeng** 기생. Made with *hanji*, just like **jisatgat**. Decorated with letters and various patterns (mainly butterflies and flowers).

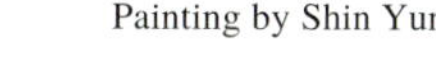

Painting by Shin Yun-bok

"Go Out of the New Year" (1921)
by Elizabeth Keith

Ayam* 아얌 -** A cold cap for women. There is a long string shaped like a ***daenggi 댕기 (pigtail ribbon) with a tassel in the center. Sometimes decorated with jewelry or gold.

Nambawi* 남바위 –** A winter cap used for both men and women A young child wears it for his/her ***doljanchi 돌잔치 (first birthday party).

***Jobawi* 조바위 –** A cold cap for women widely used from the aristocracy to the working class in the late Joseon. As *ayam* became less popular the long string at the back disappeared, and there were parts covering both sides instead.

Painting by Shin Yun-bok

***Gache* 가체** is a head ornament/wig worn by women of high social class and *gisaeng*. It first appeared during the **Unified Silla Period**, and it's assumed to have been influenced by the Tang Dynasty. During the reign of **King Seongjong 성종** of the Joseon Dynasty, some were as tall as 30 cm (1 ft) because the larger and heavier they were, the more beautiful they were perceived. Consequently, many women suffered from neck pain, and some even broke their necks!

The roof of the Seoul Arts Center building is the shape of the 갓 *gat!*

GISAENG - MULTI-TALENTED FEMALE ENTERTAINERS

Hwang Jini 황진이 (2006, KBS)

They could sing, dance, and recite poems. But most of all, they had a great store of knowledge that the upper-class enjoyed discussing current issues with them at banquets. Who were they? Renowned scholars of the time? Surprisingly, no, they were *gisaeng/kisaeng* 기생 - Korea's multi-talented female entertainers. Their origin is unclear but, according to some scholars, the victorious **Goryeo Dynasty** had to find a way to effectively manage the war prisoners they had as a result of the successful unification of the **Later Three Kingdoms**, and labelled male prisoners of war as "*no*" 노 and female prisoners as "*bi*" 비.

Among them, females who excelled in dance and music were selected separately by the state, who later established a female music band called *goryeo yeoak* 고려 여악, and supplied them for the royal and Buddhist events. During the Joseon Dynasty, *gisaeng*s were managed and supervised under the system set up by the state, and for that reason only those registered with the government could work. Once on the register, they could not escape from the status of

cheonmin 천민 (the lowest class of people, the "untouchable"), which was passed down to their children. Gisaengs had to be educated and trained for years because they had to be good at singing, dancing, playing musical instruments, writing poems, as well as calligraphy and drawing. Not only that, they learned to speak and behave in a refined and cultured manner because their clientele were mostly upper-class people. Thus there was *gyobang* 교방, a school for educating *gisaeng*s. The aspiring *gisaeng*s entered the school at an early age.

At the end of the Joseon Dynasty, *gisaeng*s were divided into three groups: *ilpae* 일패, *ipae* 이패, and *sampae* 삼패 (1st, 2nd, and 3rd class). The *ilpae gisaeng*s were a group of highly educated and trained female talents and belonged to the government, so they were known as "*yangban* (aristocracy/noblemen) *gisaeng*." They were in charge of teaching and training new *gisaeng*s for three years. On the other hand, *ipae* and *sampae gisaeng*s were strictly prohibited from performing the dance and songs of *ilpae*. Unlike *ilpae gisaeng*s, *ipae* and *sampae gisaeng*s were allowed in providing sexual services for their clientele.

However, the system which categorized and distinguished the types and roles of *gisaeng* became blurry during the Japanese Occupation period, and there's been a tendency to regard them as "high-class courtesans" mainly focusing on sexual services which *ipae* and *sampae gisaeng*s provided. As a result, the contributions they made to Joseon society have been easily overlooked. They were actually the only group of people who played the role of inheriting and transmitting female literary and traditional arts. Famed *gisaeng*s like **Hwang Jini** 황진이 excelled in many fields and left numerous works such as *sijo* 시조, traditional Korean poem, that are highly regarded as an important part of classical Korean literature.

TRADITIONAL KOREAN ENTERTAINMENT

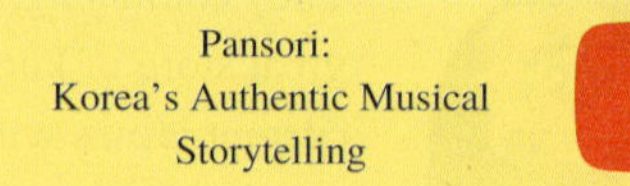

***Pansori* 판소리** – Korean Musical Storytelling. It is a type of solo opera in which a ***sorikkun* 소리꾼** (singer/vocalist) tells a story with gestures to the rhythm of ***gosu* 고수** (drummer). It was performed in a yard or concert hall, and for long stories, it could easily take over three hours.

***Samulnori* 사물놀이** - meaning "play of 4 objects." It is a traditional type of music developed based on the rhythm of ***pungmulpae* 풍물패** (Korean traditional percussion band). The 4 instruments are ***kkwaengwari* 꽹과리** (small gong), ***jing* 징** (larger gong), ***janggu* 장구** (an hourglass-shaped drum), and ***buk* 북** (barrel drum).

***Buchaechum* 부채춤 ("fan dance")** - It's the most representative group dance/performance of Korea, well known for the beautiful fans that captivate the audience with flashy dance moves. It was created by dancer Kim Baek-bong in 1954 who simplified and reinterpreted traditional Korean dances, such as the court dance, Korean Buddhist dance, and even the shamanistic rituals.

***Talchum* 탈춤** - It's a traditional play performed while wearing a mask. At first, clowns performed at court events, but during the late Joseon Dynasty, it developed into a popular culture, satirizing the feudal status society and humorously depicting the hard life of the people. ***Hahoe Byeolsingut Talnori* 하회별신굿 탈놀이** (special ritual drama to the gods mask play) and ***Bongsan Talchum* 봉산탈춤** are among the more famous.

Hahoe Tal **하회탈** (mask) is a ritual and artistic mask handed down from around the late Goryeo Dynasty in Hahoe Village in Andong, Gyeongsangbuk-do. The material of the Hahoe masks is alder tree, and they are designated as National Treasure No. 121 in 1964. It's a valuable cultural heritage representing the faces of Koreans.

Seopyeonje **서편제** **(1993)** is the story of a family of Korean *pansori* singers who are struggling to make a living in the modern world. Won the Berlin Fim Festival Honorary Golden Bear Award in 2005.

Nanta : Cookin' is a non-verbal performance that reinterprets traditional *samulnori* in a modern way which gained huge popularity through a world tour.

Wangeui Namja **왕의남자** (***The King and the Clown***, **2005**) - An acting troupe gets arrested for mocking their hedonistic king, and are given a chance to spare themselves under one condition - make the king laugh. The movie has traditional Korean play scenes including *talchum*.

WHY DO KOREANS TAKE OFF THEIR SHOES WHEN GOING INSIDE?

When you visit a Korean friend's house, you'll immediately notice something interesting the moment you step inside: a small space that's set slightly lower than the main floor. You'll probably see lots of shoes there, and just beyond the raised threshold, a few pairs of cotton slippers neatly lined up (though not every home has them).

Using your sharp instincts, you quickly figure out—you're supposed to take off your shoes!

Once inside, you'll see your friends walking around in slippers, socks, or even barefoot. What's more, your non-Korean friends have joined the club too. The same rule applies in the bathroom: it's built slightly lower than the rest of the floor, and a pair of plastic slippers is waiting for you there. That's your cue—those are bathroom-only shoes.

So, why all this division and separation between spaces? To understand it, you first need to learn about Korea's traditional floor heating system called *ondol* 온돌.

WHAT IS THE KOREAN HEATING SYSTEM - ONDOL?

The *ondol* 온돌 / *gudeul* 구들 is a traditional Korean heating system that is widely believed to have originated about 2,500 years ago in **Bukokjeo 북옥저** (ancient Korean state which was located in Manchuria and the Russian Maritime Province of Siberia, later absorbed by **Goguryeo**). Given that Goguryeo (37 BC – 668 AD) inherited the lifestyles of the Bukokjeo people, and that ondol was also passed down to **Goryeo** and **Joseon** (spread most widely during the **17th-century Joseon period (1392 - 1897)**, connecting the origin of *ondol* with the Korean people shouldn't be a far stretch.

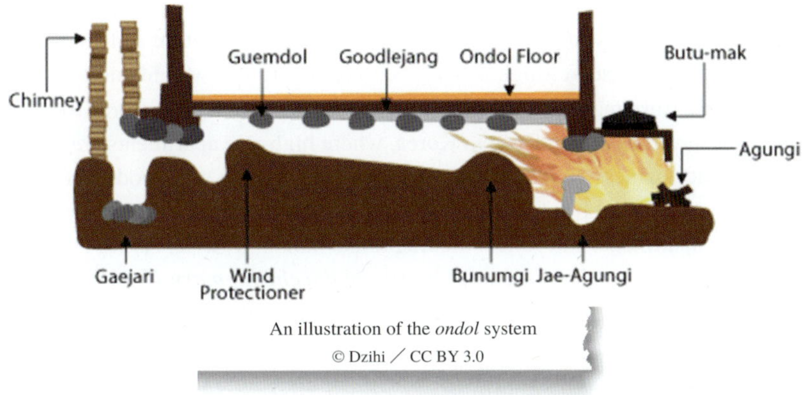

An illustration of the *ondol* system
© Dzihi / CC BY 3.0

It's similar in concept to a radiator that uses heat conduction, but the structure is different. When firewood is set on fire in the furnace called *agungi* 아궁이 (which also doubles as a cooking station), the heat generated here heats up the wide stones laid under the *jangpan* 장판 (oil/resin paper-covered floor) of the room known as *gudeuljang* 구들장, and the heat released by the hot stones makes the room warm.

In addition to heating by thermal conductivity, *ondol* combines radiant heating and convection heating, and the heat is maintained evenly from bottom to top and for a longer period compared to a fireplace or a radiator that generates heat from only one side.

And *ondol* is one of the most influential factors in the residential lifestyle of Koreans. Before the widespread use of **ondol** for residential use, Koreans had a drastically different lifestyle. Historical dramas set in **ancient Korea** to **early Goryeo period (918 - 1392)** such as **Seondeok Yeowang 선덕여왕** (*Queen Seondeok*, **MBC, 2009**), depict people sleeping in bed and sitting in chairs. But the widespread of **ondol** and the coziness it provided made Koreans prefer sitting on a cushion on the floor and sleeping on bedding laid out on the floor instead (go to a ***jjimjilbang*** 찜질방 to see for yourself - once you lie on a cozy warm floor, you won't want to get up). *Ondol* is believed to have spread rapidly in the 17th century Joseon as a means to survive the cold winter. It led to a surge in demand for firewood, and historical records say that most of the mountains were bare towards the end of the Joseon Dynasty.

In addition, *ondol* has led to the development of a single-story residential architecture style in Korea. Most of the remaining **hanok 한옥** buildings in Korea are single-story, due to the enormous weight and construction costs of ondol system. It is said that there were many multi-story buildings in ordinary houses from **Goryeo** to the **early Joseon** period before the widespread of *ondol*. Even in Korea, where high-rise apartments are the norm today, Koreans just couldn't give up the coziness *ondol* provides. Combining tradition with modern technology, *ondol* has evolved into a system where water heated from boilers is fed into and circulates in the pipes buried under the flooring. Still, modern Korean apartments still reflect the traditional *hanok* lifestyle. As we learned previously, the widespread of *ondol* (floor-heating) in the late Joseon Dynasty and *daecheongmaru* (cooling floor) played an important role in making Koreans prefer the sitting-on-the-floor over the beds and chairs which also existed in the homes before that time. Naturally, keeping the floor clean was always a top priority. Also, a word of caution - Many Korean restaurants, especially the ones with rooms, would require you to take off your shoes and sit on the floor. So it's always a good idea to inspect your socks to see if they have a hole in them before going to a Korean restaurant to avoid a surprise.

WHY DO KOREANS SIT IN A YOGA POSE?

Sitting cross-legged on the floor is commonly called **yangbandari 양반다리** ("noblemen legs"). As the name suggests, it was mainly the posture taken by superiors and elders. Although females and younger people weren't completely prohibited from this posture in front of males or elders, they also chose to sit on their knees to show respect.

JJIMJILBANG – THE SAFE ONDOL HAVEN FOR THE WEARY AND BURDENED

Traditional *hanjeungmak* (sweat house) in the Joseon Dynasty era
Painting by Kim Jun-geun

If ***jjimjilbang* 찜질방**, the Korean spa was available in the olden days, it surely would have been the safe haven for the weary and burdened. The original form of *jjimjilbang* is believed to be a sweat room called **hanjeungmak 한증막** which dates back to the Joseon Dynasty. These were small dome-shaped rooms that made use of the remaining heat from kilns used for baking charcoal or pottery.

The heated floors of jjimjilbang are inspired by Korea's traditional ondol floor-heating system—perhaps that's why Koreans love sitting and even sleeping on the floor so much.

The modern jjimjilbang, which combines a bathhouse with a steam or sweat room, first appeared in 1994, quickly spread nationwide, and evolved into a multi-purpose leisure complex offering not just rest but also entertainment.

Most jjimjilbangs operate 24 hours a day, featuring spacious sleeping areas with comfy leather sofas, recliners, and floor mats. Some upscale ones even offer mini cave-like cubicles for private relaxation! And with their relatively affordable admission fees, they make a great alternative to traditional lodging. For those who can't completely unplug, many even have PC rooms—so you can unwind and stay caught up on work (or games).

Modern version of *hanjeungmak*

But the most awesome part about jjimjilbang is definitely the food and snack facilities! You can find a wide range of options, from quick bites like instant noodles and **sundubu jjigae 순두부 찌개** (soft tofu stew), to hearty meals like **kimchi bokkeumbap 김치볶음밥** (kimchi fried rice) and fried chicken. However, the true jjimjilbang specialty lives in the snack corner. Here, you can crack open hot **maekbanseok gyeran 맥반석 계란** (eggs baked on elvan stone plates), or quench your thirst after an intense sweat session with cool treats like **bingsu 빙수** (shaved ice dessert), **sujeonggwa 수정과** (cinnamon punch), and ice-cold **shikhye 식혜** (sweet rice punch). These snacks are beloved by everyone—Koreans and foreigners alike—and are the perfect reward after hours of relaxing and sweating it out.

Boiled eggs and *sikhye* combo!

Green Tea *Bingsu*

TYPES OF SAUNA ROOMS AND THEIR SAID HEALTH BENEFITS

Disclaimer (THIS IS NOT MEDICAL/HEALTH ADVICE)

Jade Room
Constipation, Diarrhea, Indigestion, Meningitis, Menstrual Pain, Arthritis.

Herb Room
Nervousness, High Blood Pressure, Blood Circulation, Muscle Ache, Joint Pain.

Clay Room
Arthritis, Muscle Ache, Metabolism, Blood Circulation, Detoxification

Salt Room
Arthritis, Skin Rejuvenation, Blood Circulation

Germanium Room
Blood Circulation, Pain Relief, Muscle Ache, Joint Pain.

Most of the *jjimjilbang*s have sex-segregated and unisex sections. Obviously, the dressing and bathing rooms are separated, but most steam/sweat rooms and heated communal floors are unisex, though they vary from business to business. There are, however, single-sex only *jjimjilbang*s, so you might want to check before walking in.

UNIFORM

Once inside, you leave behind your everyday clothes and slip into the uniform provided by the jjimjilbang. Don't worry—it's not about stripping away your individuality. The uniform mainly prevents the facility from getting contaminated by germs or viruses you might have carried from outside. Sure, it might not be your favorite color or style, but everyone else is in the same outfit, so you instantly become part of the jjimjilbang community.

WHAT IS THE KOREAN "LAMB HEAD TOWEL HAT"?

Made by rolling up both sides of a towel and wrapping around the head, the *yangmeori* 양머리 "Lamb/Sheep Head" towel hat became popular after the main character Kim Sam-soon, wore it in a hit TV drama *Nae Ireumeun Kim Sam-soon* 내 이름은 김삼순 *(My Name is Kim Sam-soon / My Lovely Sam Soon*, **2005, MBC)**. In *jjimjilbang*, many people. regardless of age/sex. do it because it absorbs sweat and keeps the hair from going awry while adding some cuteness (you know how Koreans are obsessed with looks!).

WHY DO KOREANS SCRUB THEIR BODIES?

Throughout its life, a lobster sheds its shell up to 25 times, revealing a shiny new coat each time. Humans, unfortunately, don't have that luxury—so we rely on other methods. Cleopatra bathed in wine, Yang Guifei in milk, and in Korea, people have long relied on *ttaemiri* 때밀이, literally "body dirt scrubbing," to achieve the same effect. At most Korean public baths and jjimjilbangs, you'll find *sesinsa* 세신사, or "professional body cleansers," who guide you through the full shedding process. First, soak in warm water for about 10 minutes to soften dead skin cells. Then, let the pros work their magic with *itaeri* towels 이태리 타월—special scrubbing gloves and towels designed for the job.

All you do is turn over and follow their instructions, and soon you'll see thin dark strings falling away, like eraser shavings. That's your **ttae** 때—clumped dead skin cells being swept away. While some dermatologists warn that abrasive scrubbing can irritate the skin, countless fans—including Amanda Seyfried and Miranda Kerr—swear by it for instant results.

As for Conan O'Brien, who tried ttaemiri in Los Angeles' Koreatown… well, let's just say it looked like he was undergoing some sort of medieval punishment rather than a spa treatment.

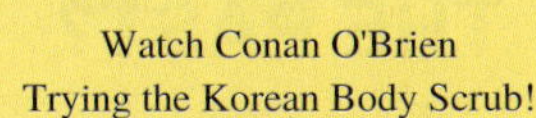

WHAT IS "ITALY TOWEL"?

Koreans have been using *itaeri* towel (Italy towel) since the late inventor Kim Pil-gon invented a durable towel using viscose rayon in the 1960s after two years of research. Before that, people used to wrap towels over a stone for buffing. The name "*itaeri*" comes from the fact that the weaving machine and dyes were made in Italy.

WHERE DID KOREANS LIVE IN THE PAST?

THE STORY OF
HANOK
한옥

Hanok 한옥 is a term that refers to the traditional Korean houses made with eco-friendly materials such as soil, clay, timber, rocks, and rice straw; therefore these homes caused no harm to our body and of course, the nature surrounding them, reflecting the environmental factors of the Korean Peninsula as well as the lifestyle of the Korean people. One interesting fact about *hanok* houses is that the difference in social status can be inferred by looking at the shape of the roof of each house. If the roof is mostly made of clay and have a rice-straw-thatched roof, it's called ***chogajip* 초가집**, and commoners and some ***yangban* 양반** (noblemen) with low income lived in it. On the other hand, when tiles called ***giwa* 기와** (made with baked soil) were placed on the roof of a house built mainly of wood and stones, it's called ***giwajip* 기와집**, and was inhabited by *yangban* and ***jungin* 중인**, the middle-class people. ***cheoma* 처마** (curvy edge of *hanok* roof) that soars high to the sky seems to represent their authority.

Clockwise from top-left: chogajip, giwa-tiled roof, cheoma, daecheongmaru

Image: *Daecheongmaru* (KOGL-O, heritage.go.kr)

The *hanok* houses have different architectural styles depending on the climate and the characteristics of the Korean Peninsula. In the northern part of the country, where cold weather is frequent, the rooms are arranged in two rows with a low roof to block cold weather from outside while maintaining warmth. In the southern part of the country, however, rooms are aligned in one straight line with a high roof, to promote natural air circulation. Earlier, we learned that Koreans were able to make it through a cold winter thanks to the *ondol* system. Then how did they survive the scorching hot summer? In the days when there was no air conditioner, *hanok* houses had a special place called ***daecheong* 대청**, which served as a natural cooling place. This space, also called ***daecheongmaru* 대청마루**, is a spacious wooden floor between rooms, where the ***cheoma*** not only keeps the *daecheongmaru* safe from the hot summer sun but by rising higher than other parts of the roof, it lifts the hot air upward, leaving *daecheongmaru* with a cool breeze. The beam, ***daedeulbo* 대들보** are the pillars supporting *hanok* houses, which is said to be safe from earthquakes because they are placed into a foundation stone, rather than the ground. It's also used as an expression that means "a very important person in the organization."

The doors and windows of *hanok* are filled with traditional Korean paper called **hanji**, made of inner barks of mulberry. The *hanji* used on the doors and windows is called **changhoji** 창호지, and they block heat and wind while letting the light in. It's also interesting to compare the different types of patterns found on the doors and the windows of *hanok* houses.

Jangdokdae 장독대 is an area outside the house dedicated to storing a series of jars called **jangdok** 장독 (or **onggi** 옹기 / **hangari** 항아리), a Korean ethnic earthenware used to ferment or simply store preserved foods, such as **kimchi**, **ganjang** 간장 (soy sauce), *doenjang* 된장 (bean paste) and *gochujang* (red pepper paste) or grains. The word **dae** means "place" or "support," so *jangdokdae* means "place for earthenware," and it's found near the kitchen. Sunshine and ventilation are key aspects of the location choice so that foods can be preserved well and kept fresh, often lasting more than several years. The similar storage area in the royal palaces was called **yeomgo** 염고 and was supervised by a court lady called **janggomama** 장고마마.

Jang - Korean Sauce And Soup Base P. 61

HOW DO KOREAN GUYS STAY COOL?
죽부인 JUKBUIN THE "BAMBOO WIFE"

Literally meaning "bamboo wife," **jukbuin** 죽부인 is a type of body pillow that was introduced from the Tang Dynasty of China. Made of thinly split bamboo trees that are hand-woven into a form similar to a sandbag. When used as a sleeping companion, the open structure provides the body with maximum exposure to cooling breezes. It was an essential item during the hot summer days in Korea. Although it was just a body pillow made of bamboo trees, it was taboo for a son to use what his father used, and when his father died, it was burned along with his clothes.

Hi there! Don't we look familiar? That's right! You might have seen us in Korean historical dramas, standing tall at the entrance of a village, making scary faces! Made of wood, we are village guardians, keeping demons and evil spirits at bay. At the same time, we double as boundary markers at the edge of a village. Usually, we're adorned with engravings describing the characteristics of the carved figures on the front of the poles.

"Male" jangseungs 장승 usually bear engravings in hangul or hanja that reads cheonhadaejanggun 천하대장군 天下大將軍 (Great General of All Under Heaven) and are decorated with headpieces worn by Korean aristocrats and scholars. "Female" jangseungs, on the other hand, wear less elaborate headpieces and bear engravings reading jihayeojanggun 지하여장군 地下女將軍 (Female General of the Underworld).

Despite our efforts to look pretty, an American Protestant missionary, Homer Bezaleel Hulbert, described us as "Village Devil Posts" in 'The Passing of Korea' (1906).

Knowing our backstory, how do we look to you now? When you visit Korea, don't be intimidated by our scary looks because we're friendly and love tourists!

WHY DO KOREAN APARTMENTS LOOK LIKE MATCHBOXES?

In the 1960s, Seoul faced a huge influx of people due to urban development policies, and housing quickly became a major issue. Apartments, which maximize the number of homes in a limited space, became the ideal solution. The government led massive construction projects, and as a result, apartments now dominate Korean housing—even in rural areas. It's worth noting that Korean apartments are closer to condominiums in the U.S., since they are mostly owned rather than rented. The interior layouts often reflect traditional hanok lifestyles: spacious living rooms and kitchens connect the rooms, echoing the courtyards and *daecheongmaru* (wooden-floor main halls) of hanok.

Furthermore, many older apartments built in Seoul and the metropolitan area during the 1970s to 1990s were constructed with wartime functions in mind, preparing for a potential North Korean invasion. Some complexes still retain structures visible today, such as underground passages allowing military vehicle access built under military orders, and firing ports where gun barrels could extend through apartment walls for shooting. Underground spaces were also designed to serve as air-raid shelters or civil defense shelters. Such building structures transcend mere housing, reflecting a unique facet of Korea's architectural culture shaped by security crises in its modern history. Despite these practical and cultural considerations, many criticize large apartment complexes for looking boxy and dull, often painted in muted colors—hence the comparison to matchboxes. While some feel they mar the city's beauty, others see them as symbols of modern Korean society. Because of this, some even call Seoul an "**apartment republic**." In addition, apartments in Korea are widely regarded as reliable investment assets. This belief gave rise to the so-called "**gap investment**" trend, in which buyers take out loans to purchase homes and profit from rising prices. As this practice spread, apartment prices soared, making it increasingly difficult for ordinary citizens to afford housing in Seoul. Although the government has introduced a series of regulations, such as heavy taxation on owners of multiple homes and stricter lending limits, housing prices have continued to climb—much like a game of cat and mouse between policymakers and investors.

JEONSE – WHY WOULD KOREAN LANDLORDS
LET THEIR TENANTS STAY FOR FREE?

Jeonse 전세, or "key money deposit," can seem very strange to foreigners accustomed to monthly rent or buying property. Under a jeonse contract, instead of paying monthly rent, the tenant gives the landlord a large lump sum deposit—usually 70–80% of the property's value—for a fixed period, often 2–3 years. The landlord can invest this deposit or use it to generate profit, effectively lending the apartment for free. At the end of the contract, the entire deposit must be returned to the tenant, which often surprises foreigners. In Korean dramas, jeonse is often used to show the hardships of families who can't afford to buy a home and must move at the end of each contract.

WHO FOUNDED KOREA?

Portrait of Dangun, Encyclopedia of Korean Culture (encykorea.aks.ac.kr), The Academy of Korean Studies

According to the founding legend recorded in the *Samguk Yusa* 삼국유사 (record of history and legends), the Lord of Heaven, **Hwanin 환인,** had a son, **Hwanung 환웅**, who descended to **Taebaek Mountain 태백산** (modern day Baekdu Mountain 백두산 area which is the highest in the Korean peninsula) and founded the city of **Shinsi 신시**. Then a tiger and a bear came to Hwanung and asked how they could become humans and they were told that if they went into a cave and lived there for 100 days while only eating mugwort and garlic **Hwanung** will transform them into human beings. Both accepted the challenge, but about halfway through the 100 days the tiger gave up and ran out of the cave. The bear, on the other hand, successfully restrained herself and became a beautiful woman called **Ungnyeo 웅녀, 熊女**. Hwanung married Ungnyeo, and she gave birth to **Dangun 단군,** who became the founding father of **Gojoseon 고조선** in 2333 BC. Today, the said legend is interpreted by scholars as a symbolic representation of a marriage with a member of a bear-worshiping tribe, rather than a literal bear-turned-human woman. The founding date, or **Gaecheonjeol 개천절** ("The Heaven Opening Day") is celebrated as a national holiday in Korea (October 3rd).

WHAT WAS THE NATIONAL MOTTO OF GOJOSEON?

홍익인간

hongik ingan

"Broadly Benefit Humanity (Devotion to Human Welfare)"

HOW OLD IS KOREA?

According to traditional Korean calendar system *dangungiwon* 단군기원 or *dangi* 단기, year 1 starts on the founding date of the first Korean kingdom **Gojoseon** (2333 BC, which means 2333 years before the Gregorian calendar was used as the global standard today). So by adding the Gregorian year, you get the current *dangi* year. For example, the year 2020 in the U.S. would be translated as the year 4353 in *dangi*. For Korean people, this number is a symbol of pride, as it means that the ancestors of the Korean people have kept their long history and tradition for 5,000 years.

Dangun Founding Legend-Inspired Dramas with Fantasy Elements
Asdal Yeondaegi 아스달 연대기 (*Arthdal Chronicles*, 2019, tvN)
Taewang Sashingi 태왕 사신기 (*The Legend*, 2007, MBC)

A classification of the period (57 BC to 668 AD) of Korean history established on the ancient Korean Peninsula with **Goguryeo** in the north, **Baekje** in the midwest, and **Silla** in the southeast and other minor states.

The map of history of Korea in 476, the moment of greatest territorial expansion of Goguryeo.
© Wikimedia Commons CC-SA 3.0

7th century Tang Dynasty painting of envoys from the Three Kingdoms of Korea: Baekje, Goguryeo, and Silla illustrates the different styles of clothes.

Three Kingdoms Period (57 BC ~ 668)

57 BC Bak Hyeokgeose founds Silla

37 BC Jumong founds Goguryeo

18 BC Onjo founds Baekje

372 Under Sosurim, Goguryeo imports Buddhism from Former Qin of China.

384 Chimnyu of Baekje officially adopts Buddhism.

392 Gwanggaeto the Great of Goguryeo begins his reign, expanding Goguryeo into a major regional power.

433 Baekje and Silla form an alliance against Goguryeo's aggression.

527 Silla formally adopts Buddhism / Martyrdom of Ichadon

553 Silla attacks Baekje, breaking the alliance.

598 Sui Dynasty attacks Goguryeo and Goguryeo-Sui War begins

612 Goguryeo repulses second Sui invasion at the Salsu.

614 Sui Dynasty defeated.

645 First campaign in the Goguryeo–Tang War.

648 Silla establishes alliance with Tang.

660 Baekje falls to the Silla-Tang forces.

668 Goguryeo falls to the Silla-Tang forces.

Unified Silla (676 ~ 935)

676 Silla repels Chinese alliance forces from Korean peninsula, completes unification of much of the Three Kingdoms.

698 The founding of Balhae by former Goguryeo general Dae Joyeong.

751 Silla, at its cultural peak, constructs Seokguram.

828 Jang Bogo establishes Cheonghaejin, a major center of trade with China, Japan, and Vietnam.

918 Founding of Goryeo by Taejo of Goryeo.

935 Silla formally surrenders to Goryeo, and Goryeo controls the Korean peninsula.

A mural from the 5th century CE Muyonchong (tomb) depicting a hunting scene.

Why Do Koreans Dominate Archery? P. 244

GOGURYEO, THE LARGEST DYNASTY IN KOREAN HISTORY (37 BC ~ 668)

Goguryeo 고구려 is said to have been founded by **Jumong 주몽** in 37 BCE and was the largest of the Three Kingdoms, which became a full-fledged aristocratic state during the reign of **King Sosurim 소수림왕**, who promulgated various laws and decrees that helped to centralize royal authority. Like other ancient Korean kingdoms, **Buddhism** was the cultural backbone, while **Confucian** education was emphasized as a means of regulating/managing the social order. Today, some of the ruins and tombs, which became **UNESCO World Heritage sites** in 2004, can be found in the far southern Jilin province in China, the territories which the Kingdom covered.

Jumong / Dongmyeongseongwang 주몽 / 동명성왕

Jumong 주몽 was the founding monarch of the Goguryeo Kingdom, the northernmost of the Three Kingdoms of Korea. His posthumous title is **Dongmyeongseongwang 동명성왕**, which literally means "**Holy King of the East**."According to the founding legends, he was the son of **Haemosu 해모수** and **Lady Yuhwa 유화부인**, who was the daughter of the god of the **Amnok River 압록강**. **Lady Yuwha** was impregnated by sunlight and gave birth to an egg, and from the egg hatched a baby boy. Jumong was known for his exceptional skill at archery, and in 37 BCE, he became the first king of **Goguryeo** and reunited all of the five tribes of **Jolbon 졸본**. **Soseono 소서노,** who was a daughter of a Jolbon chief, and his second wife, gave birth to his son, **Onjo 온조**, who later established the kingdom of **Baekje**. The kingdom of Goguryeo evolved into a great regional territory with considerable power and influence and stood for 705 years and was ruled in total by 28 consecutive emperors. Today, the descendants of **Jumong** still bear his family name "**Go**."

Gwanggaeto the Great 광개토대왕

Gwanggaeto the Great (birth name: **Go Damdeok 고담덕**), was the nineteenth monarch of **Goguryeo** Kingdom. Under Gwanggaeto, Goguryeo rose as a powerful dynasty in East Asia, making enormous advances and conquests into western Manchuria against **Khitan** tribes; inner Mongolia and the Maritime Province of Russia as well as the Han River valley in central Korea to control over two-thirds of the Korean Peninsula. He also defeated **Baekje**, which was then the most powerful kingdom of Korea. His accomplishments are recorded on the **Gwanggaeto Stele**, erected in 414 at the supposed site of his tomb in Jian, present-day China-North Korea border, and is still standing tall as the largest engraved stele in the world.

Standard portrait of Gwanggaeto the Great by Lee Jong Sang
(National Museum of Modern and Contemporary Art Seoul)
© Wikimedia Commons CC-SA 4.0

The Gwanggaeto Stele, standing tall at 7 meters (23 ft.) high.

Battle of Salsu 살수대첩 (612)

Recorded as one of the most brutal battles in world history, it was an enormous victory by **Goguryeo** over the **Sui Dynasty** of China. Led by General **Eulji Mundeok 을지문덕**, the Sui army was lured into the **Salsu River**, where the Goguryeo soldiers were preparing an attack by cutting off the flow of water with a dam in advance, and when the unsuspecting Sui troops were halfway across, they opened it. Thousands drowned and the surviving troops were killed by the Goguryeo cavalry. Over 300,000 Sui troops died while only 2,700 troops were lost on Guguryeo's side. This defeat had a major impact on the Sui Dynasty, causing them to collapse from within, leading to an eventual fall.

Baekje 백제 is said to have been founded by legendary leader **Onjo** in 18 BC in the **Gwangju 광주** area. Around the 3rd century AD, it became a fully-developed kingdom. During the reign of **King Goi 고이왕**, and during the reign of **King Geunchogo 근초고왕**, it ruled a significant portion of central Korea, including the whole Han River basin. Buddhism and Confucianism were the two pillars of the kingdom, and a large number of eminent scholars were produced. One of the most famous and distinctive artworks of the era is a Buddha statue that has a subtle and mysterious smile, known as the "**Baekje Smile.**"

Gilt Bronze Buddha (National Museum of Korea)
© KOGL Type 1 (kogl.or.kr)

King Onjo 온조

Onjo, the son of **Jumong** and **Soseono** of the **Goguryeo** Kingdom, was the founding monarch of **Baekje** which was located in the western part of the Korean Peninsula. According to the *Samguksagi 삼국사기* (a historical record of the Three Kingdoms of Korea), he was the ancestor of all Baekje kings. He was the younger brother of **Yuri 유리**, who became Goguryeo's second king, and younger brother of **Biryu 비류** who built a small state in **Michuhol 미추홀**. When Biryu died, his people joined **Sipje 십제**, which Onjo later renamed to Baekje. Onjo was able to successfully manage and stifle sporadic rebellions from other tribes, and reigned for 46 years, laying the foundations for a powerful dynasty that would last for 678 years.

Great Gilt-bronze Incense Burner 백제금동대향로

Measuring 64 centimeters (25 inches) high and 19 centimeters (7.4 inches) in diameter, it weighs almost 12 kilograms (26.5 lbs). This three-dimensional artifact, estimated to have been made in the 6th century, features realistic ornaments of the dragon and phoenix (symbol of yin and yang) and is believed to have been used for ancestral rites or other important ceremonies.

Great Gilt-bronze Incense Burner (National Museum of Korea)
© KOGL Type 1 (kogl.or.kr)

Gyeongju Bulguksa Temple from the Silla Kingdom

SILLA, THE GOLDEN KINGDOM (57 BC ~ 935)

Silla 신라, believed to have been founded by **Bak Hyeokgeose 박혁거세** in 57 BC, developed into a full-fledged kingdom as a result of the establishment of the hereditary monarchy of the Kim family. During this time, Buddhism was adopted as the national religion and flourished. The traces? Magnificent Buddha sculptures and temples can be found everywhere in **Gyeongju 경주**, where the Kingdom's capital was located. The people of Silla, especially the aristocrats, were fond of extravagant luxury. Among all, gold ornaments, such as gold crowns, belts, and various jewelry show how dexterous and artsy they were! No wonder they are called "**The Golden Kingdom**."

Bak Hyeokgeose 박혁거세

He was the founding monarch of **Silla** and the progenitor of all **Bak (Park)** clans in Korea. According to the *Samgukyusa* 삼국유사 (a collection of legends, folktales and historical accounts relating to the Three Kingdoms of Korea), leaders of chiefdoms (believed to have been refugees from Gojoseon) got together to discuss selecting a king and forming a kingdom, and at that moment in the forest, a strange light shone from the sky, and where a white horse bowed down, there was a large egg from which a boy came out of. After getting bathed, his body radiated and animals jumped with joy. The people revered him and made him king of the state named **Seorabeol 서라벌** when he became 13-years-old. He married **Lady Aryeong 알영부인**, who is said to have been born from the ribs of a dragon. The Park clans are the third-largest group in Korea today.

Seokguram Grotto 석굴암

The Seokguram Grotto 석굴암 (man-made cave) is part of the **Bulguksa Temple 불국사** complex on **Toham Mountain 토함산**, in **Gyeongju 경주**, South Korea. This awe-inspiring grotto, National Treasure No. 24, was added to the UNESCO World Heritage in 1995, along with the Bulguksa Temple complex. The grotto is situated to overlook **the East Sea** and rests 750 meters (2460 ft) above sea level. It's said to have been built by **Kim Daeseong 김대성** and originally called **Seokbulsa 석불사** (Stone Buddha Temple) whose construction first took place in 742 when he resigned his position in the king's court in 751 during the reign of **King Gyeongdeok 경덕왕** of **Silla**, which is considered as the cultural peak of the Kingdom. According to a legend, Kim dedicated the Grotto to his parents from a previous life and the Temple to his parents in his present life. The construction was finished in 774, and is acknowledged as one of the finest Buddhist sculptures in the world, and is currently one of the best known cultural destinations in South Korea.

Golden Crowns Found in Cheonmachong

This scintillating gold crown, excavated from **Cheonmachong 천마총** (Tomb No. 155, also known as "The Heavenly Horse Tomb" due to the mural of the flying horse) in 1973, is believed to have belonged to **King Soji 소지왕** or **King Jijeung 지증왕**. The crown is 32.5 centimeters (12.8 inches) in height, and three prongs are forming the Chinese character 山 "mountain" on the front of the crown. On the back, there are two prongs in the shape of a deer antler. There are also two dangling gold chains, hanging from the end of the headband, shaped as leaves. After getting designated as the 188th National Treasure of Korea, it's currently housed in Gyeongju National Museum.

Cheomseongdae 첨성대

National Treasure No. 31, **Cheomseongdae** is a Silla-era observatory located in Gyeongju. Said to have been built during the reign of **Queen Seondeok 선덕여왕** of Silla in the mid-7th century, it's the oldest existing astronomical observatory in the world and it maintains its original form without reconstruction or restoration. The use of Cheomseongdae was said to be astronomical observations, but recently different views have emerged because unlike most astronomical observatories, it was built on flat ground, and it was too narrow for people to go in and out. Therefore, some speculate that the structure may have played an astrological role in predicting the fortune of the Dynasty or served as an altar for religious ceremonies. It's still standing tall at 9.17 meters (30 ft) and 4.93 meters (16 ft) in diameter.

Martyrdom of Ichadon 이차돈

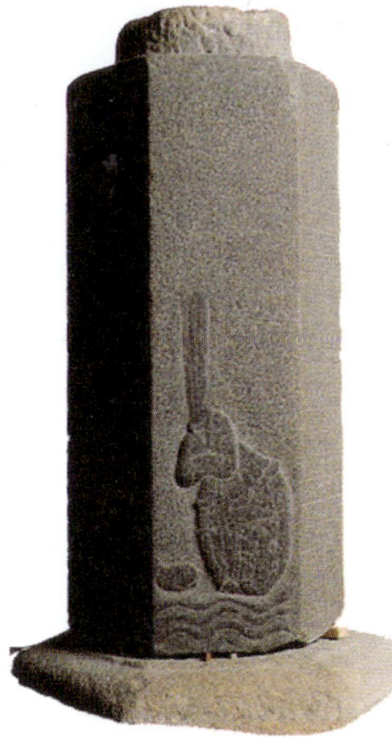

Ichadon 이차돈 (501-527) was a Buddhist monk and advisor to the Silla's **King Beopheung 법흥왕**, who desired to promulgate Buddhism as the state religion, but was facing opposition from the court officials. Ichadon devised a strategy to overcome the opposition. Convincing the king to make such a proclamation using the royal seal, Ichadon told the king to deny having made such a proclamation, and Ichadon would confess and accept the punishment of execution for forgery. He prophesied to the king that at his execution a miracle would convince the opposing court faction. His scheme went as planned, and when he was executed, the earth shook, the sun darkened, beautiful flowers rained from the sky, and white blood instead of red blood sprayed 100 feet in the air from his beheaded corpse. The omen was accepted as a manifestation of heaven's approval, making Buddhism the state religion in 527 CE. His body was then taken to the sacred **Geumgang Mountains 금강산** and buried there with respect. His martyrdom led to the construction of **Heungryunsa Monastery 흥륜사**, Silla's first state-sponsored temple.

Gilt-bronze Maitreya in Meditation

Better known as *bangasayusang* 반가사유상 (National Treasure of Korea No. 83) It's believed to be a statue of the Maitreya, the future Buddha, in a semi-seated contemplative pose, commonly referred to as the "Contemplative Bodhisattva" or Gilt-Bronze Seated Maitreya. Recognized as one of the finest Buddhist sculptures ever produced, it's housed in the National Museum of Korea as one of the most popular exhibits. The bodhisattva, sitting on a stool with his right leg crossed over his left knee, makes a thoughtful expression with his finger resting subtly on his face. The pose symbolizes an event occurred during Buddha's life before his renouncement as a prince: While observing farmers on the fields, he awakened to the cyclical nature of human suffering, and the artwork depicts the posture at this moment of awakening.

Gilt-bronze Maitreya in Meditation (National Museum of Korea)
© KOGL Type 1 (kogl.or.kr)

The Smile of Silla Roof-End Tile

This roof-end tile, (*sumakse* 수막세), which attaches to a curved tile at the edges of a roof/wall, has a smiling human face better known as "**The Smile of Silla**." Contrary to other cultures where scary faces are used (e.g., goblins), the people of Silla instead used friendly smiles to soothe all bad spirits and send them back to where they originally came from. It was the inspiration behind the logo of the Korean company **LG**.

Who Are the *Chaebols*? P. 91

190

Hwarang: The Poet Warrior Youth 화랑 (KBS, 2016)

Hwarang

Hwarang 화랑 was a mental and physical training and education organization composed of the youth of the Silla Dynasty. It was established to recruit talented people (usually children of kings and nobles, but there were no class restrictions), and the members, called **nangdo** 낭도 were united under the leadership of the leader, *hwarang*. Among the group's goals, the main role was to select talented people and have them appointed to key positions in Silla. At the same time, military training was of utmost importance. In fact, Silla in the 6th and 7th centuries, when *hwarang* was founded, continued war with neighboring countries, and national security was very unstable. For this reason, the *nangdo*s served as a reserve force and participated in battles as soldiers. **화랑도** *hwarangdo*, the ideology of *hwarang* was to serve the nation solely through individual discipline, and it was considered an honor to die in battle.

WHO UNIFIED THE THREE KINGDOMS?

The Three Kingdoms Period was a tempestuous time when three powerful kingdoms were holding each other in check and competing with each other. Over a long period, there were numerous battles and wars, both large and small, sometimes with a coalition with foreign forces to invade each other. In 648, **Silla** formed an alliance with the **Chinese Tang Dynasty** and **Baekjae** was the first of the three Kingdoms to fall in 660. In 668, **Goguryeo** fell to the **Silla-Tang forces**. When Silla repelled the Tang forces from the Korean Peninsula in 676, it finally completed the unification of the Three Kingdoms and became known as the **Unified Silla**. **King Munmu the Great** 문무대왕 was the first ruler of the expanded Dynasty, which lasted for another 260 years.

918 Founding of Goryeo by Taejo.

1033 Goryeo builds the Cheonri Jangseong (lit. "Thousand Li Wall"), a massive wall running along the northern border.

1145 Kim Bu-sik compiles the Samguk Sagi, Korea's oldest extant history text.

1231 The Mongol invasions of Korea begin.

1234 Choi Yun-ui's Sangjeong Gogeum Yemun is published, world's first metal-block printed text.

1251 Goryeo completes the Tripitaka Koreana, the most comprehensive and oldest intact version of the Buddhist canon in Chinese script.

1270 Goryeo signs a peace treaty with the Mongols, beginning an 80-year period of Yuan overlordship. The Sambyeolcho Rebellion lasts for three more years.

1285 Il-yeon compiles the Samguk Yusa, record of history and legends.

1388 General Yi Seonggye, ordered to engage China in a border dispute, turns his troops against the Goryeo court.

Maebyeong (plum bottle) decorated with
cranes and clouds
(National Museum of Korea)
© KOGL Type 1 (kogl.or.kr)

Silla, which unified the Three Kingdoms and established itself as a powerful kingdom, began to crack in the 9th century due to internal strife. As a result, Baekje and Goguryeo, which had been destroyed, were revived under the names referred to as **Hubaekje 후백제 (Later Baekje)** and **Hugoguryeo 후고구려 (Later Goguryeo)**. Eventually, in 918, **King Taejo 태조** established **Goryeo 고려** and absorbed them (Later Baekje and Later Goguryeo) to create a new unified dynasty. During the Goryeo Dynasty, Buddhism reached its zenith. It was designated as a state religion and more than 70 temples were located in the capital, enough to be called the "Golden Age of Korean Buddhism." Among many, the **Tripitaka Koreana** in **Haeinsa Temple 해인사** is a great cultural achievement, which was created with the hope of using the power of Buddha to fight against the war of invasion by the Khitan people.

Taejo of Goryeo 태조

Taejo 태조 (reigned. 918-943, birth name **Wang Geon 왕건**), was the founder and first king of the Goryeo Kingdom which unified and ruled ancient Three Kingdoms of Korea from 918 to 1392. The posthumous title, Taejo means "Great Founder," and he laid the foundation stones for his Dynasty which witnessed an unprecedented flourishing of Korean culture. The Unified Silla Kingdom (668-935) ruled over the Korean Peninsula for nearly three centuries but started to decline as rebellions broke out frequently from the peasantry and the aristocracy. During the time, **Gyeon Hwon 견훤**, a peasant leader, rose to power amid the political turmoil in 892 and revived the old Baekje kingdom. A little later in 901, **Gung Ye 궁예**, an aristocratic Buddhist monk leader who was supported by his first minister and general Wang Geon, proclaimed a new Goguryeo state. Wang Geon succeeded Gung Ye, who was killed by the hands of his people due to his fanatical tyranny, in 918. Wang Geon attacked Later Baekje, founded by Gyeon Hwon, and the declining Silla. In 935, Silla finally surrendered and Wang Geon unified the kingdoms once again, under a new name, **Goryeo 고려** (High and Beautiful), whose name implies that it's the successor of the previous kingdom, Goguryeo. He kept a large portion of the Silla institutions of government and distributed lands and high government positions to former Baekje and Silla elites. He also continued the endorsement of Buddhism and Confucianism.

WHAT DOES KOREA MEAN?

During the Goryeo Dynasty commerce flourished (commercial and natural trades alongside cultural exchanges were very active) with merchants coming from as far as the Middle East. From then on, the national name of Goryeo became widely known and it continued to become the "Korea" of today.

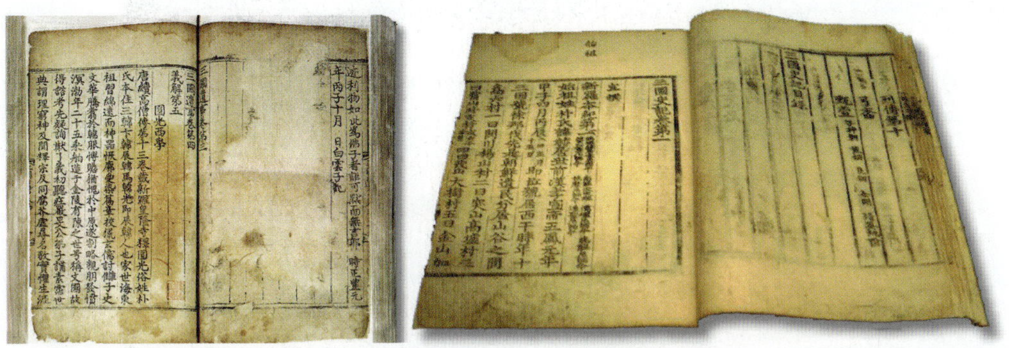

Samguksagi 삼국사기 and Samgukyusa 삼국유사

The *Samguk Sagi*, literally meaning "History of the Three Kingdoms," is a collection of historical records of **the Three Kingdoms**. It's the oldest surviving chronicle of Korean history, and the compilation project was ordered by **King Injong 인종** of Goryeo and was undertaken by the government official and historian **Kim Busik 김부식** and a team of junior scholars. The purpose of the project, which was completed in 1145, was to create a complete compilation of Korean history, whose different versions were scattered among the Three Kingdoms and lost due to the continued wars. At the same time, by incorporating in the text the Korean exemplars of Confucian virtues, it also served as an educational resource, which is considered to have helped establish Korean nationalism and identity. The *Samguk Yusa* **삼국유사**, literally meaning "Memorabilia of the Three Kingdoms," is a compilation of the history and legends of Korea, starting all the way from the founding of the very first nation, **Gojoseon**, all the way up to the Three Kingdoms Period. Written by the Buddhist Monk **Il Yeon 일연**, it differs from the *Samguk Sagi* as it covers various areas of history, with a focus on Buddhist legends and the folk tales of the Silla Dynasty, with a relatively smaller coverage on the other two kingdoms. Despite its limits, it remains an invaluable historical source and a component of Korean literature.

Mongol Invasions and Sambyeolcho 삼별초

From 1231, Goryeo was sporadically but continuously invaded by the Mongol Empire (1206~1388), who devastated a significant portion of the lands of Goryeo and its population throughout a series of invasions which lasted for nearly three decades (1231~1259). To escape from the attacks, the Goryeo government, controlled by the military regime led by the **Choi 최** family, decided to give up the land and flee to **Ganghwado Island 강화도,** where the **Mongolian horse riders** were unable to land on. Naturally, it became a resistance base against the Mongol invasion. Unfortunately, Goryeo faced frequent rebellions from its own people, and struggled internally, due to the fragile foundation of the government. In 1258, a large rebellion broke out and resulted in the establishment of **Dongnyeong Prefectures 동녕부** by the Mongols. Meanwhile, the *sambyeolcho* **삼별초** (Three Elite Patrols'), was organized by the **Choi clan** to maintain order and security on the island base by performing roles as police and combat forces. Even after the Goryeo kingdom fell to the hands of the Mongols, they continued to fight back tenaciously, moving bases multiples times, including **Jindo 진도** and **Jejudo 제주도 Island**.

Copy of a Tripitaka Koreana woodblock.
© Steve46814 via Wikimedia Commons CC-SA 3.0

Palman Daejanggyeong / Tripitaka Koreana 팔만대장경

The *Palman Daejanggyeong* 팔만대장경 or **Tripiṭaka Koreana**("Eighty-Thousand Tripiṭaka") is a compilation of the Buddhist scriptures, carved onto 81,258 wooden printing blocks in the 13th century. According to the records, the work began in 1011 during the **Goryeo–Khitan War** and was completed in 1087. During the wartime, Goryeo believed the act of carving the scriptures onto the woodblocks would bring about a divine intervention (i.e., Buddha's help), which would help the kingdom persevere through the difficult times. The original Tripitaka Koreana contained around 6,000 volumes, but they were destroyed by fire during the Mongol invasions of Korea in 1232. Seeking divine assistance once again with fighting the Mongols, **King Gojong 고종** ordered the revision and re-creation of the Tripiṭaka, and the carving began in 1237 and was completed 12 years later, and the result is the world's most comprehensive and oldest intact version of Buddhist canon in *hanja* (Chinese Characters incorporated into the Korean language) script. Surprisingly, of the 52,330,152 characters carved, there are no known errors or errata found. Each woodblock is 24 centimeters(9.4 inches) high and 70 centimeters (27.5 inches) long, as thick as 4 centimeters (1.6 inches). With over 1,496 titles and 6,568 volumes, they weigh 280 tons total (that's 140 elephants piled together!). The most amazing part is they still remain in pristine condition – no warping/deformation despite its creation 750 years ago, thanks to the special treatment the craftsmen incorporated. The production of the Tripiṭaka Koreana is a symbol of national commitment and desire to fight off the invaders. For that reason, it was designated as Korea's National Treasure in 1962 and was inscribed in the **UNESCO Memory of the World Register** in 2007. Currently, it's stored in **Haeinsa 해인사**, a Buddhist temple in South Gyeongsang Province, in South Korea.

Period Dramas Based On The History of Goguryeo
Gwanggaetotaewang 광개토태왕 (*Gwanggaeto, The Great Conqueror, 2011, KBS1*) *Jumong* 주몽 (2006, MBC)
Daejoyoung 대조영 (2006, KBS1)

Period Drama Based On The History of Baekje
Seodongyo 서동요 (2005, SBS) *Geunchogowang* 근초고왕 (*The King of Legend* 2010, KBS1)

Period Drama Based On The History of Silla
Seondeokyeowang 선덕여왕 (*Queen Seondeok* 2009, MBC) *Daewangeui Kkum* 대왕의 꿈 (*Dream of the Emperor* 2013, KBS 1)

Gyengbokgung Palace

JOSEON - THE LAND OF THE MORNING CALM (1392 - 1897)

Joseon Dynasty was founded by General **Yi Seong-gye 이성계** who brought the collapse to the Goryeo Dynasty through a military coup. Joseon Dynasty embraced Neo-Confucianism as national ideology, and Confucian culture, which still affects much of the lives of modern-day Koreans, was able to fully blossom during this period. It lasted over 500 years, from 1392 to 1897, leaving numerous cultural heritages including the creation of *hangul* 한글 the Korean alphabet until it was taken over by the Japanese Imperialists. Currently, the five grand royal palaces of the Joseon Dynasty remain in downtown Seoul.

1392 Yi Seonggye is crowned king, officially beginning the Joseon Dynasty.

1396 Capital moved to Hanyang. (modern day Seoul)

1402 The use of paper currency is initiated.

1446 The Hangul alphabet, created 3 years earlier, is promulgated by King Sejong the Great.

1592 The Japanese invasion of Korea begins under the command of Toyotomi Hideyoshi. Admiral Yi Sun-Sin employs the Turtle ship to repel Japanese naval forces.

1653 Dutch ship, with Captain Hendrick Hamel, gets wrecked on Jejudo Island.

1791 Persecution of Catholicism begins.

1864 Gojong ascends the throne with his father, Daewongun, as Regent.

1866 French Campaign against Korea.

1871 United States expedition to Korea.

1876 Kim Okgyun leads the Gapsin coup. In 3 days, Chinese forces are able to overwhelm the Progressives and their Japanese supporters.

1884 Donghak Rebellion prompts the First Sino-Japanese War and Gabo Reforms.

1895 China recognizes Korean independence in the Treaty of Shimonoseki. Empress Myeongseong was murdered by Japanese assassins.

1896 King Gojong flees to the Russian legation in Korea (Seoul).

Taejo / Yi Seong-gye 태조 / 이성계

Taejo 태조, birth name **Yi Seong-gye 이성계** (1335 - 1408), was the founder and the first king of the Joseon Dynasty, reigning from 1392 to 1398, and was the main figure in overthrowing the Goryeo Dynasty. By the late 14th century, the Goryeo Dynasty was beginning to fall apart, with its foundations collapsing from years of war against the Mongol Empire. During the time, General Yi Seong-gye gained power and was respected for pushing the Mongol remnants off the kingdom and repelling Japanese pirates. When the newly rising Ming Dynasty demanded the return of a significant portion of Goryeo's northern territory, Goryeo was split into two factions – anti-Ming who argued to fight back and those who sought peace. Yi, the latter, however, was chosen to lead the invasion. At **Wihwado Island 위화도** on the **Amnok River 압록강**, he decided to revolt and withdrew the troops, and headed back to the capital. The military coup succeeded, and he dethroned the King. He first put a puppet king, but later exiled him, and ascended the throne, and began the Joseon Dynasty.

Yukryongi nareusha 육룡이 나르샤
(*Six Flying Dragons*, 2015, SBS)

K-Drama series about
Yi Seong-gye's Military Coup &
The Beginning of the Joseon Dynasty

Yi Sun-Shin 이순신 - The Legendary Korean War Hero

Yi Sun-shin (Yi Sun-sin) 이순신 (1545 – 1598) was a Korean naval commander/admiral and is arguably the most beloved and revered figure in the entire Korean history. Famed for his incredible victories against the Japanese navy during the ***Imjin Waeran* 임진왜란 (Imjin War - Japanese invasion of Joseon 1592 – 1598)**, as well as his exemplary moral conduct on and off the battlefield. His title of ***samdo sugun tongjesa*** 삼도수군통제사 (Naval Commander of the Three Provinces) was the title for the commander of the Korean navy until 1896. Yi Sun-shin's most remarkable military achievement, which has been made into a movie as well, occurred at the Battle of **Myeongnyang 명량**, where the Joseon navy was outnumbered by 133 warships to 13, and forced into a last stand. But without losing a single ship, he led the navy to repel the Japanese force, destroying and impairing 31 of the 133 enemy warships. Behind the incredible victory was the construction of armored warship, ***Geobukseon* 거북선** ("turtle ship"), whose original design was suggested during the reign of **King Taejong 태종**. Using his creative mind, the armored ship was brought back to life and played a crucial role in defeating the Japanese. On the verge of completely expelling the Japanese force, he was mortally wounded by an enemy bullet at the Battle of **Noryang 노량** on December 16, 1598. During his last moments, he ordered the subordinates to not announce his death. After death, he was rewarded with various honors from the royal court, including a posthumous title of **Chungmugong 충무공** (Duke of Loyalty and Warfare).

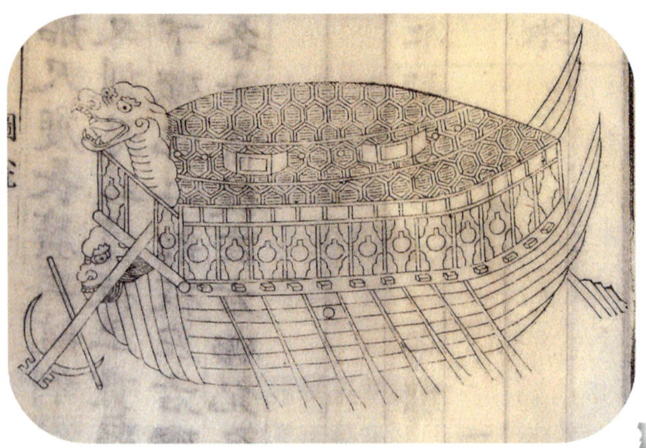

16th century Korean turtle ship in a depiction dating to 1795.
The woodblock print is based on a contemporary, late 18th century model.
© PHGCOM via Wikimedia Commons CC-SA 3.0

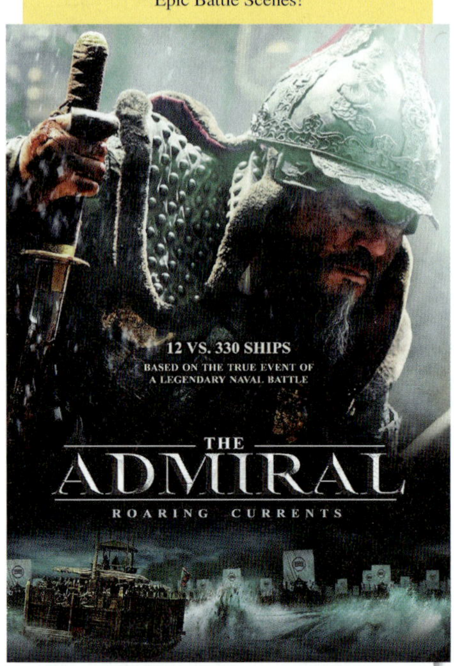

Myeongryang 명량
(*The Admiral : Roaring Currents*, 2014)

Admiral Yi Sun-sin remains a venerated hero among Koreans, and you can find his face and the turtle ship on the **100 Korean Won** and **5 Korean Won coins** today. You can also find his statue at the **Gwanghwamun Square**. Standing 17 meters (56 ft) tall with a sword in his hand is the bronze statue of the legendary war hero, Admiral Yi Sun-shin.

YI SOON SHIN - WARRIOR AND DEFENDER

The Story of Yi Soon-shin has been made
into a cartoon series by Onrie Kompan Productions

A miniature *Geobukseon*, the armored "turtle" warship, along with a pair of war drums are also found underneath. The statue was erected in 1968, after **President Park Chung Hee** ordered to "build a statue of a figure most feared and admired by the Japanese." The floor fountain is named "12.23 Fountain," symbolic of the 12 ships he fought to repel the Japanese invaders and 23 victories he achieved.

WHO ARE THE PEOPLE ON THE KOREAN CURRENCY NOTES?

Toegye Yi Hwang 퇴계이황 (1501-1570) was a leading thinker, educator, painter, and Neo-Confucianist scholar of Joseon. The painting on the back of the ₩1,000-won note is *Gyesangjeonggeodo* **계상정거도,** a work by **Gyeomjae Jeongseon 겸재 정선**, a master of landscape painting. The painting, created in 1746, depicts the surrounding landscape of **Dosan Seodang 도산서당**, where Toegye Yi Hwang stayed during his lifetime.

Yulgok Yi I 율곡이이 (1536 - 1584) was a prominent Confucian scholar of the Joseon Dynasty. If Toegye fully understood Neo-Confucianism, Yi I successfully indigenized it. On the back of the ₩5,000-won note is *Chochungdo* **초충도** (painting of grass and insects) painted by **Sin Saimdang 신사임당**, his mother. It was originally painted on eight folding screens, and on the note are a "Watermelon and Grasshopper" and a "Cockscomb and Frog."

King Sejong The Great 세종대왕 (1397-1450) is one of the most beloved and respected figures in Korea. Known as the King of humanity, he tried to develop and improve all the daily aspects of his people, including education, history, geography, politics, economy, agriculture, medicine, music, and religion. To predict nature to prevent damage to farming, King Sejong worked hard with scientists such as Jang Yeong-sil, Park Yeon, and Jeong Cho to create a device called *Honcheonui* **혼천의**, which was able to measure the location of the sun, moon, and the five planets, and it is featured on the back of the ₩10,000-won note.

Sin Saimdang 신사임당 (1504 - 1551) was a genius painter and a poet of the early Joseon period. As the mother of **Yulgok Yi I**, she was revered as a model for a good wife and a wise mother. Sin Saimdang loved *Sagunja* **사군자**, or the "Four Gracious Plants (plum, orchid, chrysanthemum, and bamboo)."The painting on the back of the note, called Wolmaedo **월매도** is not a painting by Sin Saimdang, but it is said to be the most famous and outstanding painting of plum blossoms painted during the mid-Joseon period.

HWACHA – JOSEON'S MULTIPLE ROCKET LAUNCHER!

Hwacha 화차 was a Joseon Dynasty weapon that could fire hundreds of rocket-powered arrows and iron-headed arrows out of a gun barrel at the same time!

Shingijeon 신기전 (*The Divine Weapon*, 2008)

WHY WERE KOREANS CALLED "WHITE-CLOTHES PEOPLE"?

Ernst Jakob Oppert, a German-Jewish businessman who visited Joseon, wrote in his book *Ein Verschlossenes Land: Reisen nach Corea* that "men and women, their clothes are white." Around the same period, the French Far East correspondent Laguerie also observed that "everyone is dressed in white" (1832).

Koreans often describe themselves as **baekui minjok** 백의민족, literally "the white-clothed people." However, since the term does not appear in early historical records, it likely originated from foreign travelers' impressions of Korea during the late Joseon Dynasty, when wearing white became especially common. Why did Koreans favor white clothing? Scholars offer several explanations. First, some suggest a cultural or spiritual reason: white symbolized purity and was associated with sun worship in ancient Korean beliefs. Second, there's an economic explanation. Dyes were expensive, and colorful garments—often reserved for the court or special occasions such as weddings—were beyond the means of most commoners. Naturally, white, the undyed color of plain cotton or hemp, became the default attire. During the Japanese occupation (1910–1945), white clothing took on political meaning. When the Japanese authorities encouraged people to wear colored garments instead, many Koreans saw it as an attempt to suppress their national identity. In defiance, they continued to wear white, turning it into a symbol of quiet resistance and national pride.

Royal Palaces of the Joseon Dynasty

GYEONGBOKGUNG - "Palace Greatly Blessed by Heaven"

1. **Geunjeongjeon 근정전** was the throne hall where the king formally granted audiences to his officials, gave declarations of national importance, and greeted foreign envoys and ambassadors

2. **Gyeonghoeru 경회루** was a pavilion used to hold important state banquets. The present building was constructed in 1867 (during the reign of King Gojong) on an island of an artificial lake that is 128 m (420 ft) wide and 113 m (370 ft) across.

3. **Hyangwonjeong 향원정** is a two-story hexagonal pavilion built on an artificial island of a lake.

With **Mount Bugak 북악산** as a backdrop and **Yukjogeori 육조거리** ("Street of Six Ministries" (today's Sejong-no 세종로) just outside the main entrance to the palace **Gwanghwamun Gate 광화문**, **Gyeongbokgung 경복궁** was built in 1395 (three years after the foundation of the Joseon Dynasty), in the heart of the Dynasty's capital, **Hanyang 한양** (today's Seoul) and served as the Dynasty's main palace. Sadly, it was reduced to ashes during the Japanese invasion of 1592, and was left abandoned until 1867. Today, the restored complex consists of 330 buildings, forming a labyrinthine configuration, in which the walls separate offices for the king and state officials called **Oejeon 외전** (outer court) from living quarters for the royal family and gardens called **Naejeon 내전** (inner court). Added to the extensive complex were other palaces of various sizes, including **Junggung 중궁** (the Queen's residence) and **Donggung 동궁** (the Crown Prince's residence).

In the early 20th century during the Japanese Occupation (1910 - 1945), Gyeongbokgung, the symbol of national sovereignty, was demolished and the ownership of the land was transferred to the Japanese Governor-General in 1911. In 1915, a significant portion of the buildings were torn down for an exhibition. Following the event, the Japanese built the Government-General building on the site.

The South Korean government has been making continuous efforts to restore Gyeongbokgung since 1990. The Government-General building was demolished in 1996 under the command of **President Kim Young-sam 김영삼**. **Heungnyemun Gate 흥례문** and **Gwanghwamun Gate 광화문** have also been reconstructed in their original locations. The inner court and Donggung, the Crown Prince's residence, have also been restored recently.

Gwanghwamun, meaning "spreading light," is the main and largest gate of Gyeongbokgung. First constructed in 1395, it served as a landmark and symbol of the capital **Hanyang**, but it went through recurring accounts of destruction and disrepair. It was destroyed by fire during the Japanese invasion in 1592 and was left in ruins until 1867 when it was finally restored along with the rest of Gyeongbokgung Palace. It was again deconstructed and moved to a different location by the Japanese during the Japanese Occupation so that a massive Japanese Government-General building could be built on the site. After getting completely destroyed during the Korean War, it was once again restored and relocated near the original location in 1969 and is one of the most popular spots among tourists.

On the wall outside of **Jagyeongjeon 자경전**, you can find *Shipjangsaeng* **십장생**. Meaning "Ten Symbols of Longevity," it's a traditional Korean pattern consisting of the sun, mountain, rock, water, cloud, pine tree, elixir plant, turtle, crane, and deer. Each symbol stands for longevity, but when used together it strengthens their original meaning.

Wall outside of Jagyeongjeon in Gyeongbokgung

Haechi **해치**, or *haetae* **해태**, is a legendary creature in Chinese and Korean mythology that's believed to be able to distinguish good from evil and keep justice. Since ancient times, the *haechi* have been regarded as auspicious animals that prevent fires and disasters, which is why you can find their statues at the entrance of the palaces. The Seoul Metropolitan Government selected *haechi* as the city's icon in May 2008. Since then, the Seoul Metropolitan Government has placed *haechi* statues in various parts of the city, including **Gwanghwamun Square**. Why don't you look around Seoul's historic attractions and find them all?

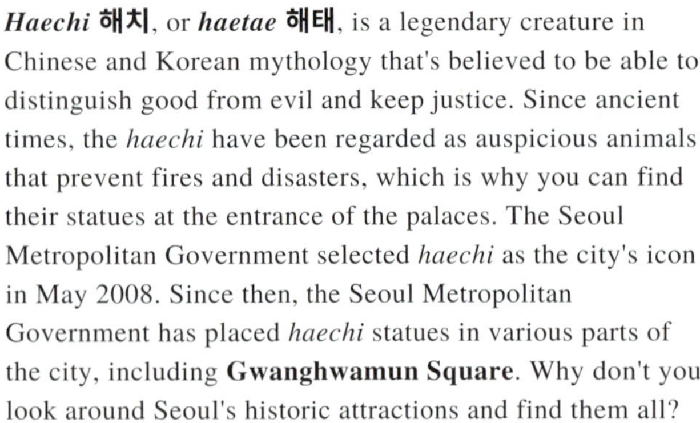

Injeongjeon 인정전, meaning "hall of benevolent ruling", was the throne hall of Palace and the most representative and dignified building of the palace. It was used for major state affairs.

Huwon 후원 ("rear garden") is a beautiful garden which incorporates a lotus pond. It was originally constructed for the use of the royal family and palace women.

Irworobongdo 일월오봉도, meaning "The Painting of The Sun, The Moon and Five Mountain Peaks," Irworobongdo is a painting on a folding screen that sits behind the king's throne. It depicts the Sun on one side and the Moon on the other, with five mountain peaks and water below them, and it was buried with the king when he died. It's said that the painting is complete only when the king is seated before it.

Eojwa 어좌, or "The Phoenix Throne" is the throne of the hereditary monarchs of Korea. The phoenix has a long association with Korean royalty.

Changdeokgung 창덕궁 is also known as **Donggwol** 동궐 (Eastern Palace) because of its location which sits to the east of the main palace, Gyeongbokgung. Changdeokgung was home to the Joseon government, as well as a beloved residence of numerous kings of the Joseon Dynasty. For this reason, it was the longest-serving royal residential palace. Its unique beauty comes from the fact that it flawlessly blends into its surrounding nature and landscape, and **Huwon** 후원, the palace's rear garden, and the only rear garden of any Korean palace, is the essence of Korean landscaping, occupying about 60% of the palace. Luckily, Changdeokgung Palace is well-preserved compared to other palaces that were damaged and destroyed throughout history and many of its original features still remain intact. It was added to the **UNESCO World Heritage List** in 1997.

Chundangji 춘당지 ("Spring Pond". Joseon kings who resided in the Palace tilled the soil with plows drawn by an ox. This symbolic ceremony was a tradition of wishing for a good harvest while promoting agriculture and share the arduous labor the farmers had to endure.

Changgyeonggung 창경궁 was built in the mid-15th century by **King Sejong** 세종 for his father, **Taejong** 태종. Originally named **Suganggung** 수강궁, it received the current name after a renovation and expansion project that took place in 1483. Like other palaces, many of its structures were destroyed as a result of the multiple invasions by Japan. It was reconstructed by successive Kings, but a significant portion was once again torn down by the Japanese during **the Japanese Occupation**, to make room for a modern park for the Japanese Empire. On the site, the Japanese built a zoo, a botanical garden, and a museum. After getting destroyed during the **Korean War**, the zoo was restocked but was eventually relocated to present-day **Seoul Grand Park**.

***Samdo* 삼도 ("Three Paths")**
Inside the palace, paths are divided into three sections. The central path, widest and
highest among them, is the royal path, called **eodo**
어도, which was used exclusively by the kings. The east path was used by civil servants
and the west path by military officials.

***Pumgyeseok* 품계석 ("Rank Stones")**
Two rows of rank stones, indicate the position
of court officials during ceremonies.

***deumeu* 드므 / *deumu* 드무**
Around the corners of the hall, there are bronze water jars with water filled up to
the brim (they are kept empty today). While they serve practical purposes of
putting out fires, their main purpose was to ward off the evil spirits of fire
because the reflection on the water inside the jars would startle them.
Interestingly, during the winter, they would keep fire around the jars to prevent
them from freezing. This is a great example of harmony between shamanistic
traditions and scientific reasoning of the time.

WHAT ARE THE MINI STATUES ON THE KOREAN PALACE ROOF?

Look up to the roofs of Korean palaces and at the peak of the roof you will find mysterious statues called
japsang 잡상, which are always placed in an odd number (the most a palace can have is 11). Their purpose
goes back to the Korean shamanic religion and they are intended to chase away evil spirits and misfortune,
similar to that of gargoyles in the Western culture, as well as to show the dignity and grandeur of a building.
The tradition is considered to have been a result of the Chinese influence during the Joseon Dynasty, as
evidenced by the fact that the first few *japsang* statues on a roof are believed to be the characters and the
deities of Earth from the Chinese classic ***Journey to the West***.

Seokjojeon 석조전 is a Western-style building and was the last residential quarter of King Gojong

Deoksugung 덕수궁 is different from other Korean palaces in style for containing a harmonious mixture of medieval and modern style architecture. For example - you will find a **Western-style garden** and a modern seal engraved on a fountain. Originally, Deoksugung was not a palace, but when the 14th king of the Joseon Dynasty, **King Seonjo** 선조, returned from evacuation during the Japanese invasion in 1592, all palaces were severely damaged, and Deoksugung was chosen as a temporary residence for the royal family. The 15th king, **King Gwanghaegun** 광해군, renamed it to **Gyeonggunung** 경운궁, and formalized it as a royal palace, and **Emperor Gojong** 고종 of the **Korean Empire** (also the 26th king of the Joseon Dynasty), stayed here and expanded it. During the Joseon Dynasty, the royal guard was responsible for opening and closing the palace gate as well as patrolling and you can see the reenactment taking place today when you visit.

(Left) **Jeonggwanheon** 정관헌, a building used for rest and entertainment.

(Above) The symbol of a deer keeping a herb of eternal youth, *bulocho* 불로초.

ROYAL GUARD CHANGING CEREMONY

***Sumunjang gyodaeuisik* 수문장 교대의식** (The Chief Gate-keeper Changing Ceremony). The royal guard system, which started when **King Yejong 예종**, the 8th king of the Joseon Dynasty who came to the throne in 1469, was conceptually the same as the national defense, as it was used as a means to strengthen the royal authority and maintain stability. The royal guard system was structured when the gate guard system and its rules were institutionalized and incorporated in ***Gyeonggukdaejeon* 경국대전** (National Code) during the reign of **King Seongjong 성종**, the 9th king. The changing ceremony of the royal guard in front of the **Daehanmun Gate 대한문** started in 1906 when the gate was designated as the main gate to the Palace.

The Order of the Changing Ceremony

1) Entrance of the officials and announcement of the ceremony
2) Delivery of the passcode and passcode response
3) First drumbeat (passing the case with the keys)
4) Second drumbeat (checking the authenticity of the token and identification of the plate which represents the chief gatekeeper, *sumunjang* 수문장)
5) Third drumbeat (implementation of the shift)
6) Closing announcement

The *yonggo* 용고 ("dragon drum"), is a barrel drum with tacked heads decorated with painted dragon designs, used in the military wind-and-percussion music called ***daechwita* 대취타**.

The construction of **Gyeonghuigung 경희궁** began in 1617 during the reign of **King Gwanghaegun 광해군**, the 15th king of the Joseon Dynasty, and was completed in 1620. It was originally called **Gyeongdeokgung 경덕궁** because Gyeongdeok was the posthumous epithet of **Wonjong 원종**, who was named king after his death. In the latter Joseon Dynasty period, Gyeonghuigung served as the secondary palace for the king, and as it was situated on the west side of Seoul, it was also called **Seogwol 서궐** (West Palace).

The secondary palace is usually the palace where the King moves to in times of emergency. From **King Injo 인조** to **King Cheoljong 철종**, about 10 kings of the Joseon Dynasty stayed here.

Before losing most of its complex to two devastating fires in the 19th century, it was of a considerable size, with an arched bridge connecting it to **Deoksugung**. During the Japanese Occupation, the remaining was dismantled to make space for **Gyeongseong Middle School 경성중학교**, which was a school for Japanese citizens. Reconstruction efforts began in the late 1990s as part of a government project, but due to urban growth and decades of neglect, the government was only able to reconstruct around 1/3 of the former Palace.

Imperial Family of The Korean Empire (Daehan Maeil Sinbo, Seoul Shinmun)

THE KOREAN EMPIRE - DREAMING OF A MODERN STATE (1897 ~ 1910)

Daehanjeguk 대한제국 (The Great Han Empire), or the Korean Empire, was the new name which the 26th King of the Joseon Dynasty, and the first Emperor of the Empire, **King Gojong 고종** renamed the Joseon Dynasty from on October 12th, 1897. In the turbulent late 19th century East Asia, the Korean Empire proclaimed itself as an independent country and promoted modernization in various fields such as the military, economy, land system, and education through the **Gwangmu Reformation 광무개혁**, but was eventually annexed by the Japanese Empire and collapsed in 1910.

1897 Proclamation of the Empire - King Gojong returns after 1 year of refugee at the Russian Legation.

1905 Korea-Japan Treaty of 1905 gives Japan complete power for Korea's foreign affairs and placed all trade through Korean ports under Japanese supervision.

1907 June - The Hague Secret Emissary Affair

July - Emperor Gojong abdicated by the Japanese Imperialists, and Gojong's son Sunjong succeeded to the throne.

1909 Ito Hirobumi (Japanese Resident-General of Korea) assassinated by Korean general and independence activist An Jung-geun.

1910 The Japan-Korea Treaty of 1910 started the annexation of the Korean Empire by Imperial Japan.

Emperor Gojong 고종 황제

Gojong, the **Gwangmu Emperor 광무대제** (1852 – 1919), was the 26th and final king of the Joseon Dynasty. During his reign, he was influenced by **Empress Myeongseong 명성황후 (Queen Min)**, and unlike his father **Heungseon Daewongun 흥선대원군,** who maintained a closed-door/national-isolation policy, he adopted an open-door foreign policy. He signed a Treaty of Amity and Trade with the US in 1882, although it was done in hopes of gaining protection from Imperial Japan, China, and Russia. While the conflict among three neighboring powerhouses was rising, Gojong proclaimed Korea an empire in 1897, and became the first Emperor, and the Joseon Dynasty ended at the same time. In an effort to maintain Korean sovereignty, he played and leveraged on the power struggle among the rivals, effectively preventing each of them from having total control over Korea. His efforts finally came to an end after the **Russo-Japanese War (1904–05)**.

Seokjojeon 석조전 in the Deoksugung Palace 덕수궁, the last residential quarter of King Gojong

Empress Myeongseong 명성황후

A portrait of Empress Myeongseong
by a Japanese illustrator

Empress Myeongseong 명성황후 (1851 - 1895) was the first official wife of **King Gojong 고종**, the 26th king of Joseon and the first emperor of the Korean Empire. The government of Meiji Japan was ambitious with overseas expansion and saw her as an obstacle, putting efforts to remove her but failed. After the first **Sino-Japanese War** which ended with Japan's victory, Joseon came under the Japanese influence. As a result, the Empress argued for stronger ties between Korea and Russia as a means to block Japanese influence. The efforts to remove her from the political arena, orchestrated through failed rebellions prompted by **Heungseon Daewongun** (an influential regent working with the Japanese), compelled her to take a harsher stand against Japanese influence. The Japanese government sent a group of *ronin*s (assassins) and assassinated the Empress. This horrendous incident ignited outrage among other foreign powers, and the Joseon people's **anti-Japanese sentiment** soared.

Eulsa Treaty 을사조약

Victorious Japan forced Emperor Gwangmu (King Gojong) to accept pro-Japanese advisors to the royal court, which in turn, led him to sign the Protectorate Treaty of 1905, more commonly known as **Eulsa Joyak 을사조약 (Eulsa Treaty)** between Korea and Japan. As a result, Korea lost its status and rights as an independent sovereign nation.

<h1 style="text-align:center">The Hague Secret Emissary Affair</h1>

Emperor Gwangmu (King Gojong) secretly sent representatives (**Yi Jun 이준, Yi Sang-seol 이상설** and **Yi Wi-jong 이위종**) more commonly known as "Hague Secret Emissary Affair," to the **Hague Peace Convention** in 1907, to assert the Korean sovereignty and to declare the invalidity of Japanese diplomatic maneuvers, including the **Eulsa Treaty of 1905**. At the convention, the representatives asserted the Emperor's rights to rule Korea independent of Japan. Sadly, the emissaries were not allowed by the nations to take part in the conference. Eventually, though, they managed to hold interviews with newspapers and spoke out about the unfairness being done by the Japanese. As a result, the enraged Japanese forced Emperor Gwangmu to abdicate and his son **Sunjong 순종** was put to the throne and ruled for just three years before the Korean Empire got annexed by Japan in 1910.

<h2 style="text-align:center">Yi Wan-yong 이완용 The Worst Traitor in Korean History</h2>

이완용 Yi Wan-yong (1858 - 1926), also known as **Ye Wanyong**, is one of the **Five Eulsa (Japan-Korea Protectorate Treaty of 1905) Traitors** and is considered the worst traitor who sold his country out to Japan. He threatened King Gojong to sign the Eulsa Treaty and changed the State Council of Joseon to the cabinet system of which he became the Prime Minister. After the Hague Secret Emissary Affair, he held King Gojong accountable and forced him to step down, and crowned King Sunjong. As the Prime Minister, he signed a **Korea-Japan annexation**.

A story of "Righteous Army (civilian militia)" during the Korean Empire period.

Mr. Sunshine (2018, tvN)

Deokhye Ongju 덕혜옹주 (*The Last Princess* 2018)

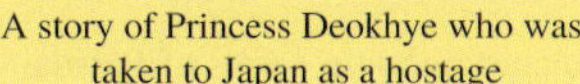

A story of Princess Deokhye who was taken to Japan as a hostage

211

For memorial of establishing Provisional Government of the Republic of Korea October 11, 1919

JAPANESE OCCUPATION - SAD HISTORY (1910 ~ 1945)

The period from 1910, when the **Korean Empire** was annexed by Japan, to 1945 when it was liberated, is one of the saddest and most painful periods in Korean history. After the annexation, Japan set up the Government-General of Joseon and systematically suppressed Koreans with administrative, legislative, judicial, and military forces in their hands, and persistently tried to plant their spirit and culture. Korean names were forcibly changed to Japanese names, and the mandatory use of the Japanese language by students, alongside the abolition of Korean language courses in all schools, were intended to thoroughly "Japanize" Koreans. Cultural property looting and economic exploitation were also frequent. This evil deed reached its peak through the **Pacific War** and **World War II**. The **Japanese imperialists** committed countless crimes against humanity, including forced labor, military sexual slavery brothels, and horrific experiments on the living bodies of the Korean people. While some argue that the Japanese colonial government's urban planning had a positive impact on the modernization of Seoul, they also acknowledge that the purpose was strictly exploitation, on the pretext of "development" and this indelible scar is why many Koreans still have anti-Japanese sentiment.

1916 The final wave of Uibyeong rebels is defeated by Japanese forces.

1919 Spurred by the sudden and mysterious death of Gojong, March 1st Movement, organized by Yu Gwan Sun and other independence activisits, began. Declaration of Korean Independence. Nationwide peaceful demonstrations are crushed by Japanese military and police forces after two months. Governor-General Hasegawa resigns.

The establishment of The Provisional Government of the Republic of Korea in Shanghai.

1920 Battle of Cheongsanri, Korean independence Army, led by Kim Jwa-jin, victory.

1932 Korean independence activist Lee Bong Chang fails in his attempt to assassinate Emperor Hirohito in Tokyo.

Korean independence activist Yun Bong Gil bombs Japanese Military gathering in Shanghai.

1945 The Empire of Japan surrenders to the Allies. According to the terms of Potsdam Declaration, Korea becomes independent.

Ahn Jung-geun 안중근 (1879 – 1910) was an independence activist and a martyr at the end of the Korean Empire. He assassinated **Prince Ito Hirobumi**, the main culprit of the invasion, and former Resident-General of Joseon, at **Harbin Railway Station** in Manchuria. **The Order of Merit for National Foundation** was posthumously awarded.

Kim Gu 김구 (1876 ~ 1949) was an independence activist and politician of the **Provisional Government of Korea** during the Japanese Occupation. After Korea's liberation from Japan's colonial rule, he tried to establish an independent and unified government but was assassinated by **Ahn Doo-hee 안두희** in 1949. *Baekbeomilji* **백범일지**, a diary written during his career in the provisional government, remains a valuable historical record.

Yun Bong-gil 윤봉길 (1908 ~ 1932) was an independence activist during the Japanese Occupation. In 1932, he threw a **bomb** at an event venue in Hongkou Park in Shanghai which was celebrating the **Japanese Emperor's birthday and victory in the war**, causing significant damage to Japanese colonial leaders. Along with Ahn Jung-geun's attack on Ito Hirobumi in Harbin, this is considered one of the greatest achievements of the Korean independence movement.

Ahn Chang-ho 안창호 (1878 ~ 1938) was an independence activist and educator at the end of the Korean Empire and during the Japanese occupation. He led educational activities to foster national competence and independence movements to regain the sovereignty of Korea. He established the **New People's Association**, **Daeseong School 대성학교**, and **Young Korean Academy**. His pen-name is **Dosan 도산**, which is also **the name of a park in Seoul** established to commemorate his achievement and legacy.

A movie inspired by the activities of the Korean Independence Fighters.

Amsal 암살 (Assassination, 2015)

But I See Koreans Speaking Fluent Japanese In Movies. How Is This Possible? P. 28

Demonstration for independence in the Park.
The Koreans are seen shouting "Mansei" with their hands up in the air. Not a single man is armed.

[Red Cross pamphlet on March 1st Movement]

Hanggeo: Yugwansun Iyagi
항거: 유관순 이야기
(A Resistance, 2019)

Ryu Gwan-sun 유관순 (alternative spelling **Yu Gwan-sun**, 1902 – 1920), was an organizer of the March 1st Movement, one of the earliest public displays of Korean resistance during the Japanese Occupation, is a symbol of Korea's fight for independence against imperial Japan. The event was a peaceful protest where thousands of Koreans gathered to cry out **"*Daehan Doklip Manse"* 대한독립만세** ("Long Live Korean Independence"), while waving thousands of Korean flags. It went on for hours until the Japanese military police started firing at the unarmed protesters. Sadly, 19 people died, including Ryu's parents. After getting arrested, she was severely tortured and interrogated, but never gave away the whereabouts of her collaborators. She later died in jail from the after-effects of torture.

WHO WERE THE "COMFORT WOMEN"?

It refers to the military sexual slavery system set up and operated by the Japanese military, which led to numerous crimes such as wartime rape and sexual abuse, committed against the women in colonies and occupied territories. It was done under the connivance and with the direct involvement of the Japanese government - during World War II, the Japanese government had to find a way to satisfy the sexual desires of their soldiers, and they set up illegal military brothels, recruited and managed women from colonies and occupied areas, including China, Taiwan, Malaysia, Vietnam, Indonesia, and even the Netherlands. The term *wianbu* 위안부 (*ianfu* in Japanese) literally means "comfort women," and was a euphemism used by the Japanese military. The so-called recruitment process had problems. Many of them were forcibly conscripted while many mothers were defrauded by a broker who guaranteed them a factory job. They were locked up against their will and sexually exploited and are still suffering from the trauma of that time. Each of the affected countries is demanding an open and sustained apology from Japan. Korean civic organizations have been installing what's known as the "Statue of Peace" *sonyeosang* 소녀상 ("statue of a girl") around the world to raise awareness of the atrocity and console the victims.

WHY DO KOREANS LIKE THE ROSE OF SHARON SO MUCH?

Emblem of South Korea and the National Assembly

"Three thousand li (unit of measurement for length) of splendid rivers and mountains, filled with *mugunghwa*." As can be seen from a passage from Korea's national anthem, Koreans have loved and cherished *mugunghwa*, also known as the "Rose of Sharon." The flower, which literally means "Flower of infinitude/eternity," is named so because the continuous blooming and fading were seen as such. Moreover, Korean people identified themselves with the flower and regarded it as a symbol of the Korean national spirit, that has survived unabated despite numerous hardships and struggles. For this reason, **Namgoong Eok 남궁억**, the president of **Hwangseong Newspaper 황성신문** and independence activist during the Japanese Occupation, established the **Mogok School** in September 1919 and made efforts to spread *mugunghwa* to the entire country. Although *mugunghwa* has never been officially designated as the national flower of Korea by law, it's customarily recognized as the national flower of Korea and is used as a symbol of the nation.

WHY ARE KOREANS SO FURIOUS OVER THE JAPANESE "RISING SUN" FLAG?

Imagine walking through the streets of Jerusalem wearing a T-shirt emblazoned with the **Nazi swastika**. Even the most daring thrill-seeker wouldn't do that—it's a symbol of racism, genocide, and the horrific atrocities committed during the Holocaust. But did you know that in Korea, there's a symbol that evokes a similar level of anger and pain? It's **Japan's Rising Sun Flag**. To many foreigners unfamiliar with the scars of the Japanese colonial era, the flag might look like a stylish variation of Japan's national flag—hence its frequent appearance on T-shirts, accessories, and even smartphone cases. However, for Koreans and other Asians who suffered under Japanese imperialism, it's far from a trendy design.

The Rising Sun Flag was the emblem of Japan's imperial army during the Pacific War, a force that invaded and exploited many Asian nations under the pretense of "liberating Asia from the West." Because of that, the flag has become a painful reminder of Japan's wartime aggression. Over the years, several foreign celebrities and global brands have faced backlash for unknowingly displaying the Rising Sun design, often issuing public apologies after receiving complaints—especially from Koreans. Even Korean idol stars have occasionally come under fire for wearing clothes or accessories featuring the symbol. Still, some scholars argue that the Rising Sun Flag is being misunderstood. Historically, it was used by the Japanese military long before the era of imperial expansion and continues to be used by Japan's Self-Defense Forces today. Technically speaking, Japan's current national flag—the plain red circle—was also in use during World War II, which makes it inaccurate to equate the Rising Sun Flag entirely with the Nazi swastika. While academics may debate whether the two symbols are identical in meaning, one thing remains clear: both evoke deep pain for the nations and people who suffered under the regimes they represent. Understanding that shared trauma is essential to fostering respect and sensitivity in a global society.

WHAT IS DOKDO AND WHAT'S ALL THE FUSS ABOUT IT?

Along with the Japanese Rising Sun Flag, another sensitive and important issue to Koreans, and a symbol of Korea-Japan conflict, is an island called **Dokdo 독도**. Dokdo, made up of two islets **Dongdo 동도** (East Island) and **Seodo 서도** (West Island), is a pair of volcanic islets located off the east coast of South Korea, next to the larger **Ulleungdo Island 울릉도**, and right in between the **Korean Peninsula** and the Japanese Archipelago. As the nickname "a lonely island" suggests, it's the easternmost territory belonging to South Korea. But as irony would have it, it's far from being "lonely," because Japan has been tenaciously claiming sovereignty over the islands. Japan claims that Dokdo (**Takeshima** is the Japanese name) was a terra nullius (nobody's land) before the Japanese annexation of Korea (1910), meaning that Korea never had control of the island. Therefore, when they discovered and used it as a temporary lighthouse during the Russo-Japanese War, Japan was the first to incorporate it as its territory. Hence, Japan claims that South Korea is illegally occupying Japanese territory now. However, in 1905, Japan forcibly seized Dokdo, then part of Joseon (1392-1910). After the end of World War II, Japan, as one of the defeated countries, was forced to return all territory seized under imperialism to the rightful owners. Nevertheless, Japan still insists that Dokdo is Japan's territory – they even changed their original argument from claiming that no country possessed Dokdo before they occupation in 1905 to new assertions in 1953 that Japanese diplomatic documents marked Dokdo as Japan's indigenous territory.

Even Japan's public documents such as 'The Tottori-han's Submission' (1693) and 'The Dajokan Order' (1877) emphasize that Dokdo is not part of Japan. These documents directly contradict Japan's current claim that Dokdo was an unclaimed territory. Moreover, Supreme Commander for the Allied Powers Index Number (SCAPIN) 677 in 1946, a memorandum that sealed the range of territories that would be changed after the end of the Second World War, excluded Dokdo from its administrative and governmental district. These documents add to the evidence that Dokdo is not under the dominance of Japan and that such fact has been globally acknowledged, even by Japan.

Official documents from Korea and Japan along with international statements from events such as the Potsdam and Cairo conferences reflect the Japanese government's unjust claim on Dokdo. Despite the evidence, the Japanese government still denies Korea's claim to Dokdo. Japan's current assertions on Dokdo can be explained as [a] threat to Korea's sovereignty and a repetition of the imperialism that triggered World War II in the past." (maywespeak.com)

The Korean government's position on the island is firm. "Dokdo Island is not a subject for territorial dispute. Dokdo is an integral part of Korean territory, historically, geographically and under international law. No territorial dispute exists regarding Dokdo, and therefore Dokdo is not a matter to be dealt with through diplomatic negotiations or judicial settlement. The government of the Republic of Korea exercises Korea's irrefutable territorial sovereignty over Dokdo."(dokdo.mofa.go.kr/eng/dokdo/government_position.jsp)

Why is Dokdo important? First of all, Dokdo is sitting in the middle of the **East Sea**, a repository of a vast amount of **natural resources**. In particular, it's estimated that there are about 600 million tons of solidified methane hydrate, which could generate 10 trillion won (about 8 billion USD) in profits over the next 30 years. But there is a very special reason why Koreans have a strong emotional attachment to the "lonely island." It's because the pain of having the country taken over by the Japanese Imperialists still lingers in everyone's minds. Dokdo was the **first part of Korean territory to be incorporated into the territory of Japan** in 1905, just a little before the Japanese Occupation began. Thus, for Koreans, loving Dokdo is a pledge not to repeat the **pain and shame of the past**, and a **symbol of patriotism**. Koreans have been residing in Dokdo since March 1965. As of March 2017, 25 people (24 households) are registered as residents. There are about 40 Dokdo guards, 3 Dokdo lighthouse keepers, with 2 working in the Dokdo management office.

WHAT'S THE NATIONAL ANTHEM OF KOREA?

During the Japanese Occupation and before the founding of the Republic of Korea, Korea didn't have an official national anthem, and they made a makeshift national anthem, where they set the song's lyrics to the tunes of a Scottish folk song, "Auld Lang Syne." Later in 1935, the lyrics were set to the melody composed by **Ahn Eak-tai** (alternative spelling, **Ahn Ik-Tae) 안익태,** and was adopted as the national anthem of the Provisional Government of Korea, which existed from 1919 to 1948. *Aegukga* 애국가, literally meaning "The Patriotic Song," has four verses, but on most occasions, only the first one is performed at public events.

Verse 1: 동해 물과 백두산이 마르고 닳도록 하느님이 보우하사 우리나라 만세.
(Until that day when Mt. Baekdu is worn away and the East Sea's waters run dry,
May God protect and preserve our country!)

Refrain: 무궁화 삼천리 화려강산 대한 사람, 대한으로 길이 보전하세.
(Hibiscus and three thousand *ri* (Korean unit of measurement) full of splendid mountains and rivers;
Great Koreans, to the Great Korean way, stay always true!)

Verse 2: 남산 위에 저 소나무 철갑을 두른 듯 바람서리 불변함은 우리 기상일세.
(As the pine atop Namsan Peak stands firm, unchanged through wind and frost, as if wrapped in
armor, so shall our resilient spirit.) / **Refrain**

Verse 3: 가을 하늘 공활한데 높고 구름 없이 밝은 달은 우리 가슴 일편단심일세.
(The autumn skies are void and vast, high and cloudless;
the bright moon is like our heart, undivided and true.) / **Refrain**

Verse 4: 이 기상과 이 맘으로 충성을 다하여 괴로우나 즐거우나 나라 사랑하세.
(With this spirit and this mind, let us give all loyalty, in suffering or joy, to love our nation.) / **Refrain**

Translation from wikipedia.org/wiki/Aegukga

WHY IS KOREA DIVIDED?

When the trembling voice of the Japanese Emperor Michinomiya Hirohito declared Japan's complete surrender over the radio on Aug 15th, 1945, World War II, the most destructive war in human history, finally came to an end. At the same time, the 35 years of pain and suffering brought upon the Korean people as a result of the Japanese Occupation (1910 - 1945) was also over. Korea was finally liberated. But the joy didn't last long. Fundamental shifts in global politics and ideological split among the Koreans led to the division of Korea into two occupation zones - the U.S. administering the southern half and the Soviet Union the northern half of the 38th parallel. Over the next three years, 1945-1948, a communist regime supported by the Soviet Union was set in the northern part of Korea above the 38th

1945. 08. 15 Japan surrenders following the WWII defeat. As a result, the Japanese occupation ended and Korea was liberated.

Fundamental shifts in global politics and ideology leads to the division of Korea into two occupation zones - the US administering the southern half and the Soviet Union the northern half of the 38th parallel.

1945. 06. 25 At the dawn of June 25, 1950, North Korean forces began the sudden invasion of South Korea, triggering the Korean War

1945. 06. 27 President Harry Truman deploys troops, hoping to stop the spread of Communism to South Korea.

1950. 10 The Communist China, which bordered North Korea, starts to worry about protecting themselves, and sends a massive amount of troops, making important victories that pushed the UN troops back acorss the 38th parallel.

1951.07.10 With the battling at a stalemate, peace talks began, but it will take two years for the opposite sides to reach an agreement.

1953.07.27 Armistice agreement ends a 3-year-long brutal war between two Koreas.

1954.04 US and Chinese representatives meet to discuss the terms to reunite Korea but fail to reach an agreement, leaving Korea divided.

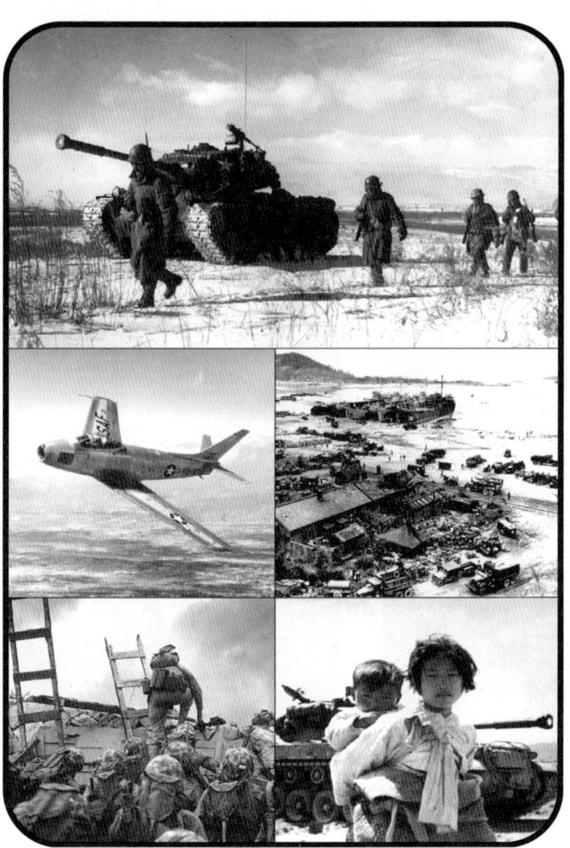

Montage of images from the Korean War. Clockwise from top: U.S. Marines retreating during the Battle of the Chosin Reservoir, U.N. landing at Incheon, Korean refugees in front of an American M-26 tank, U.S. Marines, led by First Lieutenant Baldomero Lopez, landing at Incheon, and an American F-86 Sabre fighter jet.

parallel, while a democratic government was set up and supported by the **United States** below the 38th parallel. The Korean Peninsula became the chessboard on which the intense **Cold War** power struggle between the U.S. and the Soviet Union was played.

In 1948, a United Nations-sponsored vote was held to let the people of Korea decide their own future, but all the efforts went for naught when North Korea refused to participate. South Korea took the initiative and said checkmate by forming its own provisional democratic government, with Harvard and Princeton educated Dr. **Syngman Rhee** as the first South Korean president. North Korea quickly reacted by forming their own socialist government led by a former communist guerrilla **Kim Il-sung**. This historical moment was the last time Korea was ever together as one.

At the dawn of June 25th, 1950, North Korean forces began a sudden invasion of South Korea with the operation code name *pokpung* 폭풍 (storm), triggering the Korean War. Immediately after the blitz, **President Harry Truman** deployed the U.S. troops, hoping to stop the spread of Communism to South Korea, but it wasn't enough to stop North Korea who was backed by the Soviet Union's full military support and carefully planned to invade the South. South Korea was not only over-powered but also caught off-guard. North Korea was able to seize the capital city of the South, Seoul, just three days after the outbreak of the war. Then the North kept on marching, all the way down to Busan, the final defense line of the South.

Just when South Korea was on the verge of falling to the hands of the communists, tables turned when the United Nations forces, under the command of **General Douglas MacArthur**, launched a series of massive counterattacks, starting with the "**Incheon Landing Operation (Operation Chromite)**" on September 15th. As a result, the forces were able to reach the North's capital city of Pyongyang on October 10th and all the way up to the northernmost **Amnok River**. They were just a few kilometers away from victory.

But in mid-November, Kim Il-Sung of North Korea, on the brink of defeat, sent a series of urgent letters to **Mao Zedong**, the **Chairman of the People's Republic of China** for reinforcement. Mao responded by sending a massive (over 300,000 soldiers) force of the Chinese army known as the "**People's Volunteer Army**." With the intervention, the tide turned again. The Chinese army found out that the weakness of the South - U.S. army traveled only by road, the UN forces' superior air power wasn't a big threat during nighttime, and most importantly, the South Korean force was the weakest link. The Chinese army bypassed the roads and took the mountain route, attacked the Korean troops at night to block the supply route, and cut off the retreat.

As a result, the South Korea-UN forces were pushed back, giving up Seoul on January 4th, but reclaimed it on March 15th. With the battling at a stalemate, peace talks began on July 10th, 1951, but it would take two years for both sides to reach an agreement. Finally, on July 27th, 1953, armistice agreement was signed and it ended a 3-year-long brutal war between two Koreas. A year later, the representatives from the U.S. and China met to discuss the terms on uniting the two but failed to reach an agreement, leaving the Korean Peninsula **divided in half at the 38th parallel**.

Some of the Best Korean War-Inspired Movies

Incheon Sangrykjakjeon 인천상륙작전
(Operation Chromite, 2016)

Taegeukgi Hwinallimyeo 태극기 휘날리며
(The Brotherhood of War, 2004)

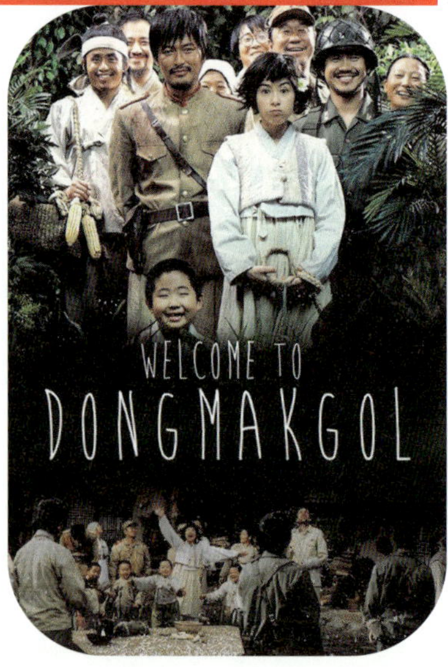

Welcome To Dongmakgol
웰컴투동막골, 2005

thank you to all the fallen heroes from around the world who lost their lives for the freedom of the Republic of Korea.

1960	April Revolution overthrows the autocratic Rhee administration. Rhee resigns and goes into exile. Yun Bo Seon becomes the President.
1961	General Park Chung Hee, overthrows the government through a military coup and becomes President.
1962	Start of the Five-year plans of South Korea.
1964	South Korea joins Vietnam War.
1970	Start of the government-operated New Community Movement.
1976	The Axe Murder Incident in Panmunjom, Joint Security Area, triggers the North Korean leader Kim Il-sung's first official apology to the South.
1977	South Korea celebrates 10 billion dollars gained by exports.
1979	President Park Chung Hee is assassinated by chief of KCIA (Korean Central Intelligence Agency), Kim Jaegyu.
1980	General Chun Doo Hwan gets military power through a coup and becomes the President. Gwangju Uprising. Martial Law is declared throughout the nation.
1987	June Democracy Movement overthrows the autocratic Chun regime. The ruling party of Fifth epublic, Democratic Justice Party, declares democratic elections.
1988	24th Summer Olympic Games held in Seoul.
1991	North Korea and South Korea join the United Nations (UN).
1992	South Korea's first satellite, KITSAT-1, 우리별 Uribyol is successfully launched.
1993	Test of Rodong-1, a single stage, mobile liquid propellant medium range ballistic missile by North Korea.
1994	Kim Jong Il takes control of North Korea upon the death of his father Kim Il-Sung. Start of the Arduous March.
1999	North Korea promises to freeze long-range missile tests.
2000	The first summit between North Korean leader Kim Jong Il and South Korean President Kim Dae Jung is held.
2002	The 2002 FIFA World Cup jointly held by Korea & Japan. North Korea pledges to extend moratorium on missile tests beyond 2003.
2006	Test of Taepodong-2 missile.
2007	The second summit is held, with Roh Moo-hyun (South) and Kim Jong Il (North) representing each side. North Korea fires short-range missile into the East Sea.
2010	North Korea launches missile and attacks Korean Pohang class corvette, ROKS Cheonan. In November, North Korean army rains artillery fire on Yeonpyeongdo island.
2011	Kim Jong Il dies, Kim Jong un takes over as the Supreme Leader of North Korea.

Rhee Syngman 이승만

Rhee Syngman 이승만 (March 26th, 1875 – July 19th, 1965), was the **first president of South Korea**. In his early years, he was forced to live in exile in Hawaii and Shanghai because of the nationalist activities he participated in against Japan during the Japanese Occupation. While in the U.S., he studied at George Washington University, Harvard, and Princeton University. Rhee originally served (1920 - 1925) as president of the **Korean Provisional Government in Shanghai**, until he was expelled by **Kim Ku**. From 1934 until 1944, he zealously campaigned in New York and Washington D.C., to with international support for **Korean independence.** Capitalizing on his closeness and familiarity with the United States, Rhee soon built up a mass political organization. As a result, Rhee was able to be elected as the first president of South Korea in 1948 and was re-elected for three consecutive terms following that. His presidency remains controversial among historians today because of his authoritarian government but is also highly regarded for his achievements as a strong anti-Communist, and for leading South Korea through the Korean War. His presidency ended in resignation following the **April Revolution**. He died in exile in Hawaii.

APRIL REVOLUTION

The April Revolution was a **large-scale uprising** led by labor and student groups, triggered by the discovery in **Masan Harbor** of the body of a high school student **Kim Ju-yul**, killed by a tear-gas shell during his participation in demonstrations against a fixed election by then ruling party of Korea in March 1960. As a result, a series of protests led to the eventual resignation of the Rhee administration and the transition to the Second Republic of South Korea.

Park Chung Hee 박정희

Park Chung Hee 박정희 (November 1917 – 26 October 1979) was a South Korean politician and general who served as the president of South Korea from 1963 to 1979, after seizing power through a **military coup** he led in 1961. Before he took over the control and became president, he was a military leader in the South Korean army and served as the chairman of the Supreme Council for National Reconstruction (1961 – 1963). Park's successful coup ended the interim government (Second Republic) and started the Third Republic. During his reign, he declared martial law and amended the constitution into a highly authoritarian form, termed the *yushin* 유신 **(reformation) Constitution**. Park led a series of monumental campaigns that transformed the devastated nation into an economic powerhouse, which is better known today as the "**Miracle on The Han River**." Despite the economic success, there was a political discourse among the people in the office, and Park was assassinated by **Kim Jae-gyu**, the then director of the **Korean Central Intelligence Agency (KCIA)**. After his death, South Korea's economic growth continued thanks to the strong foundations established under his leadership, but some also criticize that they were achieved at the expense of civil liberties.

WHO ARE THE "KIM DYNASTY"?

From Left: Kim Il-Sung, Kim Jong-Il, Kim Jong-Un

The "**Kim Dynasty**" is a tongue-in-cheek expression that refers to the absolute power of the **North Korean leadership**, which has been passed down for three generations, termed so because it's something you'd see in the dynastic era. Ever since he was named the first leader of the provisional communist government set up in the North by the Soviet Union after the division of Korea in 1945, he never gave up his ambition to unify Korea under a communist government.

As a result, he started the Korean War and committed numerous atrocities against the South, including military provocations and terrorist attacks on civilians. Domestically, he showed outstanding ability in political maneuvering. He further consolidated his absolute power through the reign of terror and ruthlessly purging political opponents who threatened his throne. Through *Juche Sasang* 주체사상 "Juche Ideology," which adopted and modified the communist ideology to be in line with North Korea's situation, the North Korean society developed a cult of individuality and worshipped him by calling *suryongnim* 수령님 ("Great Leader"). When he suddenly died in 1994, his body was embalmed and placed in a public mausoleum at the **Kumsusan Palace of the Sun 금수산 태양궁전** as has been the case with many other idolized communist leaders.

As a result of Kim Il-sung's death, his son Kim Jong-il was named leader after him, and was revered as *widaehan yongdoja* 위대한 영도자 ("Great Leader"). Kim Jong-ile was determined (or does it run in the family?) to carry on the late father's grand ambition to communize the South with force, and made numerous provocations such as terrorist attacks against the South Korean civilians (a Korean Air Flight 858 exploded in mid-air by a bomb set up by 2 North Korean spies), launching missiles, as well as developing nuclear missiles.

After Kim Jong-il's unexpected death was announced in 2011, his son Kim Jong-un, took over power and was immediately revered as a *choego yongdoja* 최고 영도자 ("Supreme Leader"). And because he studied in Switzerland as a child and experienced capitalism and freedom, people expected that he would lead North Korea to eventually open up, but instead, he chose the path of ruthless dictatorship like his ancestors. As of 2019, North Korea is recognized as a "de facto nuclear power" by the international community, which the three-generation regime has been using as a tactic to maintain its existence. In 2018, Kim Jong-un had an Inter-Korea summit with South Korea's **President Moon Jae-in 문재인** to discuss the official ending of the Korean War. The same year a U.S.-North Korea summit with President Donald Trump took place to discuss the possibility of completely abandoning nuclear weapons in return for massive economic aid while guaranteeing the existence of the Kim Jong-un regime. Permanent peace on the Korean Peninsula seemed to be within reach, but due to the wide disagreements on the terms, no tangible results have come from the negotiation at this time.

WHAT IS THE "BAEKDU BLOODLINE"?

Bakedu heyoltong 백두혈통 ("Baekdu Bloodline.") The term "**Baekdu**" comes from **Baekdusan 백두산** ("Mount Baekdu,") a sacred, and the tallest mountain, on the Korean Peninsula, which North Korea claims to be the base of **Kim Il-sung**'s anti-Japanese activities, as well as the birthplace of **Kim Jong-il**. However, critics claim that these words were entirely made up by Kim Il-sung's son, Kim Jong-il, to justify the succession of power within the family. In 2013 the Ten Principles for the Establishment of a Monolithic Ideological System proclaimed,"The supreme leader in North Korea can only be of Baekdu Bloodline," and **Kim Jong-un**'s power is expected to remain for a considerable amount of time.

DID YOU KNOW THAT KOREA IS STILL AT WAR?

Although the Korean Armistice Agreement was signed on July 27th, 1953, no peace treaty was signed, which means technically, South and North Korea are still at war. In 2018, the leaders of South and North Korea met at the **Demilitarized Zone (DMZ)** to discuss the matter.

WHY DO KOREAN MALES HAVE TO GO TO THE MILITARY?

All Korean males, including your favorite K-Pop idols and K-Drama actors, who have reached the **age of 18** and meet a certain level of physical, mental, and academic requirements, are required to serve in the military for a **minimum of 18 months** (more for the Navy and Air Force). The timing of enlistment may be deferred for reasons permitted by law. Also, if you win an international competition or sports event (such as the Olympics or an international music competition) or receive a certain level of prize set forth by law, you are exempted from military service—though you are still required to receive basic military training for four weeks. If it's difficult to serve in the regular military for various reasons, alternative service can be performed, such as working as public service personnel or at a designated enterprise selected by the Commissioner of the Military Manpower Administration.

As of 2025, a Private Second Class receives ₩750,000 per month (about $535 USD), a Private First Class receives ₩900,000 (about $640 USD), a Corporal receives ₩1,200,000 (about $855 USD), and a Sergeant receives ₩1,500,000 (about $1,070 USD) per month. For a Sergeant First Class, the total monthly income can reach ₩2,050,000 (about $1,465 USD) when including the government-supported Soldiers' Future Preparation Savings Fund. South Korea's 2025 minimum wage is ₩10,030 per hour. Based on a 40-hour workweek, this translates to a monthly wage of approximately ₩2,096,270 (about $1,495 USD). The Sergeant's total monthly income of ₩2.05 million (about $1,465 USD) is about ₩46,000 (about $33 USD) lower than the minimum wage monthly salary.

However, considering the unique circumstances of fulfilling mandatory military service, it is viewed as significant progress that soldiers' pay has effectively reached the minimum wage level. For comparison, in 2020, a Sergeant's monthly salary was about ₩540,000 (roughly $385 USD), which was only about 30% of the minimum wage at the time. This change reflects the government's growing commitment to improving social compensation for military service. While in the military, anyone—including entertainers—cannot engage in commercial activities such as appearing on TV or performing at concerts, which can cause significant career setbacks for those at their prime (though, of course, it affects all Korean men alike). Fans of globally renowned K-Pop bands have even petitioned the government to grant exemptions for achievements that elevate national prestige, arguing they should be treated on par with winning international competitions, but to no avail.

Mandatory military service also brings several social issues. Some of the rich and powerful have been criticized for using dishonest methods to have their sons exempted from enlistment, sparking public outrage over fairness and privilege.

WHAT IS DMZ? THE SCARIEST PLACE ON EARTH!

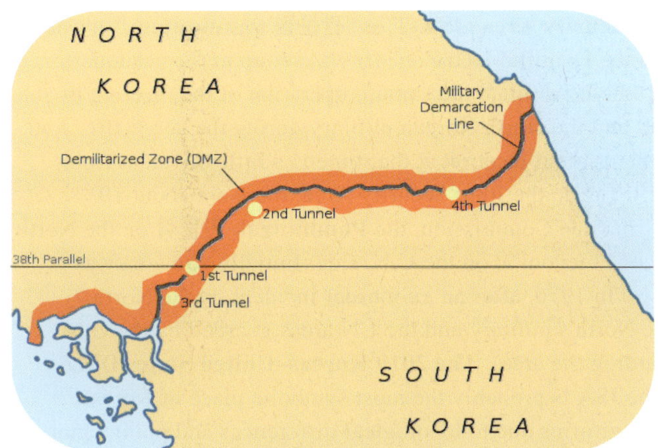

The Demilitarized Zone in Korea

What is the scariest place you can think of? A haunted house? That's cute. According to Bill Clinton, the **Demilitarized Zone (DMZ)** is the scariest place on earth. The DMZ is a 4 km-long (up 2 km north and down 2 km south from the **Military Demarcation Line (MDL)** neutral zone created as a result of the armistice agreement in 1953 and is the most heavily-guarded border on Earth. While military activities of any type are strictly prohibited here, this is where one of the Earth's most intense confrontations is taking place, even at this very moment. The descendants of the sworn enemies - North Korean soldiers, South Korean soldiers, and the United Nations forces, are watching each other around the clock, separated by a massive minefield and barbed wire fences. The tension and stress are so enormous that a single mistake could easily trigger a shootout and lead to a full-blown war. Anyone standing here would agree with what Bill Clinton said.

Three ROK soldiers watching the border at Panmunjeom in the DMZ between North and South Korea.

DMZ viewed from the North

Gongdong Gyeongbi Guyeok JSA 공동경비구역
(*Joint Security Area*, 2000)

JOINT SECURITY AREA – SLEEPING WITH THE ENEMY

Called the "**Military Armistice Commission Joint Security Area (JSA),**" or "**판문점 Panmunjom,**" it's an area located along the Military Demarcation Line in the Demilitarized Zone. It was set up at the headquarters of the Military Armistice Commission in October 1953 to facilitate the smooth operation of the meeting by the U.N. Forces, the Chinese People's Assistance Force, and the North Korean military during the cease-fire. And this is where the armistice agreement was signed (the original location at that time is a little different from now because it was located slightly above the MDL). Inside the Joint Security Area, there are about 10 buildings, including the main hall of the Military Armistice Commission, the **Panmungak 판문각** on the North Korean side, and the **Jayueuijip 자유의집** ("House of Freedom"), on the U.N. side. Initially, the area was jointly guarded by the U.N. and North Korean forces. In 1976, after an ax-murder incident by the North Korean military, the North areas are guarded by the North's military and the UN areas guarded by the U.N. forces (since 2014, South Korea is in charge of guarding the area). **The 2019 Koreas–United States DMZ Summit** was also held at the House of Freedom. The JSA is probably the most symbolic place of Korea's division where Koreans are put in different military uniforms due to ideological differences and point a gun at each other. It's possible to visit the JSA through a group tour, but for those who can't, I highly recommend watching this amazing movie titled ***Gongdong Gyeongbi Guyeok JSA* 공동경비구역** (*Joint Security Area*, **2000**) as an alternative.

CAN NORTH KOREANS AND SOUTH KOREANS UNDERSTAND EACH OTHER?

Yes and no. Essentially, both South and North Korea speak Korean, with only minor differences. Since they share the same grammar rules—including word order and sentence structure—they are not considered two separate languages, but rather different dialects of Korean. The main distinctions lie in intonation, pronunciation, and especially vocabulary. For instance, South Korean tends to adopt and use many foreign words as they are, whereas North Korean replaces them with what it calls "pure Korean" alternatives. Moreover, even shared words can differ in specific terms or expressions. The gap widens further in technical or professional language, to the point where communication can sometimes feel like speaking two different languages. In short, South Koreans and North Koreans can understand each other, but it's not always effortless.

	SOUTH KOREA	**NORTH KOREA**
Tunnel	터널 Tunnel	차굴 *chagul* "Car Tunnel"
Front Light	헤드라이트 Headlight	앞등 *apdeung* "Front Light"
Mother-in-Law	시어머니 *shieomeoni*	아고 *ago*

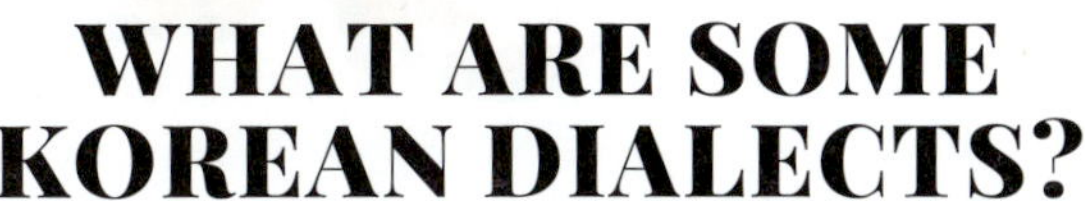

WHAT ARE SOME KOREAN DIALECTS?

Gyeongsang-do 경상도 dialect is tonal, which means the intonation or pitch in which a sound is spoken affects the meaning. Also, many sentences are spoken in a literary style and end with "*~da*" "~**다**," "*no*" "~**노**," and "*na*" "~**나**."

Chungcheong-do 충청도 dialect is perceived to be slower than other dialects, even in emergency situations. But it actually sounds like that because the end of the sentence is drawn out. Also, sentences end with "*~yeo*" "~**여**," "*~gyeo*" "~**겨**," and "*~yu*" "~**유**." For example, "*haesseoyo*" "**했어요**" ("I did") is "*haesseoyu*-" "**했어유**," with the end drawn out.

Jeolla-do 전라도 dialect has a variety of accent-heavy rejoinders, such as "*atta*" "**아따**," (boy/gee!) and "*chammallo*" "**참말로**," (really/seriously). Also, many sentences end with "*ranke*" "~**랑께**," and "*bureo*" "~**부러**."

Jeju-do 제주도 dialect is the most unique one compared to others, as Jeju Island is separated from the inland by the sea. One of the examples is the structure of an interrogative sentence. "*-haetsseo?*" "-**했어?**" "did you do it?" is "*haen*?" "~**핸**?" in Jeju dialect. *Eoseo oseyo* "**어서오세요**" "Welcome," is *honjeo opseo*" "**혼저옵서**" in Jeju dialect.

WHY DO KOREANS SAY "I GO" SO MUCH?

Why do Korean people say "**I go**" even when they are not going anywhere? What you hear is *aigo/aigoo* **아이고/아이구** , which is an interjection for "oops" or "oh, man," which can be used to show frustration, embarrassment, and surprise, like when you drop something or see someone hit their pinky toe on the furniture! It can also be used when you are scolding someone.

For example, "*Aigoo*! Did you catch a cold? Didn't I tell you to bundle up?"

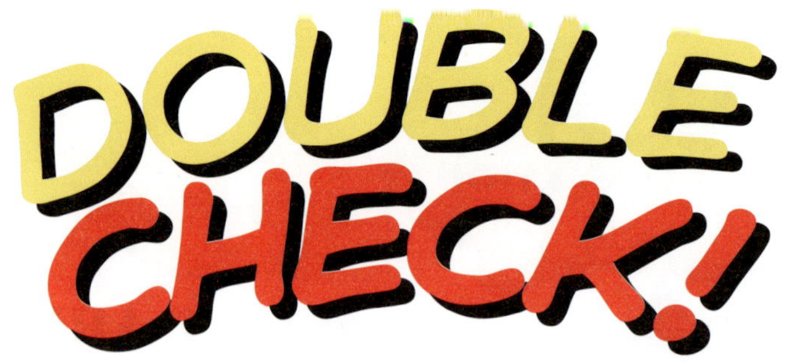

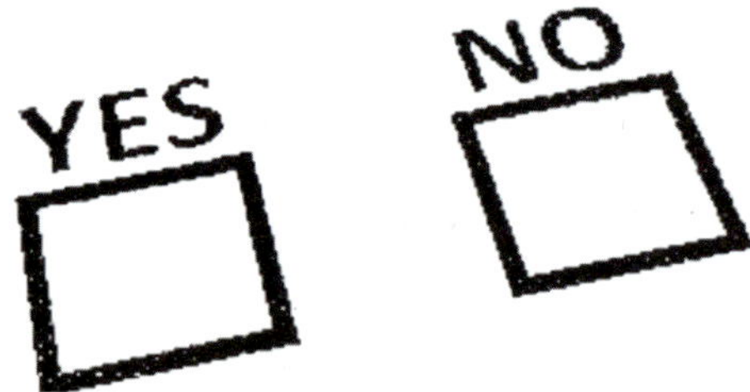

English Teacher: "You didn't do your homework?"

Korean Student: "*No*, teacher."

English Teacher: "What? You're going to fail the class then."

Korean Student: "Why? I *did* my homework."

English Teacher: "You just said you didn't do your homework."

Korean Student: "No teacher, I said I *did* my homework."

English Teacher: Okay, let's take a roll. Cheol-su? Isn't Cheol-su here?

Korean Student: *Yes*, teacher.

English Teacher: Well, I don't see him? Where is he?

Korean Student: I said Cheol-su is *not* here, teacher!

Do you see what's going on?

In the first exchange the Korean student's "No" actually meant, "No — I did do my homework."
In the second, the student's "No" answers the whole question "Is Cheol-su here?" (i.e., "No, Cheol-su is not here.") Koreans often negate or confirm the entire proposition rather than directly echoing the verb-focused short answer English speakers expect.

So when you speak English with a Korean speaker, it's wise to double-check what they meant.
Confusing? Yes? No? (Which "Yes/No" do you mean?)

"PUSAN" AND "BUSAN" AND "CHANG" AND "JANG" WHY THE DIFFERENT SPELLINGS FOR THE SAME NAME?

Until 2011, the **Pusan International Film Festival (PIFF)** was held in **Busan**, not Pusan. At first glance, it might seem like Pusan and Busan are two different places with similar names. But in reality, they refer to the exact same city — just spelled differently. So why the disparity?

The root of this issue lies in the existence of **two romanization systems** for the Korean language. The older one, known as the **McCune–Reischauer System**, was used **between 1984 and 2000**. It represented Korean consonants as follows: **K** for ㄱ, **T** for ㄷ, **P** for ㅍ, and **CH** for ㅈ. The current **Revised Romanization System**, adopted in **2000**, instead uses **G** for ㄱ, **D** for ㄷ, **B** for ㅂ, and **J** for ㅈ. Linguists argued that this new system more accurately reflects the actual sounds of Korean. When the Pusan International Film Festival was first launched in 1996, "**Pusan**" was the correct spelling according to the system then in use. However, in **2011**, the festival committee officially changed its name to **Busan International Film Festival (BIFF)** to align with the revised romanization system — finally resolving the inconsistency. You can see similar examples in other words. For instance, older English-language Korean books might write *gimchi* instead of kimchi, and Korean surnames such as **Jang** and **Jo** were formerly spelled **Chang** and **Cho**, respectively.

This coexistence of two different systems caused plenty of confusion for foreigners traveling in Korea — imagine relying on an outdated guidebook searching for "Pusan," only to discover there's no such place! Fortunately, the old system is gradually disappearing, and today, the revised version is used almost universally.

WHY DO KOREANS MAKE A FIST WHEN TAKING A PICTURE?

Remember? Koreans are known for their "can-do" spirit, and the expression *hwaiting* 화이팅 (Fighting/Let's go!) is used frequently in everyday conversation. The fist-making gesture in photos symbolizes resolution and determination, because there's nothing like saying hwaiting to promote harmony and unity among people.

YOU SAY CHEESE? KOREANS SAY *KIMCHI*!

Another popular option is saying *kimchi* when taking a picture. Just like saying "cheese" or "whisky" (or "whiskey," for your Irish readers), it naturally makes the corners of your mouth turn up, creating a bright smile.

WHY ARE KOREANS ALWAYS IN A HURRY?

When asked about the most impressive characteristic of Koreans, foreigners almost always pick ***ppali ppali*** 빨리빨리 ("quickly, quickly") as their number one answer. Besides ***hwaiting*** 화이팅, the expression of the Korean "can-do" spirit, ppali ppali represents the "Let's get it done fast" attitude that reflects the efficiency-oriented nature of the Korean people. Some say this mindset is what made it possible for the nation to recover so quickly from the scars of war. But it has its downsides, too. Because it prioritizes speed over everything else, taking shortcuts by bending rules or skipping the manual was once common—and often overlooked. As a result, it sometimes led to poor-quality work and even tragic man-made disasters. However, Koreans learned quickly from their mistakes, and such practices are now fading as compliance and workplace safety are more strictly enforced today. Now, let's take a look at some of the positive sides of the *ppali ppali* spirit—the ones that have made daily life in Korea incredibly fast and convenient.

WHY ARE KOREAN DELIVERIES SO FAST?

CHINESE FOOD DELIVERY AND THE ICONIC "STEEL CONTAINER"

Koreans had been enjoying food delivery long before smartphones existed. Among the most popular was Chinese food delivery, featuring the iconic ***cheolgabang*** 철가방—a "steel container" used by Chinese restaurants for decades. Whether you're picnicking at the Han River or gaming at a PC Bang, there's no need to worry—the cheolgabang man will find you.

QUICK SERVICE!

We may be talking about drone deliveries in the rest of the world, but in Korea, there's already Quick Service! It's a private courier system where couriers safely and swiftly deliver anything—from documents to large boxes—often within an hour or less.

TAEKBAE – 1 DAY SHIPPING

Korean ***taekbae*** 택배 (parcel delivery) is extremely fast and reliable. Place an order today, and you can expect your package to arrive the next day, delivered right to your door with a smile.

SUPER FAST INTERNET

According to DataReportal, South Korea's median fixed-internet download speed in early 2025 was 175.18 Mbps, while the median mobile internet download speed reached 148.34 Mbps.

In global rankings, World Population Review reports South Korea's average fixed broadband speed as 202.61 Mbps, placing it among the top in the world.

WHY DO KOREANS LOVE INTERNET EXPLORER?

Just up until the early 2010s, Internet Explorer (IE) was pretty much the only browser used in Korea. For this reason, many websites, including e-government systems, banking, and a majority of online games, were developed for IE using non-standard codes and ActiveX, which had died out long ago. As a result, some of those outdated pages are still causing compatibility issues and give Korean people (and foreigners!) a major headache. Even after Microsoft officially ended support for Internet Explorer in 2022, many older Korean websites continued to rely on it for several more years. Although most systems have now switched to modern browsers like Chrome or Edge, the legacy of IE still remains deeply rooted in Korea's online environment.

WHAT IS "OFFICIAL ID CERTIFICATE" FOR ONLINE USE IN KOREA?

Known as *gongin injeungseo* 공인인증서, or "Official ID Certificate," it's a type of digital ID card used for various online activities including online banking and shopping. While it sounds like an awesome way to prevent digital fraud, there were many hoops to jump through to get it. Also, maintaining it (it had to be renewed each year with a fee) and using it (sometimes you had to install the visiting site's proprietary software) were quite pesky, too. Since 2020, however, the government has abolished the mandatory use of the old certificate system, and now users can easily verify their identity with mobile authentication apps such as KakaoTalk, PASS, or Naver Certificate instead.

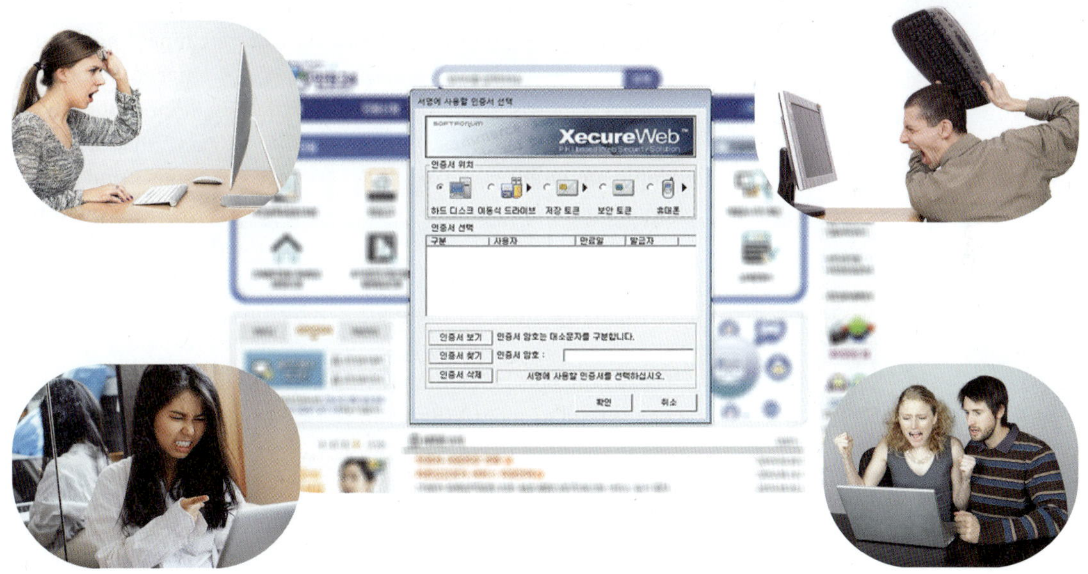

GOOGLE IT? YOU MEAN LOOK IT UP ON NAVER?

Google is a household name for an Internet search engine in the U.S., but if you say "Google it," then people in Korea will most likely whip out their smartphone, open the green app called Naver, and make a search query in the green box. Naver is still widely used because it provides localized results, blogs, and shopping links all in one place.

WHY DO KOREANS SAY THEY ARE A NATION OF "PURE BLOODED KOREANS"?

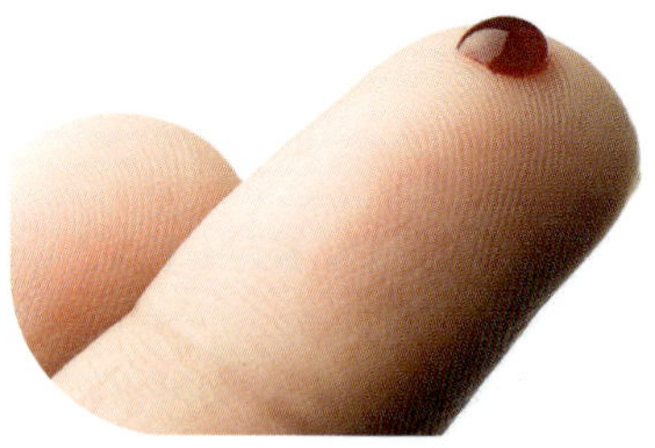

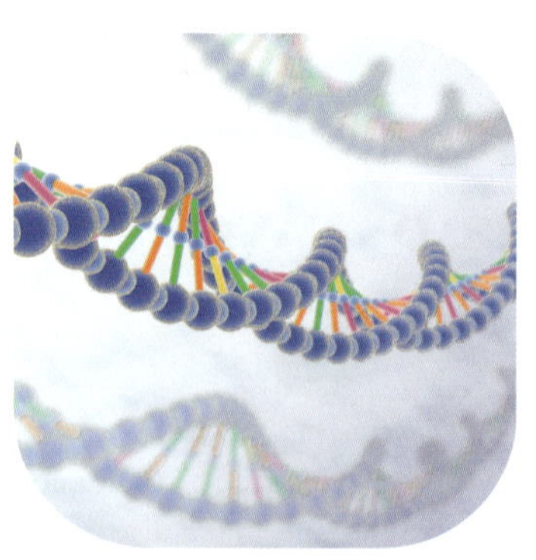

The phrase *"Korea is a single-race (homogeneous) nation"* is something most Koreans have learned in school, and it's an idea so deeply embedded that few ever think to question it. Since the country's first kingdom, **Gojoseon 고조선**, Koreans have regarded themselves as the main members of the nation, calling themselves *baedal minjok* **배달민족** — "The Baedal People" — where Baedal refers to ancient Korea. They spoke the same language and shared the same history and cultural background, unlike many other nations composed of multiple ethnic groups. Over time, this idea of a **"single-race nation"** came to be interpreted as **"pure-blooded."**

But are Koreans really "pure-blooded," made up of only Koreans?

Recent DNA research by Professor Kim Wook of Dankook University's Department of Bioscience suggests otherwise. According to genetic studies, Koreans share genotypes common among Mongolians, Eastern and Southern Siberians, as well as Southeast Asians and Northern and Southern Chinese populations. Koreans were found to be most genetically similar to Manchurian peoples in northeastern China, and partially similar to the Miao of China and Vietnamese populations. This indicates that the Korean people are largely a mixed race between the northern and southern regions of Asia — which isn't surprising considering that Korea has been invaded nearly a thousand times throughout its history.

So where did this "pure-blooded" myth come from?

These concepts, sometimes viewed as insular or nationalistic today, once served as a unifying national philosophy, holding the Korean people together like a glue during times of foreign invasion and Japanese colonial rule. Historians now suggest that it should be understood as a shared cultural lineage rather than a literal bloodline. In recent decades, Korea's immigrant and multicultural population has been rapidly increasing, giving rise to many multicultural families.

As society becomes more diverse, many argue that being Korean should not depend on one's appearance or ancestry, but rather on the culture and identity one embraces. In that sense, those who live by Korean values and participate in Korean society can also be seen as part of the "single Korean race" in a modern, cultural sense.

WHY DO KOREANS HOLD THEIR NECK WHEN THEY GET OUT OF THEIR CAR AFTER A MINOR FENDER-BENDER?

Young-mi, a college girl, zones out behind the wheel for a fraction of a second and bonk! It's a fender bender. It can't be too bad—it was more like a little push! She gets out of the car to assess the damage, and luckily, there's not even a hint of a scratch on the bumper. No need to call the police or the insurance company!

But guess what? The *ajusshi* 아저씨 from the other car gets out, holding the back of his neck, his face contorted with pain! Wait a minute… you can't be serious, right? And the ajusshi insists that he goes to the hospital and gets treated for a while.

No matter how big or small the accident is, it's a cliché scene in Korean dramas. Of course, the neck is the most vulnerable part of the body susceptible to injury in a car accident—but why the oversell in a harmless "contact" between two cars?

These people, known as **"nylon patients"** 나일론 환자—with "nylon," a type of synthetic fiber, implying something "fake"—try to receive a large amount of settlement money from the insurance company of the driver at fault by exaggerating or faking their injuries. They take advantage of a legal loophole: if a medical certificate is issued by a cooperating medical institution, the driver at fault will be held responsible even if insurance fraud is suspected. This situation tends to occur more often to female drivers, who are sometimes seen as easier targets.

DAERIGISA - DRUNK? DON'T DRIVE AND CALL THE "DRIVER FOR HIRE"

It goes without saying that drinking and driving is a very dangerous act. But in Korea, you don't have to worry too much—because there's a special service that lets you hire a driver who drives your car for you when you've been drinking. Known as *daerigisa* 대리기사, literally "driver-for-hire," this is a very convenient service that sends a driver to your location to take you (and your car) safely to your destination. You can request one through a quick phone call or a smartphone app, and they usually arrive within minutes. It's a popular after-work side job, especially in today's gig economy. Many retired people also find it a valid source of income, though it's not always easy—they often have to work late into the night and deal with drunk or unruly customers.

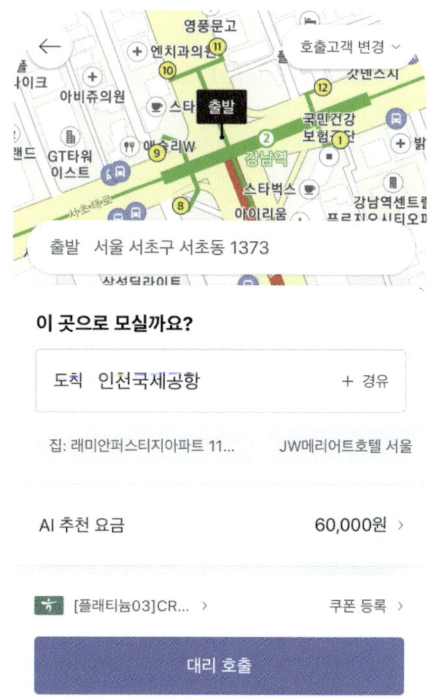

WHY DO KOREAN CARS HAVE BLUE SPONGES ON THEIR DOORS?

If you drive around Korea, you might notice vehicles with little blue sponge blocks stuck on their doors—and foreigners are often curious about them since they're rarely seen anywhere else. So, what are they?

These small blue sponges are protectors for cars that have just been released from the factory. Automakers attach them to prevent dents and scratches when opening doors in tight lots. Interestingly, many new car owners decide to keep them on even after purchase because parking spaces in Korea are notoriously narrow. It's a uniquely Korean way of being considerate toward fellow drivers—and, of course, avoiding the hassle of paying for someone else's door repairs.

WHY DO KOREANS TAKE A POOP SQUATTING?

Squats may be the king of leg exercises—but Koreans have long been doing them not in the gym, but in the bathroom! While squat toilets are now mostly found in older buildings, rural areas, or some parts of Seoul, they were once the standard across the country. Many younger Koreans—and especially tourists from the West—find it hard to adjust to this "different" defecation posture, even though squat toilets were once common in many other regions too, including Southern Europe and Africa. (They're even called "French toilets" in parts of the Middle East and "Turkish toilets" in Western Europe!)

With modernization, Western-style sit toilets have gradually replaced traditional squat toilets. There's even a running joke that the average leg strength of Koreans has declined because people no longer squat as much as they used to!

WHY DO KOREAN RESTROOMS ASK YOU TO TOSS TOILET PAPER IN A BASKET?

After doing your business (#2), it seems obvious to toss used toilet paper into the toilet and flush it. But in some public restrooms in Korea, you might spot a sign saying, "Please throw used toilet paper in the trash can." Not the most pleasant thought, right?

This practice stems from older plumbing systems. To conserve water, many public restrooms were designed with smaller tank capacities, meaning weaker flush pressure. Tossing paper into the toilet could easily clog the pipes, so people were encouraged to use the trash bin instead. However, this method isn't exactly sanitary or visually pleasant. Nowadays, most public restrooms use dissolvable toilet paper and improved plumbing systems, so the "flush-it-all" method is becoming the new norm across Korea.

WHY ARE CLEAVAGES A NO-NO! BUT MINISKIRTS ARE OK?

What's considered "too revealing" really depends on where you're from. If you come from the West, Korea's standards might surprise you. In Korea, showing legs is perfectly fine—and the *haeuishiljong fashion* 하의실종 패션, literally "**missing-pants fashion**," or "**the full Donald**") once swept the streets among young women without much controversy. But showing cleavage? That's a big no-no. Clothes that reveal too much of the upper body are often viewed as too "racy," which is the complete opposite of Western fashion norms. Some foreign brands have even admitted to raising their V-necklines when producing clothing for the Korean market.

WHY ARE GUNS/KNIVES/TATTOOS BLURRED ON TV?

 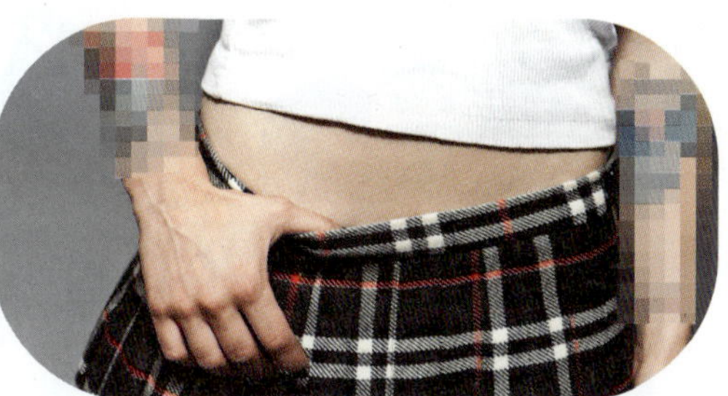

The Korea Communications Standards Commission (KCSC) sets clear rules for what can and cannot be shown on television.

- Graphic Violence:
  - Explicit depictions of beheadings, dismemberment, or brutal killings involving weapons such as guns and knives are strictly prohibited.
  - Such scenes may only appear if absolutely necessary for the plot.
- Smoking and "Decadent" Behavior:
  - Even smoking scenes are often blurred.
  - Regulations emphasize promoting "a sound civic spirit and lifestyle."
  - Content involving lewdness, decadence, drugs, drinking, smoking, superstition, gambling, or profligacy must be handled with great caution.
- Tattoos:
  - Tattoos are not legally banned, but most networks voluntarily blur them.
  - This practice is especially enforced during the "Juvenile Viewing Protection Time Zone" to protect young viewers' emotional development.

Will these restrictions last forever? Probably not. There was a time when dyed hair on K-pop idols was frowned upon, forcing them to cover their colorful styles with hats or bandanas. But those days are long gone. As modern audiences become more globalized, many now argue that over-censorship limits creativity and disrupts storytelling.

THEN WHY ARE BRANDS/LOGOS BLURRED?

Unlike violence or nudity, blurred logos have nothing to do with censorship—it's all about business. Brands and logos are masked on Korean TV to avoid unintended advertising or sponsorship conflicts. Only contracted sponsors can have their products shown on screen. This is why you'll often see a talk show table covered with drinks whose labels are carefully hidden—unless, of course, it's a **PPL (Product Placement)** deal. In that case, the product is not only visible but also strategically placed for maximum exposure.

WHY DO KOREAN TV SHOWS HAVE SUBTITLES?

"Bam!" "Whack!" "LOL!" "You gotta be kidding!"

Watching Korean variety shows can feel like reading a comic book. Speech bubbles, captions, and sound-effect subtitles pop up constantly on screen.

This style actually came from Japanese variety shows, but when Korean producers introduced it in the 1990s, audiences weren't initially impressed. Over time, though, it became one of the hallmarks of Korean entertainment TV.

These on-screen texts don't just add humor—they help viewers follow the story, highlight funny moments, and display key information like guest names or punchlines. Each program even develops its own "subtitling style," reflecting the personality of its writers and producers.

A prime example is MBC's *Muhandojeon* 무한도전 (*Infinity Challenge*, **2005**), which earned a massive fan base thanks to its clever, witty captions that elevated every joke.

WHAT IS KAKAOTALK THAT EVERYBODY USES?

Katok hae*!** 카톡해! (Kakaotalk me!) has replaced "Call me" in Korea, where everyone seems to communicate through the iconic yellow smartphone app. Originally developed as a free instant messaging service, KakaoTalk now offers numerous convenient features like voice calls, video chats, and group chats. Among all, what really sets it apart is the huge selection of emoticons that Koreans love to use to express their emotions. As of 2017, it was used by 93% of Korean smartphone owners (a de facto monopoly), and it continues to expand into new areas such as taxi-hailing, ***daerigisa ("driver-for-hire") booking, banking, and "gifticons" (electronic vouchers).

WHY DO KOREANS LOVE "KKK"?

If you have a Korean pen-pal—well, actually, a chat-pal in this day and age—you might have received a message saying "**KKK**" from your Korean friend. Wait a minute… Is this some kind of secret invitation to a notorious hate group? It possibly can't be! But then you keep seeing it again and again. One day you finally ask your friend, only to find out it's totally innocent—it's actually the romanized form of ㅋㅋㅋ, the Korean equivalent of "**LOL**." Why does your friend use it even when chatting in English? Maybe they're too lazy to switch their keyboard, or they assume you can understand Korean expressions. Either way, now you know that your Korean chat-pal is completely harmless—and just laughing out loud in Korean!

WHY DO KOREANS GET SO MUCH PLASTIC SURGERY?

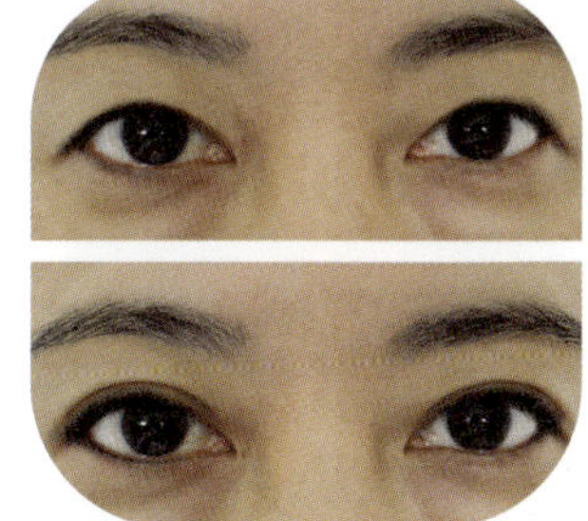

"Women are never guilty of their transformation." This famous slogan from a 1980s South Korean TV commercial captures not only the universal desire for beauty but also the Korean tendency to place great importance on appearance. As many foreigners believe, plastic surgery is indeed very common in Korea and easily accessible—even to foreign visitors who travel there for cosmetic procedures. But for many Koreans, the motivation goes beyond aesthetics. The traditional belief in ***gwansang*** 관상 (physiognomy)—the idea that the harmony of one's facial features influences their fate—still plays a role. Naturally, many people want to "improve" their appearance, and perhaps their destiny, through minor procedures before important life events like job interviews. Only God knows how much influence this truly has on interviewers, but if a new look boosts one's confidence and helps them live more fully, then perhaps their fate really does become a little brighter. The most popular procedures are double eyelid surgery and nose jobs, particularly those that raise the nose tip and bridge.

WHY DO KOREANS WEAR FACE MASKS?

WHY DO KOREANS WEAR FACE MASKS?

A world burned to the ground by nuclear war, with survivors wandering in masks—these post-apocalyptic scenes have long been a daily reality in Korea. Long before the pandemic, Koreans were already accustomed to wearing masks as part of their everyday lives. The main culprit is fine dust, or particulate matter, much of which drifts in from coal-burning factories in China, combined with pollution generated domestically and by car exhaust. Another major cause is "Yellow Dust," when dry soil particles from China and the Mongolian deserts are carried by wind, forming dust storms that sweep across the Korean Peninsula. Ironically, this long-standing habit of mask-wearing played a key role in preventing the spread of infectious diseases such as MERS-CoV and COVID-19. Even after the pandemic, many Koreans continue to wear masks—partly out of habit, partly out of courtesy when they have a cold, and sometimes simply to avoid unwanted attention or go out without makeup.

WHAT THE HECK DOES "GANGNAM STYLE" MEAN?

"Oppa Gangnam Style!" 오빠 강남스타일!

When the song **Gangnam Style** became a global hit in 2012, everyone was dancing to the famous horse-riding move, yet 99% of non-Koreans had no idea what the phrase actually meant—just like how most people danced to Macarena without understanding a word of Spanish. So, what the heck does Gangnam Style mean?

Gang 강 means "**river**," and *nam* 남 means "**south**," so **Gangnam** 강남 literally means "**the region south of the Han River**." But the term has taken on a much deeper cultural meaning—it now refers to the most affluent area of Seoul, commonly called the "Gangnam 3-gu" 강남 3구: **Gangnam-gu, Seocho-gu,** and **Songpa-gu.** These districts are known for having the highest housing prices in Korea and the largest concentration of wealthy residents, although many "old money" chaebol families still reside north of the river, in **Gangbuk 강북**.

Gangnam (not to be confused with a singer's name) represents Korean affluence and ambition. It's filled with luxury boutiques, high-end department stores, entertainment companies, and sleek office towers, often compared to Beverly Hills in the U.S. or Roppongi in Japan. It's home to CEOs, startup founders, and celebrities—people seen as the faces of success. In Korean pop culture, however, Gangnam residents are sometimes portrayed as superficial or overly obsessed with money and appearance.

Interestingly, Gangnam's development was Korea's first large-scale "planned city" project and remains the country's most successful urban transformation. One major reason the south side of the river was chosen for expansion was its distance from the Demilitarized Zone (DMZ)—a precaution against possible North Korean attacks.

So, back to the original question: when Psy sings, "Oppa Gangnam Style," he's not just saying he's from Gangnam—it's a playful boast that roughly means, *"Look at me, I'm balling!"*

HONG GIL DONG – THE JOHN DOE OF KOREA

Hong Gil-dong 홍길동 was the head of a bandit group in the Chungcheong-do area during the Joseon Dynasty, but he's more famous as the fictional hero of *Honggildongjeon* 홍길동전 (The Story of Hong Gil-dong) written by **Heo Gyun 허균**. The novel portrays him as a "righteous outlaw" who punishes corrupt officials and helps the poor—much like Robin Hood.

However, his fame today has little to do with his heroic deeds. In modern Korea, Hong Gil-dong is used as the default placeholder name on official forms and documents, much like "John Doe" in English. So, why Mr. Hong? There's no official rule designating his name, but experts suggest it's because it meets the following criteria:

- It's well-known to everyone.
- It's the name of a fictional character, so people recognize it as generic (even though a real person by that name existed, most think of the fictional one).
- It avoids real historical figures to prevent possible claims from descendants.
- It carries a positive image and doesn't cause discomfort.

Additionally, each syllable of Hong Gil-dong follows the full Korean syllable structure—consonant, vowel, and final consonant, *batchim* 받침. This makes it a perfect linguistic example as well.

And the Korean equivalent of **Jane Doe**? That would be **Hong Gil-sun 홍길순**.

What Does A Korean Name Stand For? How Can I Decode it? P. 22

SYMBOL OF LOYALTY - JINDO DOG

The **Jindo dog 진돗개**, native to Jindo Island in **South Jeolla Province**, symbolizes loyalty, bravery, and intelligence. Known for their fierce devotion, they often serve only one master—making them difficult to rehome once bonded. One famous story tells of a Jindo dog that returned to its original owner after traveling more than 300 kilometers (about 186 miles) over seven months. Their faithfulness is so admired that the Jindo breed was designated as **Natural Treasure No. 53** of South Korea in 1962.

EVERY KID'S DREAM – MAKE MONEY PLAYING VIDEO GAMES IN KOREA

It's every kid's dream: make money—not just pocket change, but a fortune—by playing video games! Sounds too good to be true, right? Well, in Korea, gaming is serious business. Video games (especially PC games) are officially recognized by the government as **eSports**, and being a professional gamer is a legitimate career that you can proudly list on your résumé.

Take **Lee Sang-hyeok**, better known as "**Faker**", the legendary **League of Legends** player. In 2019 alone, he earned over $1.2 million USD in prize money from more than 40 tournaments worldwide. Backed by his team SKT (owned by the telecom giant), his income from sponsorships and commercials made him one of Korea's highest-paid athletes. Another iconic name is **Lim Yo-hwan**, known by his in-game ID "**SlayerS_`BoxeR**", a **StarCraft** legend revered as one of Korea's first eSports heroes. At the peak of the eSports boom, Korea had multiple cable channels dedicated to broadcasting video game tournaments. Corporate-sponsored teams paid salaries comparable to those of professional sports players, and finals filled entire stadiums—like the 2014 League of Legends World Championship at Seoul World Cup Stadium, where 40,000 fans cheered live.

Though "YouTuber" may have replaced "pro gamer" as today's top dream job, eSports remains deeply embedded in Korean culture—enjoyed by people of all ages and backgrounds.

PC BANG – THE TOTAL ENTERTAINMENT HUB
FOR THE DIGITAL GENERATION

If you're an eSports fan, you may have wondered: what's the secret behind Korea's dominance in gaming?

The answer lies in infrastructure—specifically, the *PC bang* (피씨방, or "PC room"). No matter where you go in Korea, even in the smallest rural towns, you'll find a PC bang. Inside, rows of high-end gaming computers fill the space, often large enough to hold hundreds of players. While it may look like a training ground for future pro gamers, it's really a casual entertainment venue for anyone wanting to unwind, play a few rounds, or even go on a casual date.

The best part? The food. Many PC bangs serve everything from self-serve instant noodles to full meals prepared by staff—delivered right to your seat. For the average couch potato, it's gaming paradise.

Some PC bangs even offer showers and sleeping areas for overnight stays, catering to both hardcore gamers and exhausted office workers. For many, it's not just a gaming spot—it's a home away from home.

IT'S MIDNIGHT AND KIDS SHOULD BE AT HOME - "CINDERELLA LAW"

Do you know where your children are? The "Cinderella Law" (also called the "Cinderella Act") stipulated that kids under the age of 16 were not allowed to access PC games between 12 a.m. and 6 a.m., and that in-game screens must feature a warning about video game addiction.

However, this law was abolished as of January 1, 2022. Since then, the mandatory restrictions have been lifted, and instead, the government has been encouraging voluntary self-regulation among teenagers, while enhancing counseling, education, and treatment programs to help those struggling with excessive gaming.

MUKBANG - YOU CAN ALSO MAKE MONEY BROADCASTING YOUR EATING SESSION!

Becoming a pro gamer seems like a long shot because you're all fingers and thumbs? Don't give up just yet—there's another great way to make money if you love food and have a healthy appetite!

Known as *mukbang* 먹방—a compound word of *meokneun* 먹는 ("**eating**") and *bangsong* 방송 ("**broadcast**")—it refers to a **live-streamed eating show**. The host typically wows viewers by devouring huge portions of food, from instant noodles to supersized pizzas. For example, YouTuber **Tzuyang 쯔양** once ate six cups of instant noodles in 10 minutes and 170 chicken McNuggets in a single sitting!

But mukbang isn't just about eating—it's about connection. Viewers tune in for vicarious satisfaction or simply to feel less lonely while dining alone. It reflects a major lifestyle shift in Korea, where many young people embrace the *honsul/honbap* 혼술/혼밥 culture, meaning "**drinking alone**" or "**eating alone**." Through mukbang, they can interact via chat while maintaining personal space—perfect for Korea's increasingly individualistic generation. Famous mukbang streamers make serious money through YouTube ad revenue, sponsorships, and fan donations. For instance, **MoonBoki 문복희** averages more than 1.8 million views per video on her YouTube channel. The trend has since gone global, inspiring countless international YouTubers to jump on the mukbang bandwagon.

TAEKWONDO

KOREAN MARTIAL ART AND NATIONAL SPORT

"The most difficult part of traditional Taekwondo is not learning the first kick or punch. It is not struggling to remember the motions of a poomsae or becoming acquainted with Korean culture. Rather, it is taking the first step across the threshold of the dojang door. This is where roads diverge, where choices are made that will resonate throughout a lifetime."

— Doug Cook, Taekwondo: A Path to Excellence

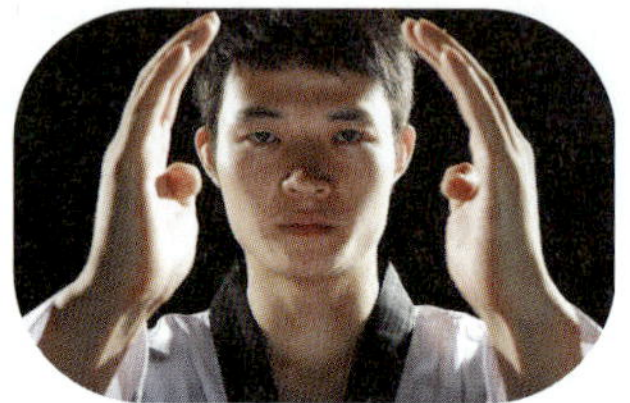

TAE

"to stomp", "feet"

KWON

"to punch", "fist"

DO

"discipline", "way"

"THE WAY OF THE HAND AND FOOT"

TAEKWONDO BY THE NUMBERS

MEMBER COUNTRIES	208
PEOPLE PRACTICING	OVER 80 MILLION
BLACK BELT HOLDERS	OVER 4 MILLION
TAE KWON DO STUDIOS IN KOREA	OVER 10,000

5 TENETS OF TAEKWONDO

COURTESY
예의 (*YE UI*)

INDOMITABLE SPIRIT
백주불굴
(*BAEK JU BUL GUL*)

INTEGRITY
염치 (*YEOM CHI*)

SELF-CONTROL
극기 (*GUK GI*)

PERSEVERANCE
인내 (*IN NAE*)

TAEKWONDO OATH

1. I shall **observe** the **tenets** of Tae Kwon Do

2. I shall **respect** my **instructor** and **seniors**

3. I shall **never misuse** Tae Kwon Do

4. I shall be a **champion** of **freedom** & **justice**

5. I shall **build** a more **peaceful world**.

BRIEF HISTORY OF TAEKWONDO

1940's
1950's

FIRST SCHOOLS ESTABLISHED
Shortly after WWII, martial arts schools, named "*kwan* appear, but each *kwan* practices their own style of martial arts.

1952

EARLY FORMATION
South Korean President Syngman Rhee urges that the martial arts styles of the *kwans* be merged and standardized

1959
1966

KTA AND ITF ESTABLISHED
Korea Taekwondo Association (KTA) is established to facilitate the unification of Korean martial arts.

In 1966, Choi Hong Hi establishes International Tae Kwon Do Federation (ITF), a separate entity incorporating his own style.

1973

WORLD TAEKWONDO FEDRATION
World Federation of Tae Kwon Do Is Established, with Kukkiwon 국기원 as headquarter.

2000

GLOBAL RECOGNITION
Tae Kwon Do becomes an official medal event at the 2000 games in Sydney

WHY ARE KOREAN WOMEN DOMINATING WOMEN'S GOLF?

Turn on any live golf tournament, and I promise you'll find at least one Korean name—if not several—on the leaderboard. As four-time LPGA champion Jessica Korda once said, "Korean women are dominating the LPGA," and the numbers back her up.

Since 1988, when **Ku Ok-hee 구옥희** became the first Korean to win on the LPGA Tour, Korean female golfers have lifted the trophy more than 200 times—and the trend shows no sign of slowing.

So, what's the secret behind their success? It all goes back to 1998, when **Pak Se-ri 박세리**, now a World Golf Hall of Famer, made history with a spectacular birdie shot to win the LPGA Championship. Her victory meant so much to the Korean people, who were then suffering from the aftermath of the Asian Financial Crisis, or the "IMF Era." Many saw her triumph as symbolic—an ordinary Korean standing tall on the world stage, winning against the odds.

Her story became an inspiration and a source of hope. Watching her rise to stardom, countless Korean parents dreamed of raising the next Pak Se-ri—and soon, the generation of **"Pak Se-ri Kids"** was born. By 2020, more than 60 Korean golfers were competing in the LPGA, compared to just one when Pak Se-ri started. Combined with Korea's famously rigorous training culture and an ever-growing pool of young talent, their continued dominance makes perfect sense.

WHY DO KOREANS DOMINATE ARCHERY?

The answer is written—literally—on the wall. The *Muyongchong Suryeopdo* **무용총 수렵도**, a mural from the Goguryeo Kingdom, vividly depicts mounted hunters shooting arrows mid-gallop. The image looks so natural that it suggests archery was once a routine part of physical and mental training. Even in ancient China, Koreans were known as the *dong-i-jok* **동이족**, or "the people good at shooting arrows." Maybe that ancient DNA carried through, because today, Korean archers reign supreme. If the U.S. basketball team is the "Dream Team," then the Korean archery team deserves an equally legendary title. They hold 12 of the 14 Olympic world records and routinely sweep gold medals at global competitions. In short, they're untouchable. Surprisingly, it wasn't always this way. Until the 1970s, Korea's archery program was fairly mediocre. But with better training methods, full support from the national association, and the athletes' relentless work ethic, the tide turned. Their training innovations became as legendary as their accuracy. To build nerves of steel, archers practiced in noisy baseball stadiums filled with cheering crowds—and even visited cemeteries at midnight. Over time, they mastered the ability to stay calm no matter the pressure.

The world took notice. At the 2024 Paris Olympics, Korean coaches led the national archery teams of no fewer than eight countries: Japan, China, France, Malaysia, Vietnam, Bhutan, Iran, and Indonesia. Furthermore, while teams from India, Kazakhstan, Uzbekistan, and Mongolia did not advance to the Olympic finals, Korean coaches played a key role in guiding them to qualification. The legacy of precision, discipline, and creative training continues to define Korea's dominance in the sport.

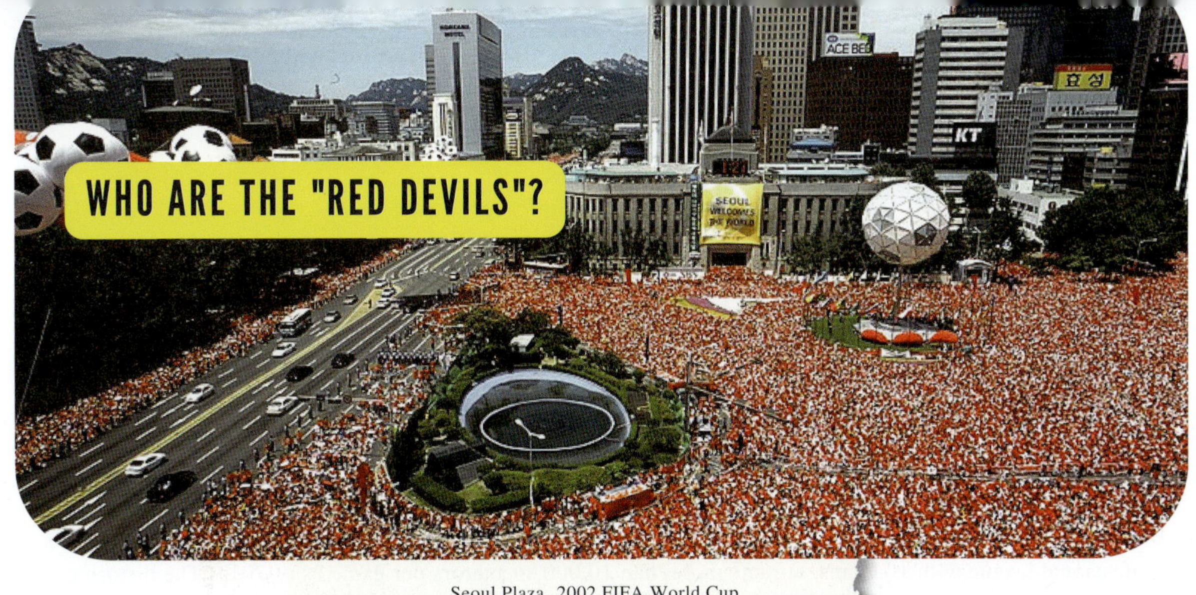

Seoul Plaza, 2002 FIFA World Cup

Founded in 1995, the original name was the 'Korea Supporters Club,' and was renamed to *bulgeun akma* 붉은악마 the 'Red Devils' in 1997. The name is said to have originated from the foreign media that used to call the **South Korean soccer team** who made it to the semifinals in a red uniform the "Red Furious" or the "Red Devils" at the 1983 U-20 World Cup (Fun fact, the nickname "Red Devils" was first used by the Belgian national soccer team). When the **2002 Korea-Japan World Cup** was held, the "Red Devils" earned the nickname the "12th player" thanks to their fervent cheering. Fueled by the Korean team's winning streak, the streets were flooded with people wearing red, and hundreds of thousands of people in red gathered at the **Seoul City Plaza** to cheer for the Korean team, creating a spectacular scene.

DID YOU KNOW THAT THUNDER STICKS WERE INVENTED BY KOREANS?

Have you ever wondered what it would be like to spend a day in the life of the hammer-wielding Norse god, Thor? With the mighty hammer Mjolnir, you can summon and control the powers of the storm. Among all his powers, the coolest special effect has to be the thunder-and-lightning combo, which daunts all adversaries with its ear-splitting thunderclap.

Well, if you envied his power, you can steal his thunder and experience it yourself. In the early 1990s, a Korean firm invented and introduced the first generation of the so-called "Thunder Sticks" (also called Cheerstix, bangers, or bambams), made of polyethylene. They were long tubes that had to be inflated using a straw. Once bent into a V shape and struck against each other, they created a noise ten times louder than clapping. Despite their novelty, they had a downside: people often discarded the straws after inflating the sticks, making reuse cumbersome and creating a huge pile of trash after events. In 2001, another Korean firm introduced a more eco-friendly version. Inspired by pool tubes, they used PVC for enhanced durability and eliminated the need for straws. To maximize convenience, air pumps were installed at stadiums so fans could easily inflate their sticks. After the event, they could simply deflate the sticks and take them home for reuse at the next game. Thunder sticks quickly gained international popularity. In 2002, the Anaheim Angels became the first Major League Baseball team to introduce them. Fans loved the noisy, fun accessory, and it became the hottest souvenir of the 2002 World Series. Today, thunder sticks are widely used at events that attract large crowds, from sports games to political rallies and protests.

Here's a fun fact about thunder sticks: in 1994, the LG Twins, the first Korean team to introduce them, won the Korean Series (the Korean equivalent of the World Series). Eight years later, the Anaheim Angels took home the World Series trophy, proving once again the mighty power of thunder!

WHY IS BASEBALL SO POPULAR IN KOREA?

Korean Baseball 101

Baseball is by far the most popular professional sport in Korea. The **Korean Baseball Organization (KBO)**, a professional league with 10 teams, attracts more than 10,000 spectators per game as of 2017. The history of baseball in Korea dates back to **1905**, when **Philip Gillette**, an **American Christian missionary**, introduced the sport to members of the **Hwangseong Christian Youth Association**. Koreans pick up new skills quickly —the Korean national baseball team won the gold medal at the 2008 Beijing Olympics, finished third in 2006, and was the runner-up in 2009 in the World Baseball Classic. At the WSBC Premier 12, they won the championship in 2015 and were runners-up in 2019. The country has also produced numerous star players who have played in Major League Baseball, many of whom still participate in the KBO.

In Korea, baseball isn't just a sport; it's a total entertainment experience. Fans sing along to team cheering songs, enjoy chicken and beer, and dance with cheerleaders' exciting moves. It's a fun way to relieve stress while enjoying the game.

WHAT IS *SSIREUM* ?

A Legendary Match!
Kang Ho Dong vs. Lee Man Ki

Ssireum 씨름 is a traditional Korean sport with ancient roots on the Korean Peninsula. On November 26, 2018, South and North Korea jointly listed it as a **UNESCO Intangible Cultural Heritage of Humanity**. The game is played by two competitors standing in a sand arena, each wearing a *satba* 샅바 (a thigh band) around the waist. The players grab their opponent's satba and try to knock or flip them over using hand, leg, or waist techniques. The match ends as soon as any part of the opponent's body, except the soles of their feet, touches the ground. Ssireum is also a sport of psychological warfare—one mistake or miscalculation can cost the match.

Traditionally, village-wide competitions were held during holidays, and national competitions were broadcast on TV. The champion, known as *cheonha jangsa* 천하장사 ("The Strongest Man on Earth"), earned fame, honor, and wealth. Popular entertainer and MC **Kang Ho-dong** 강호동 is a former cheonha jangsa. Recently, however, ssireum has lost much of its fan base. The number of professional teams has declined, and younger audiences often see it as outdated, turning instead to Mixed Martial Arts and other modern sports.

Jejudo 제주도, or Jeju Island, is Korea's largest island, located off the southwest coast of the Korean Peninsula. It's one of the most popular destinations for newlyweds, couples, and families alike. With its palm trees, volcanic basalt formations, and stunning beaches, Jeju offers a uniquely exotic atmosphere that's hard to find anywhere else in Korea.

At the heart of the island stands **Mt. Halla 한라산**, South Korea's highest peak at 1,947 meters (6,387 feet). The mountain was formed from a massive lava eruption at the end of the Tertiary (3rd) Cenozoic Era. At its summit lies a beautiful crater lake called **Baekrokdam 백록담** ("White Deer Lake"). While Mt. Halla appears calm and majestic today, it's actually a dormant volcano—its last recorded eruption occurred roughly 1,000 years ago during the **Goryeo Dynasty**.

Historically, Jeju Island was not always part of Korea. In ancient times, it was known as **Tamna 탐라**, an independent kingdom that developed its own distinct culture and engaged in active maritime trade with neighboring regions, including the Korean mainland, Japan, and China. According to historical records, Tamna first established diplomatic relations with the **Three Kingdoms of Korea**, particularly **Baekje** and **Silla**, around the 5th century. Eventually, Tamna became a **tributary state to the Goryco Dynasty** in the 10th century. **In 1105, during King Sukjong's 숙종 reign, Goryeo formally annexed Tamna, integrating it into the Korean administrative system and renaming it "Jeju" (meaning "across the sea province").** Under Goryeo and later the Joseon Dynasty, Jeju remained somewhat isolated due to its distance from the mainland, preserving much of its distinct language, customs, and folklore.

Today, Jeju's unique cultural heritage—rooted in its Tamna past—can still be felt through its myths, such as the legend of the island's three founding demigods (Go, Yang, and Bu), and its enduring traditions like the *haenyeo* 해녀 (female divers) and volcanic stone statues called *dol hareubang* 돌하르방. These features make Jeju not only a natural wonder but also a living museum of Korea's diverse history.

Hey, guys! My name is *dolhareubang* 돌하르방! (*dol* = "stone," *hareubang* = Jeju dialect for "grandfather/senior"). As the name suggests, we are statues carved from porous basalt (volcanic rock) and we can be as tall as three meters (10 ft)! Our face has bulging eyes, a long broad nose, and a hint of a smile. Like our friends *jangseung* 장승, you can find us outside of town gates, working 24/7, protecting the townspeople from the awful demons! We're very popular among women because we're a symbol of fertility - There's a myth that if pregnant women touch our nose, they will have a son. The way we place our hands has a meaning too. We rest them on the bellies, in sets of two, one higher than the other. If our left hand is higher, it symbolizes a writer/scholar, and a military figure if the right hand is placed higher. According to the *Tamnaji* 탐라지, a historical town chronicle of Jeju Island, we made a debut in 1754, and some of our friends stood outside the Eastern, Western, and Southern gates of the Jeju City fortress as guardian deities. Today, we're made into awesome souvenirs, including chocolates, miniatures, and key chains!

What Are The Huge Korean Totem Poles In Korean Folk Villages? P. 211

There is a mermaid in Jeju Island! The women in the iconic black diving suit are called *haenyeo* 해녀 ("Sea **Woman**"). Amazingly, they dive and collect seafood without oxygen tanks (there's a law set to prevent over-fishing and preserve the ecosystem, and as a result, their ability to hold their breath is outstanding). Thanks to the Jeju mermaids, we can enjoy local delicacies like abalone and sea cucumber!

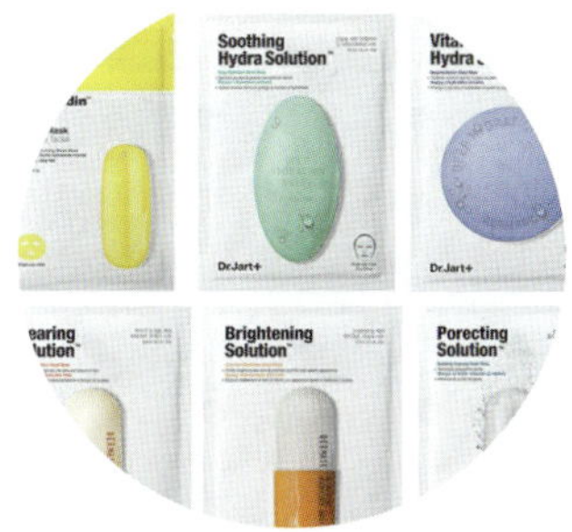

COSMETICS / BEAUTY MASKS

CHARACTER SOCKS

KOREAN LIQUOR

KOREAN SNACKS

K-POP CD/POSTERS

KOREAN RED GINSENG

KOREAN SEASONED SEAWEED

HANJI CRAFTS

HANBOK

KOREAN DOLLS

HONEY YUJA (CITRON) TEA

KEY RINGS/JEWELRY

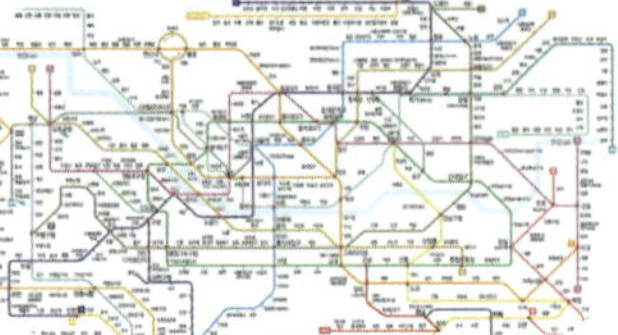

SEOUL METRO FACTS

◆ The World's Longest Multi-Operator Subway System

Seoul Metro holds the title of the world's longest urban rail system operated by multiple companies—yet it runs as a single, seamless network for passengers. Both CNN and automotive outlet Jalopnik have praised it as "the world's best subway system." Step aboard, and you'll quickly see why!

◆ One Transportation Card for the Entire Country

Unlike Japan, where different regions use separate cards, Korea's T-money card works everywhere—from Seoul to Busan, Daegu, Gwangju, and beyond. You can use it for subways, buses, and taxis nationwide, making travel smooth and effortless.

◆ 100% Platform Screen Door Coverage

Every Seoul Metro station is equipped with platform screen doors, ensuring maximum passenger safety. The doors open and close automatically with each train's arrival, reducing the risk of accidents and keeping the platforms safer and cleaner.

◆ RFID/NFC-Enabled T-money Accepted Everywhere

The T-money card uses RFID and NFC technology, allowing instant tap-and-go payments not only on subways but also on buses, taxis, and even at convenience stores. One card truly does it all.

◆ Full-Color LCD Displays with Real-Time Info

Full-color LCD screens at every platform display real-time arrival information. You can instantly see how many minutes remain until the next train—no more guessing or waiting in uncertainty.

◆ Multilingual Announcement System (Korean, English, Japanese, Chinese)

Train and station announcements are made in Korean and English, with additional Japanese and Chinese announcements at major transfer stations and tourist hubs. This multilingual support ensures a worry-free experience for international travelers.

◆ Free, Clean, and Well-Maintained Restrooms

Korea's subway restrooms are free, spacious, and remarkably clean. While many countries charge for restroom use, Seoul Metro's spotless facilities often leave foreign visitors pleasantly surprised.

INTRODUCING KOREA'S BUS SYSTEM!

BLUE (Trunk Bus)
- Travels longer distances
- Connects suburban areas to downtown Seoul

RED (Rapid / Express Bus)
- Provides fast service
- Connects metropolitan areas to downtown Seoul

GREEN (Branch Bus)
- Operates on shorter routes
- Connects major subway stations and bus terminals outside downtown

YELLOW (Circulation Bus)
- Operates within districts of Seoul
- Circulates around key areas such as business, tourist, and shopping zones

◆ Bus-Only Central Lanes & Central Bus Stops

Many of Seoul's major roads feature dedicated central bus lanes, allowing buses to move faster than general traffic even during rush hour. Some routes also include central bus stops, designed for smooth boarding and alighting right in the middle of the road—ensuring fast, efficient service across the city.

◆ Smooth Boarding with RFID/NFC Transit Cards

Just like the subway, Korean buses also accept T-money cards for easy, contactless payment. Simply tap your card on the reader when boarding, and tap again when exiting to automatically receive your transfer discount.

◆ Convenient Transfer Discount System

Bus and subway transfers are fully integrated. If you transfer within the designated time limit, you won't be charged an additional fare. With up to four transfers allowed on a single fare, Korea's public transportation system is not only convenient but also cost-efficient.

◆ Real-Time Arrival Information at Every Stop

Nearly every bus stop in Korea is equipped with a digital electronic display showing real-time arrival information. You can instantly check how many minutes remain until your bus arrives. Using Korean apps such as Naver Map, you can also track buses in real time—whether you're at a stop or walking around town.

WHAT'S THE FASTEST GROUND TRANSPORTATION IN KOREA?

HALLYU
KOREAN WAVE

WHAT IS *HALLYU* 한류 (KOREAN WAVE)?

EARLY 1990s

SEO TAIJI AND BOYS - CHANGING THE HISTORY OF KOREAN MUSIC INDUSTRY

When discussing the history of K-pop, any attempt would be meaningless without mentioning **Seo Taiji and Boys**, the pioneers who first transplanted elements of **American pop** into Korea. Their fast beats, rap, and powerful dance moves were something no one had ever tried to combine on stage before. Were they ahead of their time? When they debuted in **1992**, critics gave them discouraging reviews—but it didn't take long to prove them wrong. A massive fandom quickly formed, and imitation groups began to emerge in droves. Just like that, they became the touchstone of K-pop, and the Korean music industry was changed forever.

(*Fun fact:* **Yang Hyun-suk 양현석**, *one of the members, later became the founder of YG Entertainment.*)

Seo Taiji and Boys'
Debut Performance

THE 1990s

THE BIRTH AND BEGINNING OF HALLYU / KOREAN WAVE

The term *Hallyu* (**Korean Wave**) began to emerge in the **late 1990s**, when **H.O.T.**, one of K-pop's legendary idol groups, became popular in **China**. In **February 2000**, after H.O.T. successfully performed in Beijing, the headline "*Hallyu Hits China*" appeared in major Chinese newspapers. From that point on, "Hallyu" officially became the term for the global spread of Korean pop culture.

Meanwhile, in Taiwan, the powerful dance duo **Clon** made a huge splash, while in **China**, the pretty-boy idol group **NRG** rose to fame alongside Korean TV dramas that captivated local audiences. Back home, the three-member girl group **S.E.S.** made a meteoric rise, soon followed by **Fin.K.L**, another four-member girl group that became their biggest rival. Male groups like **G.O.D.** and **Shinhwa**, known for their strong choreography and trendy tunes, further elevated the standard for idol music and solidified the foundation of modern K-pop.

H.O.T Performs
"Candy"

FULL-FLEDGED LANDING OF KOREAN CULTURAL CONTENT IN JAPAN, THE YONSAMA CRAZE, AND DAEJANGGEUM

The next stop for the Korean Wave was **Japan**! But would it succeed there—the powerhouse of pop culture that had long dominated Asia with **J-Pop** and bubbly romantic dramas?

It was the 1999 movie *Shiri* 쉬리 that first showed the possibility. The suspense thriller, which tells the story of a romance between a South Korean intelligence agent and a North Korean spy, became a massive hit in Japan and proved that Korean cultural content could captivate Japanese audiences.

Then came *Winter Sonata* 겨울연가 (**2002**)—a melodrama that created an unprecedented boom. It generated a sensational response among middle-aged female viewers in Japan, who fell head over heels for actor **Bae Yong-joon 배용준**, affectionately nicknamed "**Yonsama**" ("**Emperor Yon**"). He was adored as the "first love" of Japanese women and welcomed like a state guest at airports, surrounded by thousands of enthusiastic fans. From then on, the word "Hallyu" entered the Japanese lexicon, and a full-blown "Hallyu Syndrome" swept across the country.

Swiri 쉬리 (1999)

Gyeoul Yeonga 겨울연가
(*Winter Sonata* KBS, 2002)

Daejanggeum 대장금 (MBC, 2003)

In the music industry, **BoA**, a teenage singer from **SM Entertainment** who had debuted in Japan at a young age, became a superstar—dominating the Oricon charts and paving the way for the soft landing of K-pop in Japan.

However, the Korean Wave content that truly captured audiences beyond Asia was undoubtedly *Daejanggeum* 대장금 (*Jewel in the Palace*, **MBC, 2003**). This historical drama, telling the story of the first female royal physician of the Joseon Dynasty, fascinated global viewers with its stunning portrayal of Korea's natural beauty, the elegance of hanbok, and the richness of Korean cuisine. Beyond its massive success in China, the drama also became immensely popular in Africa and the Middle East—particularly in Iran—and was even remade in several countries, including Japan and Turkey.

CONTINUED OVERSEAS EXPANSION OF KOREAN CULTURAL CONTENT AND THE RISE OF K-POP'S GLOBAL INFLUENCE

TVXQ's Asia Tour Concert Poster

It was **Dongbangshinki (TVXQ)** that succeeded the K-Pop craze in Japan in the late 2000s, whose sold-out concerts at mega dome stadiums were nothing to be surprised about. Idol bands with innocent, boyish charms like **Super Junior** and **SHINee** gained huge popularity, and trendy hip-hop and dance-based groups such as **Epik High**, **Big Bang**, and **Brown Eyed Girls** continued to expand their fandom overseas.

But most of all, the advent of **Girls' Generation** changed the K-Pop scene that boy bands were dominating. **Wonder Girls**, **KARA**, **After School**, **f(x)**, and **T-ara** were among the top contenders vying for the crown. And while **U-Kiss** gained popularity with their youthful charms, **2AM**, **2PM**, and **B2ST**, the boy bands with masculine charms, expanded the spectrum of the K-Pop boy band. "Girl crush" bands like **4Minute** and **2NE1** appeared and were well received by fans around the globe. At the same time, variety show programs such as *Running Man* and *Infinite Challenge* were exported overseas and received positive responses.

2NE1 Performing in New York MTV IGGY's Best New Band in the World

In the early 2010s, idol groups such as **ZE:A**, **CNBLUE**, **SISTAR**, **Miss A**, **Girl's Day**, and **APink** continued to appear and dominate the K-Pop scene. It wasn't a big step, but it was a time when the Korean Wave continued to secure fandom around the world with small but steady steps.

Gangnam Style
Music Video

At that very moment, something that no one ever expected happened — and people all over the world were suddenly captivated by K-Pop madness! That's right, it was **Psy**'s "**Gangnam Style**." The addictive melody and horse-riding dance helped the song go viral through social media, pushing it to the second place on the **Billboard chart**, an unprecedented achievement in the history of K-Pop. Including a New Year's Eve performance at **Times Square** and a collaboration stage with **MC Hammer** at the **American Music Awards (AMA)**, Psy was the busiest person in the world in 2012, and his presence helped shatter the stereotype that K-Pop is only about idol groups.

HALLYU'S CONTINUING POPULARITY AND SPREAD INTO THE GLOBAL MARKET

Taeyangeui Huye 태양의후예
(*The Descendants of the Sun* KBS, 2016)

Gisaengchung 기생충
(*Parasite*, 2019)

So far, the Korean Wave has been a huge success in Asian markets, but in North America and Europe, it had only formed a small fandom. However, from this time on, the Korean Wave finally moved beyond its geographical limits, and people around the world began to enjoy K-Pop.

The globalization of the Korean Wave continued with the emergence of talented groups such as **EXID, EXO, AOA, BTS, GOT7, AKMU, Red Velvet, Lovelyz, iKON, Mamamoo, ASTRO**, and **BLACKPINK**. The reason for this success is that K-Pop, which initially began by imitating American pop music and Japan's J-Pop idol system, has now created its own flavor through active convergence and transformation. Today, K-Pop is no longer a child of American Pop or J-Pop, but a unique brand with a "cool and hip" feeling that only K-Pop can offer.

In addition, **Korean dramas** and **movies** continued to gain international attention. *Taeyangeui Huye* **태양의 후예** (*Descendants of the Sun,* **KBS, 2016**) became a sensation across Asia and sold its broadcasting rights to numerous countries in Europe. And in 2020, director **Bong Joon-ho**'s **Parasite (2019)** surprised the world by winning four **Academy Awards**, setting a major milestone in Korean film history.

In 2021, the Netflix original series *Squid Game* topped the charts in over 90 countries worldwide, sparking a true "syndrome." Lead actor **Lee Jung-jae 이정재** won the **Emmy Award** for Outstanding Lead Actor in a Drama Series. Since then, various Korean dramas such as *Hellbound, The Glory, My Name*, and *Extraordinary Attorney Woo* have received immense global love through streaming platforms, solidifying Korean dramas as the distinct genre known as "K-Dramas." K-Pop also continues to evolve, expanding its influence on the global stage. **BTS** took the stage consecutively at the **2021** and **2022 Billboard Awards** and the **Grammy Awards**, cementing their status as global superstars. **BLACKPINK** headlined major global festivals like Coachella, further elevating K-Pop's presence. Meanwhile, new-generation artists such as **NewJeans**, **LE SSERAFIM**, **Stray Kids**, **SEVENTEEN**, **IVE**, and **aespa** are making remarkable strides, touring Europe and America and climbing to the top of global music charts.

Another cultural milestone came with *K-Pop Demon Hunters* **(2025)**, an animated film whose production was by Sony Pictures Animation. This project was especially significant—it represented a new form of **global collaboration**, backed by foreign investment, yet deeply rooted in Korean creativity. Despite being an international co-production, its Korean setting, themes, and characters captivated audiences around the world. The film's original soundtrack, featuring the hit songs "*Golden*" and "*Sugar Pop*," dominated the Billboard charts for weeks, further demonstrating the worldwide power of K-Pop. Following the film's success, Korea saw a dramatic rise in foreign visitors—not only for shopping or entertainment, but also for deeper cultural experiences. Many began exploring **Korea's historical and artistic treasures**, with destinations like the **National Museum of Korea** emerging as new must-visit cultural sites.

Today, the Korean Wave has transcended mere cultural content, firmly establishing itself as a "**lifestyle**" that extends into **fashion, beauty, food**, and **digital platforms**. Many young people around the world now recognize Korean culture as "trendy," and the number of those learning Korean due to its influence continues to grow. The Korean Wave is no longer a temporary trend; it has taken root as a powerful cultural current that people around the world resonate with and enjoy.

WHAT DOES THE FUTURE OF HALLYU / KOREAN WAVE LOOK LIKE?

While some critics hold negative views about the sustainability of the Korean Wave—claiming it's too heavily skewed toward K-Pop and K-Dramas—no one can deny that they played the most important role in sparking global interest in Korea. And now, those efforts are coming to fruition. The Korean Wave is gradually expanding its presence into various areas such as fashion, cosmetics, food, tourism, martial arts, movies, literature, and education, making the spectrum of Hallyu wider and more diverse. Experts say that K-Beauty and K-Webtoons are emerging as the golden boys of the next-generation New Hallyu, and it will be fascinating to see how the New Hallyu Wave continues to evolve.

WHAT DOES IT TAKE TO BECOME A K-POP IDOL?

"Trainee" literally means an aspiring K-Pop singer who enters into a contract with an entertainment agency and goes through a rigorous professional training course (vocal, dance, language, and so many others) with a dream to become a K-Pop idol star one day. Most of them start in their teenage years and the training period can last as many as 7~8 years, but it's not a guarantee as the entertainment companies have the right to release them if they believe their trainees don't have what it takes to become a K-Pop star. However, being a K-Pop idol is not a job for everyone, and it's ultimately a professional agency's job to determine whether the gemstone is a diamond in the rough or not, and it's also their role to process it into a sparkling diamond. But if they can make it, they have a great shot at wealth and fame. For this reason, many teenagers pick K-Pop idol as their dream job. But what happens when everyone wants the same job? Becoming a professional idol singer, let alone becoming a trainee, is as difficult as getting into an Ivy League school.

TOP K-POP ENTERTAINMENT COMPANIES

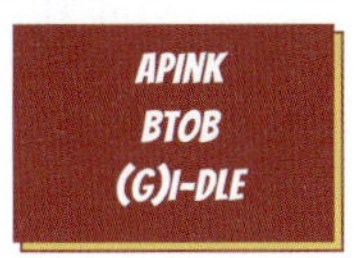

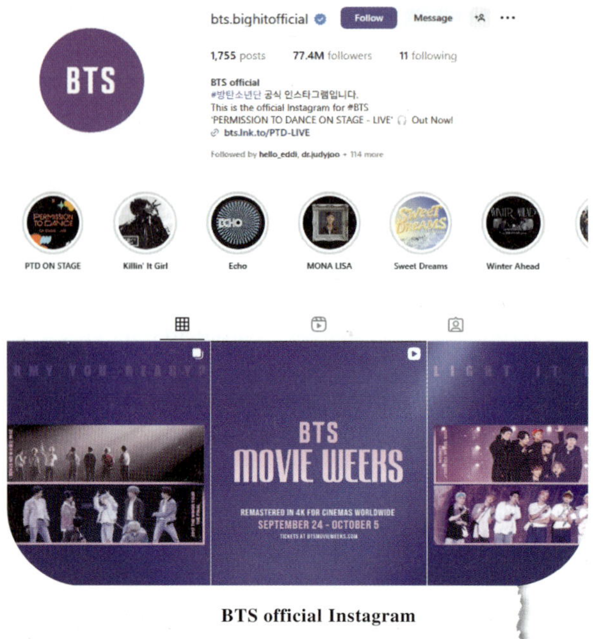

BTS official Instagram

Addictive melodies, perfectly synchronized and astonishing dance moves, trendy fashion and makeup, story-driven sensory music videos, and multi-talented idols with diverse charms—there are many reasons K-Pop captivates global audiences. But beyond all that, what truly makes K-Pop special is the emotional connection and sense of participation it builds between artists and fans.

A perfect example is **BTS**, a group that has become the face of K-Pop worldwide. BTS's fandom, **A.R.M.Y (Adorable Representative MC for Youth)**, is one of the most powerful and organized fan communities in the world. Yet, the reasons for their success go far beyond good looks or flawless choreography—qualities that many other K-Pop groups also possess. The real difference lies in how they connect.

BTS was officially named the **most-mentioned artist on Twitter** and recorded an overwhelmingly high fan engagement index compared to other celebrities. This marks a revolutionary shift in the production and consumption of popular culture. In the past, entertainment agencies created content and fans passively consumed it. But K-Pop—led by BTS and many other groups—has redefined that structure. Fans now directly communicate with agencies and artists, providing feedback and shaping the creative process from the early stages. In this new system, fans are no longer mere consumers—they are co-creators of the culture.

Social media platforms like **Twitter, Instagram, Weverse, and V LIVE** have made this possible. Fans can follow their favorite idols' daily lives, watch behind-the-scenes moments, and interact in real time. This constant exchange turns fandom into a shared experience, where artists become not just celebrities but **friends**, **mentors**, and **sources of emotional comfort**.

The messages often found in K-Pop songs—about **love**, **effort**, **self-acceptance**, and **youth**—resonate deeply with fans worldwide. This shared emotional space allows fans to feel seen and understood. They don't just listen to music; they collect albums and merchandise, attend concerts and fan signings, watch real-time live streams, and actively engage in global fan communities. Especially in K-Pop, this frequent, intimate interaction creates the feeling that fans are personally involved in an artist's journey. Some even say it feels like a friendship—or even love!

Ultimately, the secret behind K-Pop's worldwide popularity lies not only in its catchy music or dazzling performances, but in its unique culture of communication and participation. Fans and artists grow together, creating a two-way relationship that blurs the boundary between performer and audience.

That's why K-Pop isn't just music—it's a shared experience, an emotionally connected global community. From BTS to BLACKPINK, from EXO to NewJeans, this powerful fan–artist bond continues to drive K-Pop forward, making it one of the most dynamic and influential pop cultures in the world today.

Old Boy (2003) / *Old Boy* (2013)

Yeopgijeokin Geunyeo 엽기적인그녀 *(2001) / My Sassy Girl (2013)*

Janghwa Hongryeon 장화홍련 (2003) / *The Uninvited* (2009)

Shiwolae 시월애 (2000) / *The Lake House* (2006)

Geoulsokuro 거울속으로 (2003) / *Mirrors* (2018)

KARMA KNIGHT by UltramrineSoft
available on Steam Network

REFERENCES

- 「대한민국의 국기」, Wikipedia, ko.wikipedia.org/wiki/대한민국의_국기
- 「태극기의 변천」, theme.archives.go.kr/next/symbol/Korea
- 「Flag of South Korea」, Wikipedia, en.wikipedia.org/wiki/Flag_of_South_Korea
- 「조선민주주의인민공화국의 국기」, Wikipedia, ko.wikipedia.org/wiki/조선민주주의인민공화국의_국기
- 「Flag of North Korea」, en.wikipedia.org/wiki/Flag_of_North_Korea
- 「Package Design Trivia: Why is the Pepsi logo red, white, and blue?」, Core77, core77.com/posts/12821
- 「우리나라의 성씨는 몇 개나 될까?」, kostat.go.kr/file_total/nkids/kids_pp/story_pdf130603.pdf
- 「Sato most common surname in Japan」, Japan Today, japantoday.com/category/national/sato-most-common-surname-in-japan
- 「List of the 1000 Most Common Surnames in the U.S.」, namecensus.com
- 「Hangul」, Wikipedia, en.wikipedia.org/wiki/Hangul
- 「위기의한글① '반대를 위한 반대' 한글 탄생 가로막다」, 뉴스1, news1.kr/articles/?3730958
- 「"국한문 혼용으로 돌아가자...한국어 품격 높아진다"」, 동아일보, donga.com/news/Culture/article/all/20141010/67068211/2
- 「Kimchi」, Wikipedia, en.wikipedia.org/wiki/Kimchi
- 「뮤지엄김치간」, kimchikan.com, kimchikan.com
- 「김치에 대한 진실 혹은 거짓」, 서울식품안전뉴스, fsi.seoul.go.kr/webzine/seoulFood201801/2017_02_002.html
- 「Korean Confucianism」, en.wikipedia.org/wiki/Korean_Confucianism
- 「한국유교」, 성균관, skk.or.kr
- 「삼강오륜」, bupdori.com
- 「조선아동교육 남녀칠세부동석」, 한국콘텐츠진흥원, culturecontent.com
- 「삼종지도, 칠거지악」, 한국민족문화대백과사전, encykorea.aks.ac.kr
- 「경례(敬禮)와 악수(握手)」, 한국전례연구원, wooriyejeol.or.kr
- 「절하는 방법」, 네이버 백과사전, terms.naver.com
- 「여름철, 보양식, 유래는 아시고 드시나요?」, 열린창업신문, rgnews.co.kr
- 「Dog Meat」, Wikipedia, en.wikipedia.org/wiki/Dog_meat
- 「7 Proven Health Benefits of Ginseng」, healthline.com
- 「Ginseng」, Wikipedia, en.wikipedia.org/wiki/Ginseng
- 「우황청심원」, 나무위키, namu.wiki/w/우황청심원
- 「우리의 맛 장(醬) 장의 종류」, 식품음료신문, thinkfood.co.kr
- 「떡의 유래와 의미 (여러가지 떡)」, 전통문화콘텐츠연구소, noriyon.co.kr
- 「비 오는 날, 막걸리에 부침개가 당긴다...왜 그럴까?」, 연합뉴스, yna.co.kr/view/AKR20160705179300064
- 「코로나19에 "숟가락 섞지 말아야"...겸상 문화가 한국 거라고?」, 한국일보, hankookilbo.com/News/Read/202005020399057581
- 「한국인만 유독 쇠젓가락을 사용하는 '똑똑한' 이유」, heftykr.com/chopstick_culture
- 「한국의 소주」, Wikipedia, ko.wikipedia.org/wiki/한국의_소주
- 「선비들이 술을 마시는 의례 - 향음주례(鄕飮酒禮)」, dongheon.or.kr
- 「Miracle on the Han River」, Wikipedia, en.wikipedia.org/wiki/Miracle_on_the_Han_River
- 「삼신할머니」, 한국콘텐츠진흥원, culturecontent.com
- 「Mongolian spot」, Wikipedia, en.wikipedia.org/wiki/Mongolian_spot
- 「사주팔자」, 나무위키, namu.wiki/w/사주팔자
- 「[관상의 과학] 부자 관상·왕의 관상 타고나지만, 살면서 바꿀 수 있다?」, 아시아경제, asiae.co.kr/article/2018061511532486737
- 「풍수지리」, 나무위키, namu.wiki/w/풍수지리
- 「무당」, 한국민속신앙사전, folkency.nfm.go.kr

ACKNOWLEDGEMENT

Parts of the text have been adopted in full or with modification for optimal reading experience from the following sources under the CC-BY-SA license.

- 「선풍기 사망사고의 진실은?」, 연합뉴스, yna.co.kr/view/AKR20080715194900003
- 「[취재파일] '손 없는 날' 믿어야 하나?」, SBS 뉴스, news.sbs.co.kr/news/endPage.do?news_id=N1001636632
- 「혈액형 성격설」, 나무위키, namu.wiki/w/혈액형%20성격설
- 「내 얼굴, 큰 것일까 커 보이는 것일까?」, 한국경제, hankyung.com/news/article/201206055778
- 「전통장례절차」, 예다함, yedaham.co.kr
- 「장례식」, 나무위키, namu.wiki/w/장례식
- 「한국의 제사」, Wikipedia, ko.wikipedia.org/wiki/한국의_제사
- 「제사상 차리는 방법」, 서울시설공단, sisul.or.kr
- 「혼례(婚禮)」, 한국민족문화대백과사전, encykorea.aks.ac.kr
- 「신정과 구정의 차이를 아십니까...음력 설의 수난사」, 시사저널, sisajournal.com/article/173856
- 「Korean New Year」, Wikipedia, en.wikipedia.org/wiki/Korean_New_Year
- 「보신각 종, 33번 치는 까닭은?」, 한문화타임즈, hmhtimes.com/news/articleView.html?idxno=1626
- 「제야의 종」, 나무위키, namu.wiki/w/제야의_종 「삼국 시대의 복식」, blog.daum.net/yonghwan6158/1421
- 「한국 복식: 삼국시대(고구려, 백제, 신라)」, blog.naver.com/mongjja_/221099996686
- 「한복디자이너[삼국시대의 복식]」, blog.naver.com/PostView.nhn?blogId=abcde3965&logNo=50145936239
- 「[한복] 시대별 한복의 변화」, instiz.net/pt/5317188
- 「한복」, 위키백과, ko.wikipedia.org/wiki/한복
- 「Hanbok」, Wikipedia, en.wikipedia.org/wiki/Hanbok
- 「한국민족문화대백과」, 네이버 백과사전, terms.naver.com
- 「Voyage en Corée 2. (Voyage in Corea Section 2)」, anhtony.sogang.ac.kr
- 「Taekwondo」, Wikipedia, en.wikipedia.org/wiki/Taekwondo
- 「마을의 수호신 돌하르방」, 제주도청, jeju.go.kr/culture/folklore/religious/religious05/religiousHarubang.htm
- Wikipedia, wikipedia.org/wiki/Three_Kingdoms_of_Korea
- Wikipedia, wikipedia.org/wiki/Goguryeo
- Wikipedia, wikipedia.org/wiki/Baekje
- Wikipedia, wikipedia.org/wiki/Silla
- Wikipedia, wikipedia.org/wiki/Goryeo wikipedia.org/wiki/Joseon
- Wikipedia, wikipedia.org/wiki/Gyeongbokgung
- Wikipedia, wikipedia.org/wiki/Changdeokgung
- Wikipedia, wikipedia.org/wiki/Changgyeonggung
- Wikipedia, wikipedia.org/wiki/Deoksugung
- Wikipedia, wikipedia.org/wiki/Gyeonghuigung
- Wikipedia, wikipedia.org/wiki/Korea_under_Japanese_rule
- Wikipedia, wikipedia.org/wiki/Korean_War